Foreign Resources and Economic Development

A Symposium on the Report of the Pearson Commission

Edited by

T. J. BYRES

Lecturer in Economics,
School of Oriental and African Studies,
University of London

FRANK CASS : LONDON

First published 1972 in Great Britain by
FRANK CASS AND COMPANY LIMITED
67 Great Russell Street, London WC1B 3BT, England

and in United States of America by
FRANK CASS AND COMPANY LIMITED
c/o International Scholarly Book Services, Inc.
P.O. Box 4347, Portland, Oregon 97208

ISBN 0 7146 2932 4

Made and printed in Great Britain by
The Garden City Press Limited
Letchworth, Hertfordshire SG6 1JS

Foreign Resources
and
Economic Development

Contents

L00 0450918

Preface

This volume of essays has emerged from my activities as review editor of *The Journal of Development Studies*. It was decided to recognize the importance of the Report of the Pearson Commission by having it reviewed in depth, by more than one economist. One of the reviewers, Peter Bauer, suggested that I might want to edit a collection containing at least three differing reactions to Pearson. From there the symposium grew and Paul Streeten was most helpful with suggestions. Professor Bauer also proposed that an Outline of the Report would provide a useful prelude to the substantive papers and kindly prepared such an Outline. I gratefully acknowledge the help and suggestions, but full editorial responsibility is, of course, mine.

The papers which follow constitute a set of seven very different responses to the Pearson Report. All of the issues raised in the Report are not covered, and there was no attempt made to secure comprehensiveness or parity of treatment. Yet no important issue is, I think, ignored or treated scantily. An effort *was* made to ensure as wide a range of view and approach as possible, and the reader will certainly find sharp difference among authors. Authors responded in their own individual ways and not to any editorial suggestions of topic. There was no reading of one another's contributions and there is, therefore, no in-fighting. The reader will detect some cross-fire (to change the metaphor), but this is the result not of direct confrontation but of the authors' being in the field of "development economics" for some time and occupying well-known and entrenched positions. Finally, a feature of the papers is that while they are, in parts, technical the general approach is far from being *narrowly* technical. I hope, therefore, that the audience will include more than professional economists and budding professional economists.

T. J. BYRES

London
September, 1971

Introduction

Foreign Resources and Economic Development: Some of the Issues Raised by Pearson*

T. J. Byres

The central concern of the Pearson Commission was with the operation and consequences of foreign aid and with how foreign aid might more effectively contribute towards the complex business of economic development. This was its assigned writ and is what must occupy us most in our consideration of the Report. Such, indeed, is the major preoccupation of the papers which follow, though the reader will find no unanimity among authors upon the *modus operandi* or the effects of foreign assistance or upon which policy changes are desirable or likely to be implemented. The circumstances surrounding the Commission's writ are of interest and are discussed in some of the essays (see, especially, the Outline and the contributions of Byres, Johnson and Streeten). They need not detain us here. Suffice it to note that the uneasiness among international civil servants derives from a disenchantment among reluctant donors and frustrated recipients. This, in turn, is reflected in the views of development economists. The small band of *laissez-faire* economists have been joined by critics at the other end of the political spectrum, while along the spectrum it is difficult to find anyone who is happy about foreign aid. The most fervent advocates of foreign aid—members of the "aid lobby"—are profoundly unhappy about the small size of aid flows and the unlikelihood of their growing.

The Commission covered a fairly wide terrain in its deliberations —and rightly, since the repercussions and ramifications of foreign aid are widespread—and made several recommendations. The range

* **Partners in Development: Report of the Commission on International Development** by Lester B. Pearson *et al. New York: Praeger; London: Pall Mall,* 1969. Pp. xvi, 400; no index. £2.50 ($7.95) cloth, £1.10 ($3.45) paper. Mr Lester Pearson was Chairman of the Commission; the other Commissioners were Sir Edward Boyle, Mr Roberto de Oliveira Campos, Mr Wilfred Guth, Sir Arthur Lewis, Professor Robert E. Marjolin and Dr Saburo Okita. *Unless otherwise stated, references to "the Report" throughout this book refer to the above; similarly, page references unaccompanied by further bibliographical details refer to the Report.*

of the coverage and the nature of the recommendations are to be found in the individual essays and there issue is taken on a broad front. Again the details can be ignored at this juncture. What we can, however, underline is that foreign aid cannot be seen in isolation from a whole host of other factors, as the Report itself stresses. Just how wide-ranging one's analysis is to be is a matter of individual judgment. But, starting at close quarters, foreign assistance cannot be analysed without reference to private foreign investment. It is possible to view the two flows as competitive *or* as complementary. It is further possible to see them as part of a "system" which is exploitative *or* beneficent. It is necessary, however, to see them in conjunction. They both involve the transfer of real resources, though we can argue about the precise size of the transfer and the balance of net advantage. Hence our chosen title, *Foreign Resources and Economic Development*. The Report has recommendations to make with regard to private foreign investment and this area is given detailed frontal treatment in the paper by P. C. I. Ayre. Private foreign investment is also examined by Bauer and Yamey, Byres, Griffin and Johnson. Again the reader will see a marked difference of attitude among authors.

More generally, what emerges in clear fashion from most of the essays is that an adequate analysis of the problem of foreign resources and economic development cannot be conducted in narrowly technical terms (though technique—and rigour—are, of course, essential), or without reference to politics, social philosophy, social structure, and other non-economic variables. The economic and non-economic are intertwined in a causal nexus and to sever and isolate one from the other may be to mislead and distort. Political economy is the appropriate framework, however uncomfortable contemporary economists feel in such unfamiliar surroundings. And if these essays have shortcomings *as political economy* they do show that a disturbingly real problem can induce some diminution in intellectual agoraphobia.

To return, finally, to some of the crucial questions raised by the giving and utilization of foreign aid, we note issues which are considered by Pearson and which recur in the various essays. Once more we need not become enmeshed in detail, but can confine ourselves to stating the general by way of introduction. All of the authors except Ayre (who is not concerned directly with questions of foreign assistance) consider the general question: Why aid? This immediately breaks up into a series of more specific questions to which varying degrees of attention are given. Firstly, questions of *motivation*. Why have donors given aid in the past? We have differing explanations: altruism, conscience money, concern to narrow the "income gap", ties with ex-colonies of a benign nature, military and strategic advantage, economic benefit, ideology, neo-colonialism. Why should they give aid—more aid, on better terms— in future? Obviously we can have recourse to the same range of explanation in presenting our answer, with the added point of disillusionment with regard to expected returns (economic and non-economic). Johnson, most notably, is critical of the Commission's failure to provide any *new* motivation for aid-givers (and this is noted, also, by Byres and Streeten). The second set of questions follows naturally, and relates to the *impact* of aid. Does aid promote growth in poor countries? Is it, indeed, a *sine qua non* of growth? For very different reasons Bauer and Yamey, Byres and Griffin argue that its growth-promoting powers have been limited or nil. Lipton, however, provides a spirited defence of aid's ability to induce development, positing that its impact has been limited because its size has been small. Streeten points to aid's ability to generate as many problems as it solves. Thirdly, there are questions relating to the appropriate *institutional framework* for giving and receiving aid: bilateral versus multilateral aid, and so on. This is touched upon at several points. Finally, questions of *alternatives* to aid. If aid, *tout court*, does not promote development, or, a different proposition, if aid is not forthcoming in sufficient quantity to generate "respectable" growth, are there alternatives? Byres and Griffin argue that there are alternatives *within* a suitably reformed and adequately planned underdeveloped economy. Bauer and Yamey also identify endogenous forces of advance, but in terms of untrammelled private enterprise, with foreign resources being raised, where necessary, by proper, commercial loans. Johnson, concentrating on the need for foreign resources, sees the international corporation as the bringer of progress: transmitting technological advance and reallocating capital resources between rich and poor.

And so we have come full circle. The Pearson Report is important as a statement of a particular case and has received widespread attention. These essays subject it to detailed, critical scrutiny and in the process clarify, I think, some of the complex issues which it raises. They are, however, more than *ad hoc* reactions to an important public document and contribute, I trust, in a lasting way to the debate on one of the outstanding problems of our time.

PARTNERS IN DEVELOPMENT

Outline of the Pearson Report

PARTNERS IN DEVELOPMENT
Outline of the Pearson Report

The Pearson Commission on International Development was appointed by the President of the World Bank late in 1968 to conduct a grand assize on the operation and results of development assistance (foreign aid). Its Report, submitted in September 1969, was not generally available until 1970. The Report, written to secure maximum impact, is likely to prove influential, especially at a time when the value of aid is widely questioned particularly in the United States. It may set the stage for discussions on aid in the 1970s in much the same way as did the United Nations Report on Measures for the Economic Development of Underdeveloped Countries for the discussions on development in the 1950s.

According to the publisher's blurb, the Report is

the most comprehensive analysis on development aid to date. Partners in Development is also a full-scale treatment of development in the coming decades: the problems, the policies, the potential ... addressed to the full range of development problems from philosophy to techniques, the report proposes a new basis for international development, and spells out the responsibility of both donor and recipient countries ... Partners in Development is the turning point in the relations between rich and poor nations.

The Report is in eleven chapters. The first summarizes the Commission's view of the case for aid, and also presents its main proposals; chapters two and three deal with the economic development of the underdeveloped world in the last two decades; chapters four to eleven spell out the Commission's proposals and the reasons behind them. There are two annexes: one entitled "The Development Situation", which comprises staff materials (papers on various underdeveloped countries and regions); this annex is about half the length of the Report. The second annex is a statistical appendix. The opening sentence of the Report refers to "a widening gap between the developed and developing countries [which] has become a central issue of our time". To reduce this gap "has inspired the nations left behind by the technological revolution to mobilize their resources for economic growth. It has also produced a transfer of resources on an unprecedented scale from richer to poorer countries" (p. 3).

However, there is now much disenchantment with the results of aid which sets up the danger that the rich countries might "allow the structure built up for development co-operation to deteriorate and fall apart" (p. 4). This disenchantment is the outcome of misconceptions about the aid relationship, of exaggerated expectations about earlier results, and also of dispensing bilateral aid to gain political or strategic advantages, or to support military forces of the recipients, instead of directing it to the promotion of the long-term economic growth of the recipients. There is also much disillusionment among the recipients, who often have harboured misconceptions about the process of economic growth and the policies appropriate to its promotion.[1] However, by now both donors and recipients understand these problems much better: the importance of outward looking policies, of agricultural growth, and of individual incentive, and have adjusted their policies accordingly, and equally it is realized that development depends primarily not on external help but on the "national will to make the fundamental changes which are needed" (p. 6).

The Commission think that the aid relationship is now much better understood than in the past, a relationship which, if it is to be effective, must not be dominated by the interest either of donors or of recipients, but means "a set of new relationships which must be founded on mutual understanding and self-respect" (p. 6).

The prime purpose of co-operation for international development is not the removal of all inequality (which the Commission recognizes as impossible):

> It is to reduce disparities and remove inequalities. It is to help the poorer countries to move forward, in their own way, into the industrial and technological age so that the world will not become more and more starkly divided between the haves and the have-nots, the privileged and the less privileged (pp. 7–8).
> The war against poverty and deprivation begins at home but it must not end there. Both wars must be won. Both problems must be solved (p. 8).

If they (i.e. governments of rich countries) concentrate

> on the elimination of poverty and backwardness at home and ignore them abroad, what would happen to the principles by which they seek to live? Could the moral and social foundations of their own societies remain firm and steady if they washed their hands of the plight of others? (p. 8).

Moreover, this moral imperative is reinforced by enlightened self-interest. Rich countries also will benefit if the world's resources are used to the fullest capacity, if international trade expands, and if all are prosperous and secure. "If we wish that world [in which we all live] to be secure and prosperous we must show a common concern for the common problems of all people" (p. 9). Insistence on this world community leads to the same emphatic assertions. There is now a widespread awareness of a world community. This concept of world community is itself a major reason for international co-operation for development. It is an assertion of faith in the future, as well as of the conviction of the need to act now.

As with other articles of faith, certain consequences, which must also be accepted, flow from it. The most important is the obligation of every government to play its part in co-operation with all others to ensure that all people have a reasonable chance to share in the resources of the world, which should be developed for the benefit of all.

This means refusal to tolerate the extreme and shameful disparity in standards of life that now exists within and between nations.

All governments have accepted a commitment to help the impoverished nations free themselves from the bondage of want (p. 10).

In any case the developing nations are committed to economic development as part of their unfinished revolution, a commitment to achieve a better life for their children by whatever means.

The achievement of much higher standards of living and of self-sustaining growth for the majority of developing countries is plainly possible by the end of the century.

We live at a time when the ability to transform the world is only limited by faintness of heart or narrowness of vision. We can now set ourselves goals that would have seemed chimerical a few decades ago, and working together, we can reach them ... The thing to remember is that the process, global in scope and international in nature, must succeed if there is finally to be peace, security and stability in the world.

If the developed nations wish to preserve their own position in that world, they must play their full part in creating a world order within which all nations, and all men, can live in freedom, dignity and decency (p. 11).

Much has already been achieved in the post-war period in which sixty-five new nations have been created in Africa and Asia. In the 1960s the growth of the gross national product (GNP) of the underdeveloped world reached about 5 per cent p.a., which was however reduced to $2\frac{1}{2}$ per cent per head as a result of the population growth. In this progress, foreign aid, though it represented only 10 per cent of total investment in the developing countries was nevertheless very important in relieving the scarcity of foreign exchange and transferring technology.

Summary of Main Proposals

The following are the main components of the strategy of international co-operation for development envisaged in the Report. The framework of a free and equitable international trade should be created principally by the removal of trade barriers against the exports of developing countries, and if possible by their replacement by special preferences. Primary producers should be assisted by developed countries financing buffer stocks in support of commodity agreements and by supplying supplementary finance to meet persistent shortfalls in export earnings.[2] Mutually beneficial flows of foreign private investment should be encouraged. This requires removal of disincentives to private economic activity in developing countries wherever such a policy is consistent with legitimate national goals.

Private foreign investment cannot be an effective alternative to public aid. Indeed, official aid for infrastructure is often a prerequisite of private investment. The volume of official aid must be increased and this increase should be combined with better partnership, clearer purpose and greater cohesion in its administration. Official aid should be raised to 0.70 per cent of GNP of the donors (presumably at market prices) by 1975, against the average of 0.39 per cent in 1968.[3] This increase in official aid would require a major effort by some donors but "we believe this difficult and demanding challenge must be met if the basis for international community is to be secured" (p. 18). The objective of the policy is to raise the rate of growth of the GNP of developed countries from the present average of 5 per cent to at least 6 per cent. The Commission suggests that although some countries will lag behind, and will therefore need to be aided for humanitarian or other reasons, for many others this acceleration is feasible; and with growth rates of 6 per cent they should be able to increase capital formation sufficiently by about the year 2000 to be able to dispense with aid. These increases in aid should henceforth be linked closely to the economic objectives and the development performance of the recipients. The performance of the donors however also needs scrutiny, especially because recipients cannot plan ambitiously unless they are assured of continuity of external support. Thus donors and recipients should jointly review and assess performance, a dialogue which is best conducted multilaterally under the auspices of inter-regional and international organizations.

The Commission also recommends an increase in the share of multilateral aid in total aid from the present figure of approximately 10 per cent to at least 20 per cent, an increase which together with a higher total volume of aid would increase multilateral flows of aid fivefold by 1975.

Developing countries should be assisted to meet their mounting indebtedness, the legacy of past development loans and suppliers' credits. Debt relief should be considered a legitimate form of aid and future financing must be more lenient than heretofore to avoid heavy and critical indebtedness.

The organization and procedures of the international agencies need to be reviewed in view of their prospective greater responsibility. Technical assistance needs to be strengthened especially by closer integration with other forms of aid.

Energetic steps are advocated to reduce the rate of population increase which at present impedes economic and social advance. The efforts of aid recipients in this direction should be recognized in the allocation of aid. "Aid-givers cannot be indifferent to whether population problems receive the attention they require" (p. 20).

Proposals for a large expansion of official aid and for its increased multilateralization and suggestions for domestic policies by recipients deemed appropriate by the Commission, together with the grounds of these proposals, are the major distinctive topics of the Report, as has been recognized in public discussion, even though in the Report certain other matters notably international trade and private foreign investment are discussed ahead of these more distinctive and radical issues.

NOTES

1 "The nature of the obstacles which stood in the way of quick results, or the decisions which had to be taken to achieve any results at all, were not always understood. The need for export growth was underestimated, agricultural development was usually neglected. Development was also too often only seen as a consequence of decision-making at the top. The vital need to bring about mass participation in development was at times sacrificed to the enrichment of special groups of individuals" (p. 5,).

2 In particular the Commission writes: "Reasonable buffer stock arrangements in support of commodity agreements should be eligible for financial support. The discussions aimed at supplementary finance to meet sustained shortfalls in export earnings should be expedited" (p. 15).

3 It may be helpful to relate these figures to the widely publicized figure of 1 per cent of the national income as target for flow of

resources from rich to poor countries. In many discussions this 1 per cent figure includes private foreign investment; the figure of 0.39 per cent as the average in 1968 refers to official flows of grants and soft loans as percentage of GNP. It was at the UNCTAD meeting in 1968 that GNP replaced national income as basis for calculating these percentages. The Pearson Commission estimates (p. 144) that GNP at market prices exceeds the national income on average by about one quarter, so that the 1968 UNCTAD resolution in effect raised the target for the inflow of resources by about one quarter.

1

THE FUTURE OF PRIVATE FOREIGN INVEST-MENT IN LESS DEVELOPED COUNTRIES

The Pearson Report and Beyond

by

P. C. I. Ayre

School of Oriental and African Studies
University of London

THE FUTURE OF PRIVATE FOREIGN INVESTMENT IN LESS DEVELOPED COUNTRIES

The Pearson Report and Beyond

I INTRODUCTION

Publication of the Pearson Report provides a good opportunity to review the role which private foreign investment might play in the economic development of less developed countries over the next two decades or so. The Report itself devotes a chapter to this topic (Chapter 5) as well as discussing it briefly in other contexts.

Inspection of the following table reveals that private foreign investment is still an important part of the total flow of resources from developed to less developed countries:

Net Flow of Private Financial Resources to Less Developed Countries (Millions of US Dollars)

	1956	1961	1966	1967	1968	1969
Total Private Flows	2998	3098	3810	4208	5963	6280
of which:						
Direct Investment, net	2350	1986	2188	2118	2899	2566
Bilateral Portfolio	190	453	502	796	886	1260
Bilateral Portfolio	190 }	453	502	796	886	1260
Multilateral Portfolio		90	15	306	605	414
Export credits	458	569	1106	989	1579	2040
Total net flows of financial resources (private and official)	6258	9197	10348	11310	13113	13571

Sources Data for 1956 and 1961 is from the Report Table 15, p. 378.
Data for remaining years is from [34]. 1970 Table 7, pp. 178–9.
Totals may not add due to rounding.

The data show clearly that the private flow is dominated by direct foreign investment and export credits, although there has been a substantial growth of portfolio investments in recent years. This pattern may be contrasted with the situation in the years between 1850 and 1914 when private foreign investment in developing countries was dominated by portfolio investment.[1] The question of how far private foreign investment has contributed or could contribute to the economic development of the less developed countries has given rise to an active and often heated debate in recent years. This is especially true where the investment takes the form of direct investment involving foreign firms physically operating the facilities they own in the developing countries. Opinions vary from the highly optimistic view expressed in 1956 by the Research and Policy Committee of the Committee for Economic Development that "the progress of underdeveloped countries would be well served if private American investors were willing and able to supply most of the foreign capital they could usefully absorb and if the underdeveloped countries were willing and able to encourage large investments from this source" [40, pp. 15–16] to the distinctly sceptical opinions expressed by such writers as Griffin [13] [14] and Diáz-Alejandro [9].

The Report's position in this spectrum of opinion is well represented by the following quotations:

> ... in our judgment, available facts do suggest that direct foreign investment has added substantially to the real national income of the developing countries (p. 104).

> We have received the definite impression that most low-income countries would welcome a larger flow of foreign investment, sharing our belief that such flows would contribute to their faster growth (p. 105).

This distinctly favourable view of the growth promoting effects of foreign investment is tempered by a recognition that it can give rise to a number of problems, particularly when taking the form of direct foreign investment. The view of the Commission,[2] however, is that the difficulties are very largely caused by the policies of the less developed countries themselves and consequently a number of recommendations are directed at these countries. At the same time complementary policies are proposed for developed countries.

For both groups of countries two lines of policy are proposed. Firstly, trade policies should be adjusted so that the less developed countries can move from a concentration on the encouragement of manufacturing production for the home market by various protective measures towards a policy based on manufacturing production for export. For this to be possible the developed countries will have to reduce the levels of protection which they give to labour intensive manufactures in which the less developed countries have a comparative advantage.[3]

Secondly, both groups of countries are enjoined to pursue capital market policies which, if carried out, could have important implications for the pattern and volume of foreign capital flows to less developed countries. Developed countries are asked to reduce the various restrictions on access to their capital markets which limit the flow of portfolio capital. As a complement to these relaxations it is suggested that the less developed countries should take measures to improve the workings of their capital markets and eliminate some of the more obvious distortions such as interest rate controls which sometimes mean that the real return from holding financial assets (after allowing for inflation) is negative.

Capital market improvements in less developed countries are important in the context of this paper since there is some evidence that the potential for financing domestic investment from voluntary saving is much greater than is often thought. This is suggested by the fact that some less developed countries are major capital *exporters*. Residents may invest their savings abroad at least in part because there are no suitable financial assets available domestically. Again, Drake [10] has shown how local savers in Malaysia and Singapore responded strongly to the opportunity to purchase newly issued shares. So much so that many issues were over-subscribed. It is important to keep in mind that capital market improvements in both donor and recipient countries could reduce the dependence of less developed countries on external finance in the form of direct foreign investment and export credits. This possibility will be discussed below.

Let us now proceed to a consideration of the role of direct foreign investment in economic development. I shall deal first with investment in non-extractive industries, primarily manufacturing, and then with the rather special issues raised by investment in minerals and petroleum.[4] In a final section I will consider portfolio capital and export credits.

II DIRECT FOREIGN INVESTMENT

(a) *Non-extractive Industries*

The contribution which direct foreign investment can make to economic development is related to its ability to reduce specific scarcities in the countries which receive it. On the one hand it provides capital which might not otherwise be available because of a low level of domestic saving and because access to bond and other portfolio finance from developed countries has been very limited since 1930[5] (pp. 115–18 of the Report). On the other hand, and perhaps more importantly, direct foreign investment brings with it a complementary package of inputs, notably managerial and marketing expertise, knowledge of technical processes not easily obtainable by other means, scarce labour skills and, in some cases, facilities for training local workers in a variety of skills.

Despite these apparent advantages, this form of investment has been the subject of quite severe criticism. Leaving aside the more xenophobic varieties of this criticism, it is possible to distinguish a number of themes in the literature.[6] Firstly, it is argued that foreign firms create enclaves which have little connection with the rest of the economy and do not give rise to any significant "spillover" effects on the local economy.[7] Secondly, remittances of profits and capital can be argued to cause balance of payments difficulties for the host countries. Thirdly, it is argued that foreign firms often stultify the development of local enterprise. This may be because they preempt the best investment opportunities, because they borrow on the local capital market and divert funds away from domestic firms or because they take over going domestic concerns. Fourthly, it is pointed out that foreign enterprises typically do not permit local participation in ownership. Finally, a number of criticisms concern the oligopolistic nature of much foreign enterprise from which a number of disadvantages can flow: e.g. the parent firm may not permit a subsidiary operating abroad to export and prices may be maintained much above the competitive level.[8]

As the Report is concerned to emphasize, the balance between the costs and benefits of private foreign investment (and particularly direct investment) for a recipient country is intimately bound up with trade and exchange rate policy. The environment in which much recent direct investment has taken place has been one of overvalued exchange rates defended by import controls and tariffs. This environment has had a fundamental influence on the pattern and effects of direct investment. To begin with, when the exchange rate is overvalued foreign goods appear to be relatively cheap in relation to comparable domestic goods with the result that it will pay any producer, domestic or foreign, whether selling in the domestic market or exporting, to use imported materials and capital goods whenever this is permitted by the exchange control authorities.[9] It is not difficult to see that this has the effect of reducing the "linkages" of an enterprise with the rest of the economy, tending to establish and perpetuate enclaves [33].

In these circumstances producers have to be "persuaded" by the enforcement of local content requirements or the banning of imports of intermediate goods to buy their production requirements from local producers. A weaving firm, for example, will be likely to strongly resist attempts to establish and protect a spinning plant.[10] If a spinning plant is established tariff protection for the weaving firm may well have to be increased resulting in even less efficient production of cloth.

A considerable amount of direct foreign investment in the last two decades has gone into manufacturing industry,[11] the great bulk going into the production of goods for protected domestic markets.

The contribution of this investment to sustained economic growth is, however, open to question. After an initial period of rapid growth reflecting the replacement of imports by domestic production, growth in the manufactured sector of countries pursuing import substitution policies has typically slowed down considerably as further output growth becomes dependent on the growth of export earnings (required for imported inputs) from traditional agricultural and mineral products, growth which is handicapped by the disincentives created by overvaluation and protective policies for the manufactured sectors. It is unlikely that help will come from a growth of manufactured exports since heavily protected activities rarely become exporters without special incentives.[12]

Although import substitution policies have usually been initiated because of balance of payments difficulties, the contribution of these policies to reducing foreign exchange outflows may be quite small and in some cases there can be a worsening of the situation. This extreme case[13] has received a good deal of attention recently and occurs where imported inputs or exportable inputs are used to produce products whose value when measured in terms of world prices is less than that of the inputs used. Or, to put the point another way, the foreign exchange cost of directly importing the final product would be less than the foreign exchange cost of the inputs used for domestic manufacture. The existence of such cases has been documented for some industries in, among other countries, Pakistan, India and the Philippines. [27, p. 186].

While investment in protected activities by domestic firms can cause net foreign exchange losses investment by a foreign firm introduces another dimension, namely profit remittances. It is now possible that even though the production of the commodity domestically saves foreign exchange the addition of profit remittances to the foreign exchange cost of inputs brings about a net loss to the balance of payments.

This point can be made clearer by a very simple numerical example. Assume that a country has an official exchange rate of one peso per dollar and that the rate is significantly overvalued, being maintained by tariffs and other import restrictions. Assume that a product whose world market price is $100 is produced in the country by a foreign owned firm. The domestic price is P160 with protection (if no tariff were applied and importation were permitted it would obviously be P100). It is by no means impossible that imported materials to the value of $80 would be required to produce the output domestically. Suppose that domestic labour, which would otherwise be unemployed, costing P50 is used, leaving a profit of P30. (A profit share in value added of between 30 per cent and 40 per cent is not unrealistic.) Assuming that all profit is remitted at the official exchange rate, and ignoring taxation, domestic production of the output leads to a worsening of the balance of payments by $10.[14] Although extremely crude, this example shows that it is quite possible that the balance of payments can be worsened by foreign investment if this occurs in a protected sector.

On the other hand, of course, if a foreign firm establishes itself in direct competition with imports there cannot be a worsening of the balance of payments because the sale price must be equal to or below $100, so that whatever profits are remitted one cannot ascribe foreign exchange difficulties to remittance (except in the naive sense of saying that the balance of payments would be improved if everything else remained constant but the profits were not remitted!).

The percentage of total output produced by foreign firms is typically high in just the sectors which have a high degree of protection. This is usually true, for example, of consumer durables, cosmetics and pharmaceutical products. The reasons for this are varied, but technical complexity, high capital intensity and branding and trade marks are probably the major explanation. These are industries where specialist technical knowledge is often of considerable importance and, what is more, the knowledge may be patented or for some reason not easily available to domestic firms.[15] Indeed, to the extent that foreign firms have developed the knowledge by their own research and development they may be unwilling to make it available to other firms on any acceptable terms because they fear that such firms may compete with them in third markets. It has already been pointed out that some writers argue that the transmission of specialist knowledge is the main function of direct investment—the knowledge comes as part and parcel of the project.

How far this knowledge is of value to the host economy is, however, debatable. The point has already been made that foreign firms are often unwilling to divulge it, especially to a competitor in the same market. One cannot, therefore, expect much "spinoff" to domestic firms in less developed countries (though one could stress the demonstration effect of foreign firms in improving management techniques). Even if domestic firms do obtain knowledge of the production techniques because of the presence of foreign firms it is questionable whether the techniques will be optimal from the point of view of the resource endowment of the country. Research intensive activities originating in the requirements of capital rich countries are unlikely to be the most efficient activities for countries with a relative abundance of unskilled and semi-skilled labour.

Another point relevant in this context is that the subsidiary of a foreign firm operating in a protected market is likely to have very little incentive to engage in continuous technical improvement and advance.[16] The firm may continue to produce the same goods with the original technique despite improvements in its parent company's operations. The foreign investment may, therefore, bring about a once-for-all transfer of knowledge embodied in production techniques rather than provide a path through which new knowledge continuously enters the economy and is diffused through the system. If such is the case the foreign firm could with justification be called an enclave.

Industries which have attracted a lot of foreign investment in less developed countries have tended to be more capital intensive than those where domestic firms predominate.[17] This reflects a special advantage of foreign firms over domestic firms since they usually have access to capital on more favourable terms especially where the capital requirements are large.[18] Once again, it can be questioned how far such activities are desirable at all in a less developed country and the fact that foreign firms have an advantage in these activities is certainly not a good enough reason for fostering direct foreign investment.

Finally, many of the products produced by foreign firms in protected markets are branded goods where familiar names are a great asset. The domestic firm is often at a distinct disadvantage vis-à-vis the foreign firm in such industries. Given that consumer preferences in this area are accepted it may be argued that direct importation is preferable to the subsidization of production by foreign firms, the subsidization being implicit in the higher price which consumers have to pay as a result of protection.

The unique advantages possessed by foreign firms investing in manufacturing[19] appear on examination to be in large part related to the protective policies of which the Report is critical. It is therefore important to consider how far direct foreign investment would continue to play a substantial role in the economic development of the less developed countries under somewhat different trade policies. Before considering this problem, however, an aspect of direct foreign investment neglected by the Report will be examined.

The tenor of the Report's analysis of direct foreign investment is that the protective measures taken by less developed countries towards manufacturing have been the result of their own policy decisions, which then induced domestic and foreign investment in the protected sectors. In actual fact, it appears that this has not always been the case and that the role of foreign firms has sometimes been to encourage governments to introduce (or increase) protection.

This is suggested by Kilby's study of Nigerian industrialization

[22] in which he concludes that a substantial part of the increase in tariffs which occurred in that country in the 1960s was brought about as a result of pressure by foreign investors who were already established there. Diáz Alejandro, reviewing Latin American experience, believes that "tariff setting was probably not free from pressures arising from foreign investors in new activities" [9, p. 326]. Of course, one should point out that these investments may have taken place in anticipation of protection being granted once the firms were established—not perhaps a very unreasonable expectation in the 1950s and early 1960s.

It is, in fact, probable that a good deal of foreign investment, not only in manufacturing but also in extractive industries, takes place not so much as a result of a careful balancing of profitabilities in different countries and activities and between exporting to a country and producing there but rather as an outcome of the world-wide strategies of multinational oligopolists. If one firm establishes production in a country, rivals are fearful that it may be given tariff or other protection, so closing the market to their exports. It is even possible that the firm established in the country has discovered a genuine productive advantage there which will enable it to threaten established positions in other markets. Given these uncertainties, Vernon [44, p. 377] has argued that there is an important asymmetry facing the rival. If it enters and both are successful the world-wide balance of the firms is maintained. If both are wrong they may be in a strong position to pass on the cost of the error by gaining protection. On the other hand, if the first firm is successful and the rival does not enter, its world-wide position may be threatened.[20]

It is not difficult to see how such a process can lead to the establishment of a large number of foreign-owned plants operating below capacity and with little prospect of ever becoming exporters.[21] Indeed, the subsidiaries of multinational firms are sometimes forbidden by their parents to export. The market structure within the country tends to be oligopolistic and similar to that in the countries of origin of the investment. This market structure tends to militate against competitive price policies by the firms concerned. Furthermore, to the extent that there are economies of scale or foreign firms have special technical advantages there may be little possibility of entry by domestic firms to share in the profits of the industry. In these circumstances less developed countries would certainly be wise to view pressure by foreign firms for protection with considerable suspicion.

Even without formal protection adverse consequences can result from the foreign ownership of facilities which form part of an international oligopoly. This possibility is well illustrated by the example of oil refining in consumer countries.[22] It has been shown by Das gupta [7] that the foreign-owned refineries in India in the 1950s typically transferred crude oil into India at a higher price than the price at which oil was available from independent sources of supply, notably the Soviet Union at that time. Most of the oil, of course, came from the company's own production facilities and the companies were interested in the overall profitability of their whole vertically integrated operations. But from the Indian point of view the transfer price set is an important determinant not only of foreign exchange outgoings but also of tax revenues since company taxes are based on profits which can be ascribed to refinery and distribution activities and these profits are obviously affected by the price set for the raw material. The establishment of a domestically operated refinery in such a situation may substantially reduce foreign exchange outgoings.

It should not be thought from the foregoing that some specific encouragement for manufacturing is never justified. Little, Scitovsky and Scott [27] have recently argued an elegant case for such a policy but this case implies that equal encouragement should be given to production for the export market and production for the home market. There should not be the discrimination against exporting inherent in import substitution policies of recent vintage.

It is, for example, quite conceivable that as a consequence of a "learning" process which takes time a firm which is not competitive initially may become so later. Labour efficiency as well as entrepreneurial ability may improve as a consequence of practice. As is well known from the literature on the infant industry argument such a situation does not as such justify protection since the perfectly foresightful firm with access to capital resources to finance the initial losses would invest so long as discounted future returns exceeded discounted future costs. But real world firms are unlikely to operate in this somewhat rarified atmosphere. Or, at least, domestic firms in less developed countries are not likely to be in this situation. Some special encouragement to these "infants" can be justified and this might take the form of tariff or other protective measures, though ideally policy measures should be directed at the source of the learning and should take the form of production subsidies if learning is related to output, or a subsidy on employment if the source of the gain over time lies with the number of workers employed. This is not the place to go into the intricacies of these arguments[23] but it does seem prima facie that foreign firms will be doubtfully eligible for special encouragement since they are in a much better position than domestic firms to carry short-term losses.

In addition, one of the main aspects of their operations where domestic firms are likely to have to pass through a learning process is in the development of export markets [3, p. 13], and this is just where the foreign firm is likely to have an initial advantage. Special incentives for *domestic* firms to help them to overcome an initial period of disadvantage is sensible providing they can eventually stand on their own feet. Since entrepreneurship is at least in part a learning process the essence of which is doing [39, p. 104], the only way to get real entrepreneurship established may be to provide it with some initial assistance *vis-à-vis* foreign firms.

A perfectly justifiable exception to this argument is where the foreign firm generates some benefits for other parts of the economy as when a firm trains people who take skills to other sectors (providing the firm does not "finance" this training by paying the trainees less than their marginal product to the firm). Some foreign firms do play a significant role in training workers who eventually work elsewhere in the economy,[24] though this may be part of an overall deal with the firm involving bargaining over the returns from the surplus earned on mineral or petroleum resources.[25] As a general rule, however, it may be suggested that it is very difficult to justify any form of protection for foreign firms.

(*b*) *The Implications of the Report's Recommendations for Direct Foreign Investment in Non-extractive Industries*

Having suggested that there are reasons for being somewhat sceptical concerning the contribution which direct foreign investment in non-extractive industries has made to self-sustained growth in recent years, let us now consider how an adoption of the Report's trade and capital market policy recommendations by developed and less developed countries would alter the situation.

It will be recalled that the Report recommends the less developed countries to pursue more outward looking, less protective policies while the developed countries are enjoined to reduce their tariff and non-tariff[26] protection, particularly on the products of labour intensive manufacturing activities.[27] There are very good reasons for believing that if the developed countries were to reduce the protection which bears particularly heavily on the products of labour intensive manufactures produced by less developed countries those countries (or at least the relatively more developed among them, like Brazil, the Philippines, and Taiwan; it is likely that for some time to come the smaller, less advanced countries will continue to remain highly dependent on agricultural and mineral exports) could expand their production of a wide range of products for export to developed countries. The sort of products in which less developed countries appear to have a comparative advantage range from toys and sports equipment to wood products and some types of electronic goods. Lary [25, especially Chapter IV] has examined this subject in considerable detail and has shown that a wide range of industries could become viable exporters providing markets are opened for them in developed countries. This view is supported by the fact that in the last decade countries like Taiwan and Pakistan have substantially increased their exports of manufactures despite the relatively high levels of protection ruling in developed countries.

What one could hope for is that over the next two decades developed countries will put into operation a programme aimed at eliminating over a 15–20 year period the trade barriers on those products of special interest to the less developed countries. Such a policy would have the great advantage of not tying the growth of demand for the products of less developed countries to the growth of incomes in the developed world but, by enabling the poorer countries to replace high cost production in developed countries with competing products, would provide a basis for a substantial growth of output [25, Chapters 4 and 5; and 19, Chapters 3 and 6]. It may be pointed out that this policy would also tend to increase the growth of real incomes in the developed countries by encouraging a transfer of productive factors to those sectors which are most efficient in relation to the factor endowments involved so further increasing the size of the market for poor countries' products and, incidentally, increasing the demand for the products of those countries which remain basically dependent on mineral and agricultural exports—always assuming agricultural protection in the developed world is not even further increased from present levels.

It seems to the present writer that unless a re-orientation of trade policy along these lines takes place the growth prospects of the developing countries will not be bright. At the same time, if growth continues to be based on indiscriminate import substitution policies in those countries the value of foreign investment to them in the protected sectors is questionable.

What would be the situation if the trade policy recommendations of the Report were adopted? The interesting possibility which emerges now is that foreign enterprise might well not be competitive with domestic enterprise in a wide range of activities. To see why this might be so it is necessary to remember that foreign firms tend to have disadvantages *vis-à-vis* domestic firms because of the familiarity of the latter with the political, social and economic environment in which they operate. To be successful they must have

3—FRAED * *

22 FOREIGN RESOURCES AND ECONOMIC DEVELOPMENT

special advantages to offset this general disadvantage.[28] These special advantages which, as we have intimated above, can be very decisive in industries like automobiles and consumer durables, lie in the more favourable terms and ease with which foreign firms can raise large amounts of capital, their superior management techniques when operating relatively large scale plants involving co-ordination both within the plants and between them and in their access to specialized knowledge not easily available to entrepreneurs in less developed countries.

If one accepts Lary's argument that the less developed countries could become important exporters of relatively labour intensive products and if their future growth were based on an outward looking strategy it does seem that many of the advantages of foreign firms would tend to disappear. This is particularly so if capital market improvements in developed and developing countries permit a greater flow of portfolio capital to less developed countries and allow domestic and foreign savings to be more efficiently allocated within the less developed countries. But even if this does not occur the fact that small firms in labour intensive industries are often as efficient as large ones greatly reduces the importance of access to large amounts of capital funds. I have already referred to Morley and Smith's findings concerning Brazil. In that country there are no foreign enterprises in the wood, furniture and clothing industries which are among the ones singled out by Lary as being particularly promising from the point of view of export potential.

Similar arguments apply to the other special advantages of foreign firms. Technical knowledge is frequently available as part of the purchase price of machinery and foreign technicians can usually be hired for short periods to teach local operatives to operate the sort of machines and processes likely to be important in labour intensive activities. Foreign managers can also be hired on short-term contracts, but it is worth stressing that local entrepreneurs may have a particular advantage in the management of local labour. It is not fortuitous that foreign firms tend to be more capital intensive than domestic firms even when operating in the same industry. Their advantage lies in managing processes rather than men.[29]

As far as access to research information is concerned it is likely that with the growth and development of labour intensive manufactures in less developed countries that these countries would also have the advantage from the point of view of improving techniques and developing new ones. These improvements very frequently emerge as part of a general learning process related to the operation of an activity and the solution of ad hoc problems on the job.

One area in which foreign firms have a particular advantage is in their knowledge of export markets. What might be more fruitful in these circumstances would be a joint operation where the local partners provide skills related to the local production situation and where foreign partners provide overseas marketing expertise. On the other hand, it is possible that the foreign expertise would be supplied more efficiently through general marketing firms rather than through links with individual production units.

The general import of the preceding argument is that if the recommendations of the Report concerning trade policy were put into effect the level of direct foreign investment in non-extractive activities might decline.[30] Nevertheless, in some activities it would remain a profitable use of foreign firms' capital[31] and it is therefore necessary to consider whether or not any disadvantages accrue to an economy from foreign investment even when it is not protected. It will become apparent that the answer to this question is not unrelated to the state of the domestic capital market.

Arguments that direct foreign investment may be disadvantageous even in the absence of protection are typically related to its effect on the development of local entrepreneurship. Unfortunately, this is an aspect of the problem where evidence is hard to come by. Those who are dubious of the value of foreign investment tend to assume that it is always competitive with local entrepreneurship and, in addition, that investment opportunities are strictly limited. Now, while this is by no means an inaccurate description of the state of affairs when foreign investment flows into import substitute activities which are heavily protected, it is much less likely to be the case when foreign firms receive no protection.[32] In this case the foreign firm is likely to have an advantage which is extremely scarce in the recipient country or else to be taking up investment opportunities which would otherwise not be taken up because of a shortage of domestic entrepreneurs or saving.

Nevertheless, some writers such as Griffin [13 and 14] tend to take the view that foreign investment simply displaces domestic investment. Whether this would occur in a relatively open economy is doubtful for the reasons already suggested, but the outcome would seem to depend on the answers given to the following questions:

(1) To what extent is the level of domestic saving "determined" by domestic investment opportunities both for entrepreneurs to reinvest profits and for individual savers to find suitable outlets for their savings? How far, in other words, do domestic capitalists save and invest so as to carry out all projects

yielding some minimum rate of return which is similar to the minimum rate of return acceptable to foreign investors?[33]

(2) How are domestic investment opportunities affected by the establishment of foreign firms? For example, does foreign investment break important bottlenecks, opening up new opportunities for local capital,[34] or does it preempt the best opportunities because of its access to larger capital resources with adverse effects on the development of local entrepreneurship?

The most likely set of circumstances where direct foreign investment could have the effect of basically substituting for domestic investment would be where local firms are constrained by a lack of capital and this capital is not available from local savers because of capital market imperfections. Lack of institutions which issue acceptable paper to savers may well mean that savers are legally or illegally accumulating foreign assets while firms which are perfectly capable of competing with foreign firms cannot obtain capital. This possibility underlines the potential importance of improving domestic capital market institutions. Not least important, these institutions might serve as a basis for attracting a greater flow of portfolio capital from abroad for use by domestic firms (pp. 115–18 of the Report).

A special situation exists where domestic saving is not directly convertible into foreign exchange.[35] Normally a rise in domestic saving can be expected to release resources which can produce exportable goods (or import substitutes) or to reduce the demand for imports. However, it is possible that this does not occur. One well recognized case is where the foreign elasticity of demand is less than unity so that an increase in exports leads to a fall in foreign exchange receipts. Another situation is where a reduction in demand occurs for goods which are not exportable and have very low import content and where the factors which produce them cannot produce exportables or import substitute goods. No doubt such cases do exist and if they do domestic investment—which typically has quite a large import content—will not be able to take place unless foreign exchange inflows increase. In this case foreign investment will be especially valuable since it will provide employment which domestic firms are unable to do and if the foreign firm is an export industry which yields the government tax revenue or a genuine import saver foreign exchange inflows will increase and domestic investment will be able to expand.

(c) Investment in Extractive Industries

The preceding discussion has been largely concerned with direct foreign investment in non-extractive industries (though the last few paragraphs have dealt with some of the factors relevant to an assessment of investment in the extractive industries) reflecting the belief that it is here that the major impact of the implementation of the Report's recommendations would be felt since implementation would change the whole pattern of incentives affecting foreign investment in manufacturing. It is time, however, to look briefly at the rather different situation likely to exist in the extractive industries.

Since virtually all foreign investment in extractive industries is concerned with the production of materials for export and the level of protection on these products (at least in unprocessed form) is usually very low in developed countries, adoption of the Report's trade policy recommendations cannot be expected to change the environment in which foreign investment in this sector takes place too drastically. However, a reduction in the degree of over-valuation of exchange rates in less developed countries could contribute to a useful encouragement of purchases of locally produced commodities and services by foreign firms. At the moment these firms often have a substantial incentive to import as much of their requirements as possible, since the exchange rate at which they can convert foreign currency earnings into the domestic currency needed to purchase local products is often very unfavourable to them. Such increases in local purchases would serve to reduce the much criticized enclave characteristics of firms operating in the extractive industries.[36]

Extractive activities tend to be in fields where local enterprise is very likely to be at a relative disadvantage, at least in the early stages of development of the resources. This relative disadvantage arises from the high degree of technical and organizational complexity of some of these activities and the very large amounts of capital which are required and which often have to be invested for a number of years before returns begin to be realized. In addition, the stages of exploration and development are characterized by high risk and multinational enterprises operating in many countries are probably in a better position to bear these risks than individuals or even Governments in relatively poor countries.

For all these reasons one might predict the continued importance of direct foreign investment in extractive industries, but the prime reason for its likely continued importance lies in the market structure in which the firms concerned operate in industries like copper and bauxite mining and petroleum production. This structure can be loosely described as vertically integrated oligopoly. This market structure characteristic, more than anything else, probably explains the dominance of multinational corporations in this field and why they can be expected to remain important on the scene.

The fact that a great deal of the mineral and petroleum output of the world moves through the channels of vertically integrated organizations rather than being traded on the open market presents any independent producer of the raw material with substantial risks. He is dependent for market outlets not so much on independent processers as on processers who are typically part of firms which also produce the raw material. Even if capital were available and experts could be hired the investment might be somewhat precarious.

This situation has been vigorously criticized by a number of writers[37] who correctly argue that less developed countries may suffer as a result of these arrangements. Girvan [12, p. 13], for example, points out that if a multinational corporation which is extracting minerals from a less developed country were to build a processing plant in, say, Canada, it would not be likely to make a subsequent processing investment in the less developed country even if the Canadian investment proved to be much less efficient than one which could, in the light of new information, be made in the less developed country. If the mineral were being mined by an independent producer, however, a processing plant could be established if sales could be made in an open market. Again, the level of output (and, hence, tax receipts) may be restricted by the owner of a concession because he has only limited marketing and processing facilities but does not want to sell to rival firms who compete with him in final markets.[38]

Nevertheless, less developed countries which are exporters of minerals and petroleum may on balance be net gainers from the system of which they are a part. This would be the case if the oligopolists are successful in maintaining prices at a higher level than would otherwise be the case and if demand for the products is relatively inelastic. Furthermore, the prices on which tax payments are based may be significantly higher than prices which could be realized on the open market.[39]

Although one can predict the continued importance of direct foreign investment in the extractive industries, the terms on which it takes place are already changing substantially. The Governments of less developed countries are becoming aware of the fact that in the past sales of concessions and very long leases have meant that on successful ventures foreign firms have reaped extremely large profits. Present leasing arrangements are usually for much shorter terms and frequently provide for additional payments by foreign investors if output turns out to be greater than initially predicted.

The contracts which have been made between oil companies and the Indonesian authorities illustrate the sort of arrangements which may become widespread in the extractive industries.[40] In these contracts, which are for thirty years, the foreign firm is viewed as a contractor of the State petroleum company, Pertamina. When a concession is granted the company accepts the risks of exploration and initial development. It is typically allowed 40 per cent of the crude oil produced as an offset against past and current expenses. The remaining 60 per cent of crude oil is divided 35/65 in favour of Pertamina. Provision is usually made for additional payments if output exceeds certain levels. These may be either fixed money amounts or else a reduction in the company's share of crude on the marginal units of output. Finally, it is worth stressing that the valuation of oil is based on "open market prices", i.e. prices obtainable in arms length bargaining with independent refiners rather than the tax reference prices used in many Middle East contracts [16 p. 98] so that the Indonesian authorities share with the companies the gains and losses resulting from price fluctuations.[41]

Contracts such as these go a long way towards ensuring that less developed countries obtain maximum return from extractive activities carried on within their boundaries while at the same time benefiting from the special advantages which foreign firms possess in these industries. In the Indonesian case, the foreign firm bears the risks of exploration and development and puts up the capital for investment. At the same time, the marketing facilities of the company are available to the Indonesian authorities if they choose to sell their share of the oil abroad rather than use it for domestic purposes.

III FOREIGN ENTERPRISES AND THE DOMESTIC CAPITAL MARKET

(a) Local borrowing by foreign enterprises

Foreign enterprises are often heavily criticized for borrowing in the local capital market so, it is argued, reducing the supply of funds available to domestic firms. There is a certain degree of paradox here in that foreign firms are also criticized for not becoming integrated into the local economy—specifically in this context, not allowing local equity participation in their undertakings.

The Report recognizes that local borrowing can be undesirable when interest rates are kept artificially low by Government policies, usually creating a substantial excess demand for funds which naturally tend to be lent to enterprises with the highest credit ratings—very often foreign-owned companies. The remedy is to have a more sensible capital market policy, one which will encourage local savers to invest in domestic financial institutions by allowing them a realistic return which will also tend to deter foreign firms from borrowing. It is rather ludicrous that capital scarce economies should often have lower interest rates than capital abundant ones.[42] This recommendation, of course, again reflects the Report's view that there is a great deal which less developed countries can do to avoid any disadvantages which may result from the presence of foreign firms operating within their boundaries.

Kindleberger [24, p. 99] has pointed out that if a country is well integrated with the world capital market and looking at the problem from the vantage point of general equilibrium there is no reason why that country should deter borrowing by foreign enterprises. If foreign firms increase their borrowing, interest rates will rise and capital will flow in from abroad. There is no presumption that there is a fixed quantity of funds available for investment. Nevertheless, one may question whether the interest elasticity of capital flows to less developed countries is sufficiently great to allow this problem to be completely dismissed.[43] Particularly if it is thought undesirable to change interest rate policy in line with the Report's recommendation restrictions on the access of foreign firms to local funds may be desirable.

However, the general equilibrium perspective is valuable in clarifying thought on these matters. Consider, for example, the balance of payments effect of the issue of equity shares to local investors.[44] While it is possible that this merely draws funds away from domestic firms it is by no means impossible that the funds used would otherwise have been invested abroad. Local firms may be unwilling to issue shares because they wish to retain the ownership of companies in family hands so that the issue of shares by foreign firms introduces a type of financial asset not previously available in the country. So far, therefore, there may be a balance of payments gain. But the foreign firm might very well have invested anyway. In this case a reduced capital outflow will be offset by a reduced inflow and the short-term balance of payments effect is zero.[45]

Whatever the short-term situation, the long-term balance of payments effect is not zero since future profit repatriation depends upon the division of ownership of the foreign firm (or subsidiary) between nationals and foreigners. It is here that the demand for local participation, the value of which the Report is somewhat sceptical about, has force. There will be long-term gains to nationals if the company's shares earn a higher rate of return than alternative foreign assets which individuals could hold. It is not the same thing that nationals may be able to purchase shares in the parent company since the local branch may be the most profitable part of the corporation [24, p. 30].

These considerations naturally lead to the question of the eventual operation of a foreign enterprise by nationals. A major criticism of the failure of most foreign enterprises to gradually extend local ownership by issuing shares in the local branch is that it makes it extremely difficult for any group of domestic entrepreneurs to gain control of the operation. This is true even if they could operate the firm more efficiently than the foreign entrepreneurs and so would be willing to pay a price for the assets of the company beneficial to the foreign shareholders. The reason why this is so is that without shares being issued giving ownership in the local plant there is no direct contact between a potential purchaser and foreign shareholders. Domestic interests wishing to purchase a controlling interest in the local plant must negotiate with the management of the parent company and, within limits, the management is likely to be unwilling to dispose of the plant (and hence of control of some top managerial posts) even if this would be in the interests of the shareholders. This situation can be expected to be a cause of considerable embitterment in the relationship between foreign investors and the local government and business community. "Expropriation" may be the only way in which a transfer of ownership, and more importantly, operation can take place.

(b) *Takeovers of Domestic Firms by Foreign Firms*

In the previous section we have examined the problems of a domestic firm or group taking over a foreign subsidiary. But the problem which has concerned a number of less developed countries is the reverse. Local firms are being taken over by foreign ones. This is a topic not considered by the Report yet is a matter on which there are extremely strong feelings.

One can, of course, argue that apart from the situation where a takeover strengthens or establishes a monopoly position there is nothing to be feared. The owners of the firm presumably get a higher price than from any potential domestic purchaser. There is an inflow of foreign currency (or a reduction in outflow if retained earnings are used to purchase the firm) which gives rise to a future outflow. The domestic sellers of the firm may conceivably invest elsewhere in the economy in an activity more suited to their talents and abilities. Some of the advantages which accrue to the economy from direct foreign investment such as demonstration of superior techniques and assistance to suppliers and users of the product will occur almost as much in this case as when completely new facilities are established.

However, one cannot help feeling that this is not the whole story. Morley and Smith [32, p. 134] cite the experience of Brazil in 1964–6 when local firms, hard pressed by a liquidity crisis induced by monetary policy aimed at stabilizing the price level were purchased at knock-down prices by foreign firms who had access to credit abroad. It would seem to be at least open to question whether such a transfer of ownership meant a shift of assets into the hands of more efficient entrepreneurs. Had Brazilian entrepreneurs been able to reschedule their liabilities by having access to foreign capital on equal terms with foreign firms it is at least possible that they would have been unwilling to sell. It must not be forgotten that from the vantage point of the economy as a whole the fact that a company suffers from a liquidy squeeze may not reflect poor management so much as an inadequately developed capital market which forces domestic firms to rely on relatively high cost, short-term credit.[46] To counterbalance this market imperfection which gives a false impression of the real productivity of resources under domestic and foreign management, some restrictions on takeovers at least in times of general monetary stringency and stabilization can probably be justified. This is, of course, especially true if the firms concerned operate in a protected market where foreign ownership increases the possibility of net loss to the economy.

Dunning [11, pp. 324–7] has suggested a further reason why takeovers of domestic firms by foreign firms might not be desirable. His argument is that if foreign firms are significantly larger and have more diversified interests than domestic firms they may well be willing to pay a higher price for a domestic firm than any domestic purchaser because they are able to accept a higher degree of variance about a given expected value of an asset. But variance matters much more to the individual firm than to the economy as a whole. Consequently there is a divergence between social and private benefits and some restrictions on take-overs of domestic firms by foreign firms might be justified.

IV PORTFOLIO CAPITAL AND EXPORT CREDITS

It would appear to follow from the foregoing discussion of direct foreign investment, always assuming that policy changes in both developed and less developed countries permit the growth of export based manufacturing, that some change in pattern will occur over the next two decades. The continued presence of foreign firms in extractive industries is likely because of the magnitude of the capital required, the risks involved and the market structure of the industries concerned. As far as manufacturing is concerned, however, it is likely that the relative importance of direct foreign investment will decline and be increasingly replaced by a greater emphasis on managerial contracts involving foreign management for limited periods of time and by direct purchases of technical information by firms in less developed countries from firms in developed ones.

Although the successful prosecution of an outward looking growth strategy by less developed countries may be possible with relatively little direct foreign investment in the manufacturing and service sectors, it is nevertheless the case that in many countries the pace of development would be accelerated if firms in these countries had access to the private savings of developed countries. In the early stages of the establishment of a new firm it may require foreign exchange to purchase capital equipment as well as to pay for foreign managerial and technical advice. Although the scarcity of domestic savings can be exaggerated, some supplementation of these will often be useful.[47]

At the moment flows of portfolio capital, largely restricted to bond financing, are limited both by a lack of credit worthiness of most firms in less developed countries as far as world capital markets are concerned and by restrictions on access to these capital markets. Bond financing is, indeed, dominated by the borrowings of the Governments of the relatively advanced less developed countries such as Mexico.

Relaxation of restrictions on access to capital markets in developed countries is desirable, but it is doubtful how far relaxation of restrictions alone would contribute to increasing the flow of funds to less developed countries. There would appear to be more scope for the development of schemes which permit savers in developed countries to take equity positions in less developed countries indirectly through the purchase of the paper of financial intermediaries. What would seem to be required is the further development of private development banks in less developed countries and the establishment of mutual funds in developed countries which would invest in the development banks and also, perhaps, in some companies (pp. 117-8 of the Report). These institutional developments would go some way towards improving the capital markets of the less developed countries by providing a much needed source of equity finance for domestic firms and encouraging the development and expansion of a type of institution which can provide outlets for domestic savings as well as a channel through which funds of foreign origin can flow to domestic firms.

A number of private development banks have already been established. The Private Development Corporation of the Philippines is a good example of an institution which is playing an important role in financing and project appraisal in the private sector. Region wide institutions such as the Private Investment Company for Asia are also being formed. These organizations have the advantage of local knowledge which enables them to assess investment prospects much more easily than individuals or institutions based in developed countries.

The establishment of mutual funds in developed countries which would invest in the paper of development banks and perhaps take equity positions in some firms in less developed countries along the lines suggested by Grubel [15] would provide a link between the private investor in the rich countries and the private firm in the developing world.

Improvement in the channels through which equity and loan capital can flow between developed countries and undeveloped countries is desirable as such. But it can also be suggested that it would be highly beneficial to the latter if firms there could directly or indirectly borrow more from developed countries in the form of portfolio capital. This might reduce the importance of supplier credits in the private capital flow to less developed countries, a form of capital flow which is giving rise to some concern (pp. 118–22 of the Report).

Reference to the table on page 1 will show that net supplier credits have been expanding very rapidly in recent years and in 1969 were four-fifths the size of net direct investment. The great bulk of this flow represents credits which are guaranteed in whole or in part by Government agencies in the supplier countries as well as often being provided on subsidized terms. For a number of less developed countries export credits are a major source of foreign exchange funds and for Argentina, Peru, South Korea, Yugoslavia, Ghana and a number of other African countries they are more than 25 per cent of total external debt outstanding (p. 119 of the Report).

A number of disadvantages are believed to follow from the large scale use of export credits. It is argued that they have caused major debt service problems for a number of countries, necessitating in some cases a rescheduling of debts. But it is worth pointing out that the countries, which the Report cites (p. 119) in this connection, i.e. Argentina, Brazil, Chile, Ghana, Indonesia and

Turkey, are all countries which have pursued import substitution policies and to a greater or lesser degree neglected export and agricultural activities (often synonymous). One suspects that in these circumstances any form of capital inflow requiring repayment and servicing in foreign currency would be likely to cause difficulties (pp. 119–20).

Export credits have, in addition, been used to finance some questionably viable public sector projects which could not obtain finance from other sources (p. 120). Once again this is an area where the only real solution lies in policy changes within less developed countries themselves. But it is none the less true that Government sponsored guarantees in lender countries, by reducing the risks to the supplier of the equipment, contribute to the encouragement of such activities. If credit were supplied on the basis that the lender bore all risks one would expect a more careful vetting of the viability of particular projects as well as the country's overall economic position by lenders before they agreed to supply equipment on a credit basis.

It is frequently argued that while the competitive provision of export credit by supplier countries may have reduced the interest charges to users this has been at the expense of competitiveness in price and quality. The Commissioners (p. 119) seem to accept this argument and there is little doubt that cases do occur where the most favourable credit terms are not supplied by the most efficient producer of equipment. This tendency may be strengthened to the extent that the most favourable credit terms are available only if the whole of a project's equipment requirements are supplied by a single firm or country. Access to credit untied to equipment purchases would enable less developed countries to buy in the cheapest market.

Supplier credits may also contribute to a higher import content of investment than is strictly necessary. A firm in a less developed country may find that credit is more easily available and perhaps cheaper when it is purchasing new equipment from abroad than if it wants to borrow domestically for the purchase of domestic materials or imported secondhand equipment. This situation might lead, for example, to the use of imported steel for building construction in place of wood and bricks produced domestically. Again, if credit were available which was untied to new equipment purchases the firm could "shop around" and might find secondhand equipment which was both cheaper and more suited to the factor endowment of the economy. Improvements in the channels through which portfolio finance can flow to less developed countries would clearly be beneficial in this context.

Unless progress is made in the direction of improving the flow of untied portfolio capital to less developed countries it seems reasonable to predict a continuing and growing importance for supplier credits in the total of private capital flows to less developed countries despite their second best nature as compared to loan or equity capital which is freely spendable on world markets.

V CONCLUSION

In this paper my concern has been to give a broad survey of the sort of considerations relevant in assessing the impact of private foreign investment on the development of relatively poor countries. Using the recommendations of the Pearson Report concerning trade policy and capital market policies in both developing and developed countries as a starting point, it has been argued that implementation would be likely to reduce the importance of direct foreign investment in non-extractive activities while opening up opportunities for a profitable exchange of managerial and skilled labour on a short-term basis. Greater access to the capital markets of the developed countries for the purpose of raising portfolio capital would tend to reduce the importance of supplier credits and direct foreign investment and would be likely to have beneficial effects on resource allocation in less developed countries. On the other hand, failure to implement in particular the trade policy recommendations of the Report will render the contribution of private capital inflows in any form somewhat limited.

NOTES

1 For a general review of capital movements this century, see [11, Chapter 3], and for a review of the period down to 1913 see [43].
2 It should be pointed out that while the Commissioners agreed on this recommendation, there was not unanimity of agreement with the detail of the arguments used to support these recommendations. See p. 104 of the Report.
3 For a detailed study of the commodities involved and demonstration of the comparative advantage of the less developed countries in them, see [25].
4 Plantation investments are not explicitly considered. New foreign investments in this sector are now extremely small and in a number of years since 1945 there has been net disinvestment in this sector.
5 Some writers, for example Dunning, consider this the major contribution of direct foreign investment.

6 The Report deals with most, but not all, of these criticisms in varying depth. In particular, it does not consider the problem of the take-over of local firms by foreign firms and only gives cursory attention to the implications of oligopolistic market structures in industries dominated by multinational firms.

7 What spillovers there are may be damaging, as when high wages paid by foreign companies give rise to the establishment of minimum wage laws based on levels unrelated to the opportunity cost of labour in the economy.

8 On the last two points reference may be made to [21, esp. Chapter 6].

9 For an excellent theoretical analysis of this, the reader is referred to [41] and, for a survey of the effects of this environment on resource use in a number of countries, to [27, Chapter 5].

10 An interesting case study of the textile industry in the Philippines illustrates this point—[42].

11 The Report makes reference to only 27 per cent of direct foreign investment being in manufacturing in 1966. This is a little misleading as the overall figure is heavily weighted by the relative unimportance of manufacturing investments in the Middle East and the dominance of petroleum investment there [38, p. 100]. Reference to the most recent data shows that for 1967–8 foreign investment in manufacturing in the less developed countries of America was over 50 per cent of the total foreign investment in that area, while for Asia and Oceania it was almost 40 per cent (p. 78 of the Report).

12 See [27, Chapter 5] for elaboration of this theme.

13 See, for example, [6, pp. 50–5], and references cited there.

14 In this example the effect of employing the labour on import demand has been totally ignored. In fact, foreign exchange losses would very likely occur as a result of the labour spending its income on exportable goods, or on imports.

15 See [18] for a discussion of direct foreign investment as one means of transferring knowledge.

16 Rapid technical progress in a protected industry may be disadvantageous to the economy. Johnson has shown that technical progress in a protected industry may reduce real income. This occurs when the increase in the efficiency with which resources are used is outweighed by the adverse effect of resources being drawn into the relatively inefficient sector [20].

17 Morley and Smith, in a study of Brazil, find a rank correlation of 0.66 between capital intensity and the share of foreign firms in an industry [32, p. 131]. It is interesting to note that in relatively labour-intensive activities like wood manufacture, Morley and Smith find a total absence of foreign firms.

18 Domestic firms in less developed countries are often limited to capital raised within the family and to bank borrowing.

19 Some writers, notably Hymer [17] argue that foreign firms need some special advantages to offset their disadvantages which are inherent in their operation in relatively unfamiliar surroundings. For a discussion of Hymer's and other views, see [24, pp. 11–24].

20 Davies and Lindert in reviewing the experience of UK and US firms respectively in Singapore stress that a main reason for establishing plants was the fear that either local or foreign firms might be afforded protection [8, p. 57] and [26, p. 161].

21 The Report cites the Latin American car industry as an example (p. 114).

22 For a discussion of the price structure in the international oil industry and the experiences of consuming countries see [36, Chapters 6 and 8].

23 See [3] for a lucid discussion of these matters.

24 There are reasons to believe that foreign firms may be more efficient at training some types of labour than trade schools, Universities and similar institutions. A recent OECD report [34, 1967, p. 66] points out that the number of people trained by foreign private enterprise at its own expense probably substantially exceeds the number trained under the various official aid programmes. It suggests that aid might be directed towards subsidizing private training facilities. For a similar view, derived from a study of the Philippines, see [28, pp. 92 and 102-3]. Some foreign firms seem to train substantially more people than they require because of difficulties of selection at the pre-training state. The partially-trained "drop-outs" are often able to fill vacancies elsewhere in the economy.

25 A number of recent oil concession agreements contain clauses providing for the training of nationals.

26 For details of non-tariff protection see [2].

27 See Chapter 4 of the Report for an examination of the case for these policy changes.

28 Caves has recently pointed out that direct investment will not take place in the absence of special advantages possessed by foreign firms even if tariffs are in operation. As he puts it, "a tariff protecting a purely competitive industry with *unimpeded entry of domestic capital* [my italics] would foster no direct investment; a foreign entrepreneur contemplating entry could expect only transient windfall profits to stack against the innate disadvantages of being a foreign entrepreneur" [4, p. 9]. It seems likely that in labour-intensive activities the innate disadvantages of the foreign entrepreneur may be quite significant.

29 It is interesting to note that in his discussion of the product cycle theory of international trade which stresses that the less developed countries may be good locations to produce standardized, relatively simple products, Vernon finds little evidence that foreign investment is located to take advantage of relatively low-cost labour [44, pp. 204-5].

30 This must be qualified to the extent that it is believed that capital shortages are a major problem for less developed countries and access to the capital markets of the developed countries remains restricted. In these circumstances foreign firms might have an advantage because of having access to capital markets in their home countries.

31 Import-export merchanting activities may be a field where this is true. Foreign firms with special knowledge of foreign markets and of co-ordinating the marketing of a number of small firms may be able to contribute significantly to economic development and be highly complementary to the activities of domestic firms. This would also seem to be the case where foreign firms have established themselves to co-ordinate the production and marketing of small farmers' products. See [1] for discussion of a French case and [9, p. 342 n.] for reference to Central American experience.

32 In reviewing Philippine experience, Power and Sicat state that in the heavily-protected environment of the last two decades "foreign capital

was seen not as a supplement to Philippine resources nor as a complement to Philippine labour, but simply as a substitute for Philippine capital" [38, p. 103]. Investment opportunities in Philippine manufacturing became increasingly limited once the initial phase of rapid import substitution had passed.

33 If foreign investors have lower risk premia than domestic entrepreneurs or access to cheaper capital, then the total level of investment will be higher if foreign investment is permitted than if it is not. It may be, however, that because of the unfamiliarity of the environment foreign entrepreneurs typically require higher risk premia than domestic ones.

34 It is interesting to note that this is sometimes the effect of investment in the extractive industries. For example, the infrastructural investments or tin mines and rubber plantations in Malaya in the early part of this century gave an important stimulus to local investment.

35 Reference should be made in this context to the literature on the two-gap approach to the evaluation of foreign aid, for example [5, 29].

36 For more detailed reviews of the current situation and likely future developments in the mineral and petroleum industries, the reader is referred to [31].

37 Girvan [12] presents a particularly well-developed argument.

38 Professor Penrose has shown how joint ownership of oil concessions by a number of oil companies can result in a restriction of output and investment on the concession [37].

39 On the other hand, it seems that some countries still allow companies to determine their own transfer prices at which raw materials are transferred to processing affiliates. This transfer price is a critical determinant of tax revenues for the Government of the raw material-producing country [12, p. 5].

40 For a full text of a representative contract see [35].

41 See [16] for a further discussion of Indonesian contracts.

42 The paradox which so worries Griffin [14, p. 242] that countries are often large exporters of capital while at the same time they are receiving direct foreign investment and other capital inflows may in large part be explained by the fact that real rates of interest on savings held in the form of financial assets are frequently negative in less developed countries as a result of interest rate controls and inflation.

43 But neither should it be assumed that this elasticity is zero. A rise in domestic interest rates on bank deposits and similar assets may serve to reduce capital outflows and bring about some repatriation of savings held abroad.

44 The cases of Malaysia and Singapore suggest that local investors can be keen buyers of the shares of foreign companies [10].

45 Clearly, this is only one possibility among many. There is also the possibility that the issue of shares by a foreign firm will increase the total flow of saving.

46 This is not always the case. Domestic firms sometimes have access to capital from banks or Government institutions on extremely favourable terms.

47 Griffin [13] has argued that foreign savings tend to displace domestic savings. Some replacement is a predictable consequence of any reduction in the domestic rate of interest as a result of an increase in the

supply of savings from abroad on the assumption that the substitution effect of a fall in the rate of interest on domestic savings outweighs a possible negative income effect. But complete replacement requires that the supply of domestic saving be perfectly elastic at the current rate of interest. On the other hand, it may be that easy access to foreign capital will reduce the incentive of the local government to improve the domestic capital market and/or tax system as has recently been implied by Mamalakis [28, p. 414]. Nevertheless, it can be argued that the same institutional arrangements which would facilitate flows of portfolio capital to less developed countries would also tend to improve their domestic capital markets.

REFERENCES

[1] B. Balassa, "American Investment in the Common Market", *Banca Nazionale del Lavoro, Quarterly Review*, June 1966.

[2] R. E. Baldwin, *Non-Tariff Distortions of International Trade*, Washington, 1970.

[3] J. Bhagwati, *The Theory and Practice of Commercial Policy: Departures from Unified Exchange rates*. Special Papers in International Economics No. 8, Princeton, 1968.

[4] R. E. Caves, "International Corporations: The Industrial Economics of Foreign Investment", *Economica*, February 1971, pp. 1–27.

[5] H. Chenery and A. Strout, "Foreign Assistance and Economic Development", *American Economic Review*, September 1966, pp. 679–733.

[6] W. M. Corden, *The Theory of Protection*, London, 1971.

[7] B. Das Gupta, "The Supply and Price of Imported Crude Oil to India", *Journal of Development Studies*, April 1967.

[8] G. Davies, "United Kingdom Investment" in H. Hughes and You Poh Seng *Foreign Investment and Industrialisation in Singapore*, Canberra, 1969, pp. 46–61.

[9] C. F. Diáz-Alejandro, "Direct Foreign Investment in Latin America" in C. P. Kindleberger (ed.), *The International Corporation*, Cambridge, Mass., 1970.

[10] P. J. Drake, "The New Issue Boom in Malaya and Singapore, 1961–64", *Economic Development and Cultural Change*, October 1969.

[11] J. H. Dunning, *Studies in International Investment*, London, 1970.

[12] N. Girvan, *The Caribbean Bauxite Industry*. Studies in Regional Economic Integration Vol. 2 No. 4, Institute of Social and Economic Research, University of the West Indies, Jamaica, 1967.

[13] K. Griffin, "Foreign Capital, Domestic Savings and Economic Development", *Bulletin of the Oxford Institute of Economics and Statistics*, May 1970, pp. 99–112.

[14] K. Griffin, "The Role of Foreign Capital" in K. Griffin (ed.), *Financing Economic Development in Latin America*, London, 1971.

[15] H. G. Grubel, "A proposal to provide development aid through equity investments and mutual funds", *Economic Record*, March pp. 86–95.

[16] A. Hunter, "Oil Developments", *Bulletin of Indonesian Economic Studies*, March 1971, pp. 96–113.

[17] S. Hymer, *International Operations of National Firms—A Study of Direct Foreign Investment.* Unpublished PhD. dissertation, Massachusetts Institute of Technology, 1960.

[18] H. G. Johnson, "The Efficiency and Welfare Implications of the International Corporation" in C. P. Kindleberger (ed.), *The International Corporation,* Cambridge, Mass., 1970, pp. 35–56.

[19] H. G. Johnson, *Economic Policies Towards Less Developed Countries,* London, 1967.

[20] H. G. Johnson, "The Possibility of Income Losses from Increased Efficiency or Factor Accumulation in the Presence of Tariffs", *Economic Journal,* March 1967, pp. 131–4.

[21] M. Kidron, *Foreign Investments in India,* London, 1965.

[22] P. Kilby, *Industrialisation in an Open Economy: Nigeria 1945–1966,* Cambridge, 1969.

[23] C. P. Kindleberger (ed.), *The International Corporation,* Cambridge, Mass., 1970.

[24] C. P. Kindleberger, *American Business Abroad,* New Haven, 1969.

[25] Hal B. Lary, *Imports of Manufactures from Less Developed Countries,* New York, 1968.

[26] P. H. Lindert, "United States Investment" in H. Hughes and You Poh Seng, *Foreign Investment and Industrialisation in Singapore,* Canberra, 1969, pp. 154–76.

[27] I. Little, T. Scitovsky and M. Scott, *Industry and Trade in Some Developing Countries: A Comparative Study,* London, 1970.

[28] M. Mamalakis, "The Contribution of Copper to Chilean Economic Development, 1920–67: Profile of a Foreign owned Export Sector" in R. F. Mikesell (ed), *Foreign Investment in the Petroleum and Mineral Industries,* Baltimore, 1971, pp. 387–420.

[29] R. H. Mason, "Some Aspects of Technology Transfer", *Philippine Economic Journal,* First Semester 1970, pp. 83–108.

[30] R. I. McKinnon, "Foreign Exchange Constraints in Economic, Development and Efficient Aid Allocation, *Economic Journal,* June 1964, pp. 388–409.

[31] R. F. Mikesell (ed.), *Foreign Investment in the Petroleum and Mineral Industries,* Baltimore, 1971.

[32] S. A. Morley and G. W. Smith, "Import Substitution and Foreign Investment in Brazil", *Oxford Economic Papers,* March 1971, pp. 120–35.

[33] H. Myint, "Dualism and the Internal Integration of Underdeveloped Economies", *Banco Nazionale del Lavoro Quarterly Review,* June 1970, pp. 128–56.

[34] Organization for Economic Co-operation and Development, *Development Assistance, Annual Review,* Paris.

[35] Organization of Petroleum Exporting Countries: "A Typical Indonesian Production Sharing Contract" in *Selected Documents on the International Petroleum Industry 1968,* Vienna, 1969, pp. 81–105.

[36] E. T. Penrose, *The Large International Firm in Developing Countries: The International Petroleum Industry,* London, 1968.

[37] E. T. Penrose, "Vertical Integration with Joint Control of Raw Material, Production: Crude Oil in the Middle East", *Journal of Development Studies,* April 1965, pp. 251–68.

[38] J. Power and G. Sicat, *The Philippines: Industrialisation and Trade Policies,* London, 1971.

[39] Report of the Task Force on the Structure of Canadian Industry. *Foreign Ownership and the Structure of Canadian Industry*, Ottawa, 1968.

[40] Research and Policy Committee of the Committee for Economic Development. *Economic Development Abroad and the Role of American Foreign Investment*, Washington, 1956.

[41] R. R. Rhomberg, "Private Capital Movements and Exchange Rates in Developing Countries" in J. H. Adler (ed.), *Capital Movements and Economic Development*, London, 1970, pp. 411–40.

[42] L. D. Stifel, *The Textile Industry—A Case Study of Industrial Development in the Philippines*, Cornell University South East Asia Program Data Paper No. 49, 1963.

[43] "The Historical Record of International Capital Movements to 1913" in J. H. Adler (ed.), *Capital Movements and Economic Development*, London, 1970, pp. 3–32.

[44] R. Vernon, "International Investment and International Trade in the Product Cycle", *Quarterly Journal of Economics*, May 1966, pp. 190–207.

[45] R. Vernon, "The Future of the Multinational Enterprise" in C. P. Kindleberger (ed.), *The International Corporation*, Cambridge, Mass., 1970.

2

THE PEARSON REPORT: A REVIEW

by

P. T. Bauer and B. S. Yamey

London School of Economics and Political Science

THE PEARSON REPORT : A REVIEW

I THE CASE FOR AID

(a) Aid in Retrospect

The central theme of the Pearson Report is the uncompromising advocacy of a large and sustained expansion of intergovernmental aid to less developed countries (ldcs), to enable them to achieve self-sustaining growth by the end of the century and thus to become independent of aid. The developed countries are urged to provide the necessary resources, partly as a matter of moral obligation, and partly as a matter of political and economic self-interest.

The central theme that aid promotes growth significantly is advanced confidently. Yet the Report does not examine systematically or in any detail the economic effects and other repercussions of aid since its inception some twenty years before the appointment of the Commission. The neglect of these central issues is especially unexpected because the World Bank, which sponsored the Report as a Grand Assize on aid, specifically asked the Commission to "study the consequences of twenty years of development assistance" and to "assess the results" (p. vii).

The Commission makes large claims for two decades of foreign aid and the national development efforts it has supported. "The experience which we have gained in the last two decades bears out the premise—and the promise—of the effort that has been made. Economic growth in many of the developing countries has proceeded at faster rates than the industrialized countries ever enjoyed at a similar stage in their own history" (p. 3). The impression is given unmistakably that foreign aid played a crucial and material part in this achievement. Yet a subsequent five-page section entitled "The Contribution of Foreign Aid" (pp. 48–52) is more cautious in parts. "The correlation between the amounts of aid received [by individual countries] in the past decades and the growth performance is very weak" (p. 49). The Commission goes on to attempt to explain this unpromising result; but in doing so it refers to so many and such diverse possible factors in operation that one might well question whether any relation between aid and growth can be established from the record: "results will depend on many variables" and "the growth process is still mysterious" (p. 52). After a discussion which notes a few of the difficulties of assessing the effects of aid, the Commission observes that "nonetheless, it is clear that aid . . . has helped to make possible a good record of development in the past two decades" (p. 52). So far from this conclusion being clear, the statement is a simple *non sequitur* on the showing of the Commission's own discussion.

Establishment of the effects of aid on the rates of progress in the economies of the recipients raises complex issues of method, and analysis would have to be conducted on a level of discourse different from that of the Report. The difficulties reflect primarily the familiar problem of establishing causal relationships among specified variables, where a situation or a process is affected simultaneously by numerous past and present influences which, moreover, operate with various time lags. These difficulties are especially great in attempts to relate the progress of a whole economy to the operation of a specific variable such as the inflow of foreign aid. The economic performance and progress of an economy is an aspect of its general historical development which is affected by numerous factors, many of which do not readily lend themselves to economic analysis.

The Commission boldly assumes that aid promotes growth in the sense of raising per capita incomes; that it is indeed indispensable for achieving tolerable or acceptable rates of growth; and that increased aid will bring about the self-sustaining growth of most developing countries by the end of the century. In advancing these assumptions or conclusions the Report does not even attempt to examine the relative performance of ldcs which did and those which did not receive appreciable volumes of aid. It also does not so much as mention the arguments that foreign aid and the policies it has supported may have obstructed rather than promoted development of the recipients.

(b) The Central Theme

The central theme assumes axiomatically that aid promotes development and is, indeed, indispensable for a reasonable rate of material progress in ldcs because without it the volume of investment expenditure which is said to be a necessary and largely a sufficient condition for material progress cannot be secured without painful or even intolerable reduction in consumption. The derivation proceeds as follows: faster growth requires more investment expenditure; an increase in investment expenditure is necessarily at the expense of current consumption, and is therefore constrained by the low level of economic achievement in ldcs where a reduction in consumption implies severe hardship; foreign aid relaxes the constraint by providing additional resources to augment investment expenditure without subtracting from consumption. Each of the several links in the chain of causation is invalid.

Investment expenditure (especially when on a scale implying material depression of living standards) is neither necessary nor sufficient for the economic development of ldcs.

First and foremost, investment must be unproductive in the absence of the necessary co-operant factors, both in the form of a supply of labour with suitable skills, and also in the wider sense of the presence of appropriate abilities, attitudes, motivations and institutions. Moreover, investment will be unproductive unless there is a market for ensuing products. The presence of these required favourable conditions cannot legitimately be taken for granted. These considerations are especially likely to be ignored when it is believed that all expenditure termed investment is productive or indispensable for development, and when those who decide on the volume and direction of investment expenditures do not spend their own resources.

Second, productive investment or an increase in investment need not call for appreciable reduction of consumption. Highly productive capital formation is often not at the expense of consumption but at the expense of leisure, especially in that phase of economic development when subsistence production and customary methods give way to production for the market. This conclusion applies for instance to that large volume of direct investment, especially in agriculture, which has often contributed greatly to economic development in many countries, but which is neglected or understated in statistics of capital formation. Further, incomes can often be increased considerably without additional investment through more efficient use of resources with the aid of simple changes in techniques, or under the impact of new market opportunities. Moreover, some types of investment bring about changes which economize in capital or promote its more efficient use in other activities. For instance, investment in transport often promotes reduction in the requirements of working capital.

Third, the notion that an increase in investment expenditure implies reduction in consumption involves an inappropriate simplification; two categories of expenditure are treated as competitive when they often are complementary. An increased supply or greater variety of consumer goods has often served as inducement to improved economic performance, through additional effort or more effective deployment of resources; and the improved performance has made possible higher levels both of capital formation and of consumption.[1] More generally, an increase in national income brought about by a more efficient use of resources, including their re-allocation to benefit from changing market opportunities, is likely to promote both higher consumption and increased capital formation.

It is therefore, not surprising that many ldcs progressed rapidly between the last quarter of the nineteenth century and the middle of the twentieth century without either foreign aid or depression of living standards: on the contrary, economic progress went hand in hand with improvements in general living standards. (Had this not been so, one would not have referred to the development as economic progress.) The many examples include Japan, Hong Kong, Thailand, Malaysia, Gold Coast-Ghana, Nigeria and Mexico. Nor did the rapid material progress of western Europe and North America in the eighteenth and nineteenth centuries necessitate reductions in general living standards.[2] Nor does it follow that their economic progress would have been faster had governments enforced reductions in current consumption to promote higher investment expenditure.

Enforced current austerity in no way ensures future prosperity. The economic effects of an investment programme depend on the productivity of the expenditure, and also on the repercussions of the collection and disbursement of funds. We have already noted that the productivity (that is a return in excess of cost) of a piece of expenditure should not be taken for granted. Moreover, such investment expenditures usually require additional taxation, frequently accompanied by the imposition of specific controls, and these measures tend to retard economic development. To note but one obvious effect, the taxation required to finance these expenditures has substantial disincentive effects on saving and enterprise, which can offset any increase in income flowing directly from the additional investment. These disincentive effects are likely to be especially pronounced in economies with a large subsistence sector.

The Report nowhere suggests that governments in some ldcs may have damaged both the current and the prospective performance of their economies by accelerating the rate of investment expenditures, financed through taxation. Although there are criticisms in general terms of details of policies and their implementation (especially in Chapter 3), the impression is clearly conveyed that the raising of the rate of investment expenditures, or the maintenance of a high rate, is necessary, laudable and obviously beneficial. The fact that in the 1960s "poor countries ... have in fact mobilized the bulk of their investment capital" is hailed as a "dramatic achievement since a high savings rate accomplished at low levels of income means a heavy sacrifice", "usually through taxes" (equated with "putting aside income") (p. 30). The Commission regards it as self-evident that the sacrifices were worthwhile and indeed necessary. The economic effects of this taxation are not considered, and the productivity of the expenditures financed by it is assumed or asserted but not demonstrated. In accordance with the Commission's belief in the efficacy of investment expenditure, its own criteria for the allocation of aid include prominently the achievement of "adequate and sustained increases in the ratio of domestic savings to national income" (p. 132).

Suppose it were true, however, that economic progress could be materially accelerated by increases in investment expenditure beyond the capacity of the countries in question to finance from domestic resources. It would not even then follow that foreign aid would be necessary to achieve the desired result. Additions to a country's domestic resources can come from abroad in the form of loans from foreigners negotiated by domestic borrowers, whether individual, firms or governments, or of direct investment by foreigners.

The Report suggests that the need to finance infrastructure investments specifically calls for aid because foreign investors will not make direct investments in such forms (pp. 16 and 122). But if such investment promises to be productive, the government can borrow abroad commercially and service the loans. Moreover, historically direct foreign investment has included substantial additions to investment in infrastructure, as is in fact noted in the Report (p. 101).

(c) Repercussions of Aid

Foreign aid is thus not indispensable for the economic progress of ldcs; the rate of their advance is not determined by investment expenditure; and the latter is not constrained decisively by their poverty. Foreign aid does, however, represent a net inflow of resources without charge, or else on terms substantially below commercial terms. But it does not follow from this consideration that aid necessarily promotes the development of the recipients. There are many reasons why in practice it may retard development rather than promote it; none of these reasons is mentioned in the Report. This highly important and complex subject cannot be developed in detail here, but it is easy to see that aid does not necessarily promote economic development simply because it is a subsidy or a gift. Here are some of the reasons why this is so.[3]

Investment expenditures made possible by foreign aid may have a negative productivity. The project or programme may in time absorb a greater volume of domestic resources than the value (to the economy) of its output. This can happen where the domestic resources necessary to maintain or continue the operations of a plant or project have been under-estimated, and where for reasons of prestige the venture cannot be jettisoned. That such an outcome is not improbable is suggested both by the total failure of numerous aid-financed projects in South Asia and in East and West Africa and also by the instances in which effective protection of manufacturing industries in developing countries has been found to exceed 100 per cent (which means that the activity absorbs domestic resources in excess of the value of the net output).

But foreign aid can and often does set up much wider and pervasive adverse repercussions.

Foreign aid means that additional resources are made available to the government of the recipient country. It enlarges the resources of the government relatively to the rest of the economy. It increases the centralisation of power, especially in countries in which comprehensive economic planning is practised. Because the attainment or maintenance of political control is consequentially more important, political tensions are exacerbated, and regional and ethnic conflicts of interest become more pronounced. The greater the volume of resources at the disposal of the government, the higher are the prizes of political power. The increase in the weight or scope of government diverts the energy of able and ambitious men from economic activity to political pursuits. All these tendencies are likely to retard economic progress.

The expectation that aid will be forthcoming to help bail out a country which has got into economic difficulties has also tended to encourage the pursuit of policies likely to endanger or retard economic progress. This encouragement has been the more powerful where the policies in question have a political appeal because of their attractiveness to influential groups.

Policies of extravagant government expenditure or of wasteful protection of particular industries have been more easily instituted and implemented where there has been a reasonable expectation that the adverse economic effects would be counterbalanced, at least in part, by future inflows of aid. Where such policies led to balance-of-payments difficulties, the case for further aid could be made to appear stronger, especially when, as has been the tendency, such payments difficulties have come to be regarded, mistakenly, as an indication that a vigorous, purposeful and effective development policy has been followed.[4] For the same reason foreign aid programmes have strengthened the inclinations of some governments to avoid changes and policies which might have encouraged highly productive direct investment by foreign firms, which would not only provide foreign exchange but also introduce necessary co-operant factors, notably administrative and technical knowledge and skills.[5] Again, the availability of aid makes it less likely and urgent for governments to resist the introduction of policies which, however politically popular they may be among some sections of the population, are bound to reduce economic growth. Such policies include the expropriation of private firms, the expropriation of landowners, the restriction of the economic activities of minority groups or their expulsion, and the establishment of statutory monopolies in activities in which there are no significant scale economies. The Report does not refer to such policies which have been significant features in several ldcs in the period covered by its review.[6]

It is not suggested here that such policies, inimical to long-term economic progress, might not have been pursued in some countries but for the receipt and expectation of foreign aid. But there can be no doubt that foreign aid programmes have encouraged such policies to be more ambitious and to be continued for longer periods (and therefore to be more disadvantageous) than they would otherwise have been. Moreover, in some major instances the donors have not only encouraged the pursuit of such policies but have made it clearly understood that their adoption or intensification would be considered a favourable feature in the allocation of aid.

Thus the major theme in the Report that foreign aid has contributed significantly to the progress of ldcs, and that its sustained and large-scale expansion is necessary for the acceleration of their economic progress so as to reach an acceptable level, is untenable. While foreign aid may well promote or accelerate growth, it certainly does not necessarily achieve this effect and often has not achieved it. It may have a favourable effect in countries where the conditions necessary for economic progress are present and where appropriate policies are followed. In such situations, however, absence of aid would not prevent growth because foreign resources would in the circumstances be made available on commercial terms.[7] At best, then, the contribution of foreign aid would be the saving in the cost of servicing loans.

The Commission proposes an increase in official aid from the 1968 level of 0.39 per cent of the GNP of donors to 0.70 per cent by 1975, that is an increase by more than three-quarters.[8] This increase is said to be required to raise the rate of growth in the GNP of the underdeveloped world to 6 per cent from the current level of 5 per cent per annum.

We have shown that aid does not ensure the promotion of growth and may well retard it. It follows from this that by linking the volume of aid to the attainment of specific increases in the growth rate of the ldcs, the Commission's proposals would involve the donors in undertaking an open-ended commitment. Whatever the merits of the Pearson proposals, they cannot possibly suffice to ensure a specified target rate of growth. Moreover, even if such a growth rate were attained, there can be no assurance that it will be sustained. It is obvious from the phenomenon of economic decline that there is no such thing as self-sustaining growth. Further, the Commission envisages continued aid until self-sustaining growth is achieved without balance-of-payments difficulties. Yet such difficulties can arise and can be brought about at any level of growth rate or level of economic attainment. Indeed, governments of ldcs will be tempted to ensure payments difficulties if these can be invoked as evidence of need for aid. Thus, again, the commitment is seen to be open-ended.

This list of grounds why the proposals of the Commission imply an open-ended commitment is not comprehensive but is sufficient to make the point.

(d) The External Constraint

The Commission's central argument that aid is required to provide investible resources obtainable otherwise only at the cost of prohibitive sacrifices is buttressed by a subsidiary argument. This argument is that without aid the ldcs could not import sufficient equipment and consumer goods which they need for adequate development.

This argument, although it is secondary to the Commission's main argument for aid, is nevertheless important because it is required to reconcile a major contradiction. On the one hand, the Commission urges that without aid economic development would require heavy sacrifices for the financing out of domestic resources of the necessary investment. On the other hand, the Commission itself suggests that foreign aid is small in relation to the total income or even to the total investment of the recipients. This contradiction would be resolved at least in part if aid could be shown to fulfil a crucial role in which its contribution cannot be expressed appropriately in quantitative terms. The Commission writes: "Foreign exchange is a crucial resource in development planning. All developing countries are forced to rely on imported equipment and, to a large extent, on imported raw materials and spare parts without which their own resources cannot be pressed into service" (p. 69). And: "The experience summarized in Annex I bears out our belief that there are many specific instances in which foreign exchange constraints impede [here this must mean "have impeded"] development efforts" (p. 78).

But this reasoning is no more valid than the principal thesis linking aid to investment expenditure and to development. To begin with, many ldcs have progressed, often rapidly, without payments difficulties, both in the recent and in the more distant past. (And, of course, payments difficulties are not a prerogative of ldcs but are unfortunately often experienced in advanced countries.)

The Commission's argument based on the external constraint implies extreme immobility of domestic resources, whether as the result of the specificity of resources or as a result of an inability or unwillingness to follow policies promoting or even permitting changes in the deployment of resources. It implies that resources cannot be shifted from production for the home market to production for export or for import substitution. If a country's resources were so immobile its development prospects would be bleak, so much so that aid would make little difference even if used optimally and without adverse side effects. Further, even if at a particular time lack of some specific imports retarded development, aid would not be indispensable as it would then be worthwhile for the government to borrow abroad commercially.

There is no external constraint on the development process distinct from and additional to that of the limitation of domestic resources. The frequent payments difficulties of many (though by no means all) developing countries are usually corollaries of the pursuit of government policies which result in a volume of monetary demand which brings about claims on resources in excess of the value of current output (augmented by the inflow of foreign capital and drafts on reserves at the rate considered safe). This source of payments difficulties is recognized at one point in the text of the Report, where it is noted that inflationary policies of some countries have been "at the core of their balance-of-payments problems" (p. 75).[9] These difficulties are not corollaries of rapid economic development, nor evidence of such development or of effective policies of development.

Both the volume of imports (including so-called required imports) and also the volume of exports are largely affected by government policy. The payments difficulties of ldcs which derive from inflationary monetary and fiscal policies have often been intensified by various other policies which have impaired their trade and payments performance. Notable examples include the maintenance of over-valued exchange rates (over-valued in the context of the financial and fiscal policies pursued); heavy taxation of agriculture; and expensive subsidization of manufacturing industry and of state enterprise. Foreign aid has encouraged the pursuit of policies which expand the volume of imports required to sustain sectors favoured by government while at the same time they impair the expansion of exports. Indeed, aid is often regarded as necessary for the pursuit of just these policies.

This conclusion is borne out by certain observations in a recent perceptive study by Professor H. Myint: [10]

> The advocates of domestic industrialization policies tend to underrate the potentialities of internal economic policies and seek to relieve the effects of domestic distortions in the allocation of resources[11] by means of external aid. Thus it is paradoxical to describe such policies as "inward-looking" when their main underlying emphasis is on economic aid (and trade concessions) to be administered from outside . . .

> Aid is treated here [in certain influential circles] as a means of providing the underdeveloped countries with strategic imports which they are supposed to require in fixed proportions as technical inputs for the expansion of their domestic manufacturing sector.

Thus the alleged presence of an external constraint does not remove the basic inconsistency in the Report which we have noted. Nor does it supply an argument for aid. The reverse is more nearly true, as aid has encouraged policies leading to payments difficulties.

The need for technical aid is related to the external constraint and provides another subsidiary argument for aid in the Report. However, although the advocacy of aid under this heading is emphatic, the Commission does not make large claims here, as is suggested by the following passages:

> Only too often the transfer of knowledge and know-how becomes a mechanical projection of the rich countries' own view of technology and education, while low-income countries need new and different solutions to their unique problems (pp. 179–80).

> Experience indicates that technical assistance often develops a life of its own, little related either in donor or recipient countries to national or global development objectives (p. 180).

> Low-income countries have increasingly come to realize that technical assistance, ostensibly a grant, may, in fact, represent a considerable cost to the recipient (p. 182).

> The supply of competent people from the donor countries for overseas work is limited . . . In very general terms—and allowing for some notable exceptions—most developing countries seem increasingly dissatisfied with the quality of technical assistance personnel (p. 184).

The changes required for material progress of most developing countries are not those which require transfer of technology, or which would be brought about by its attempted transfer. The changes of primary importance in this context are those which imply modernization of the mind, that is a change in attitudes, motivations and mores, and also related changes in institutions and political arrangements. Such changes are much more likely to be brought about by perceptive and patient domestic government policy, including attention to the essential well-recognized appropriate functions of government, and also through the operation of a large number of dispersed external contacts, than they can through a transfer of technology and educational techniques financed from abroad. In so far as technical expertise from abroad is useful, Japanese experience suggests that it is more likely to be effective when financed by the host countries from their own resources and on their own initiative since it is then most likely to be geared to their own requirements.

(e) The Performance Test for Aid

The Commission urges that, more so than in the past, "aid should be linked to performance" (p. 127) chiefly because it believes that "with improved assessment and reporting procedures, meaningful judgments with respect to the development performance of aid recipients are feasible. Only if additional aid is increasingly allocated in light of such judgments can it reasonably be expected to progress toward self-sustaining growth" (p. 133).[12] It is clear from the context that here the Commission is advocating the allocation of additional aid resources, administered on a multi-lateral basis, to recipients according to their assessed development performance.

The notion is attractive of treating preferentially recipients of aid who use it effectively. But it is clear from the Commission's own discussion of criteria of allocation, and from the setting within which these criteria are to be applied, that the Commission's proposals will not promote efficiency in the use of aid.

"If ... [the] purpose [of economic aid] is movement toward financial independence [of aid], it has only two *direct* manifestations; namely, adequate and sustained increases in the ratio of domestic savings to national income and in the ratio of exports to imports. The first of these ensures that the country will sooner or later be able to finance its own development from domestic sources, while the second moves to eliminate the balance-of-payments constraint" (p. 132). We have already examined the validity of the underlying ideas; and, as we shall show shortly, there is no likelihood that these criteria will be applied. However, we may note here that countries with successful development experience and sound prospects could fail on either of these criteria. For example, an ldc which is growing rapidly in the course of a large-scale shift from leisure and/or subsistence to more effort-intensive and specialized agricultural production for commercial markets is likely to have a low ratio of domestic savings or capital formation to income (as usually measured). Again, a country with a good record and prospects may be able to attract much private foreign capital: its favourable position and prospects may be accompanied by a lower ratio of domestic savings to national income and of exports to imports than if it were less able to attract, or less willing to accept, private foreign capital.

The Commission proceeds to undermine such value as its tests or criteria might have:

> Of course, use of statistical indicators of this kind must be conditioned by the knowledge that the national accounts of many developing countries are not so reliable, particularly with respect to capital accumulation, that they can be taken as more than circumstantial evidence.[13] Also, such items as export growth are in large part responsive to factors outside the control of most developing countries. Thus sensible judgments cannot rely solely on these indicators and must also take into account the specific obstacles to change, political and social as well as economic, which are faced by the particular country in question (p. 132).

The Commission nevertheless believes that "satisfactory criteria for judging performance can be worked out", and that "those who allocate funds will have little difficulty in distinguishing between good, mediocre, and bad performance" (p. 132). However, the Report does not provide operationally applicable criteria for allocation of aid, a situation which is recognized in the Commission's references to the need to take into account social and political obstacles to change, obstacles which it does not define.

And even if the Commission had proposed operationally applicable criteria, it appears as if it would not have wished to see these enforced. Thus it writes that some countries will "continue to lag behind" and "will continue to receive aid for humanitarian and other reasons" (p. 17). Moreover, in practice it is unrealistic to suppose that, so long as there is an aid programme, aid will not continue to be given, or even be increased, when a country has payments difficulties, regardless of the reasons behind them. Further, the Commission urges donors not to interfere with the domestic policies of recipients: "The formation and execution of development policies must ultimately be the responsibility of the recipient alone, but the donors have a right to be heard and to be informed of major events and decisions" (p. 127). There is no mention here of withholding aid.[14]

Altogether the references in the Report to the conduct of aid recipients are vague but conciliatory; they frequently note the presence of political and social obstacles to development; and the Report allows sympathetically for national aspirations and sensitivities even when these issue in policies obstructing economic development. On the other hand, the recommendations addressed to donors are specific, direct, peremptory, or even stern, as for instance in the recommendations on debt relief, trade policies, and especially the volume and types of aid to be supplied.

The proposal for increased multilateralization of aid is partly based on the view that multilateral agencies will be more ready to apply economic allocation criteria than individual donor countries and that they will be less subject to political pressures. However, the international agencies are unlikely to do better than the Commission in defining sensible and practicable performance tests for the allocation of aid. Nor are they likely to withhold aid from governments pursuing policies adverse to development. In practice almost any allocation decision can be both challenged and defended, at least with superficial plausibility, once it is laid down that social and political obstacles facing growth in the recipient ldc should be taken into account.

The multilateral distribution of aid under the auspices of the international agencies must of necessity be primarily political decisions involving the staffs of these agencies and the representatives of the donors and recipients of aid. The recipients of aid will always find arguments for asking for more money, and especially so if all stigma of receiving it is removed, as it is in the Commission's insistence on equal partnership between donors and recipients. The level of the demands by ldcs, the extent of the support for it by international organizations, and the strength of the resistance by representatives of donors (in so far as they resist it at all) will be determined by the play of political forces, not by the state of knowledge on economic development nor the dictates of economic criteria.

There is indeed no possibility of removing aid from the political arena. It would not be appropriate to do so. Nor is it appropriate to attempt or pretend to do so. Foreign aid is taxpayers' money collected through the political process; and in principle, at any rate, its allocation should take into account the political interests of the donors. And in the recipient countries aid necessarily has various political repercussions, whatever the criteria of its allocation.

Indeed, in one respect transfer of responsibility from national governments to multilateral agencies is likely to reduce further what little effectiveness aid may have as an instrument of development. Such a transfer would sever all connections between the supplier of capital and its user, with the result that the economic effectiveness of expenditure so financed would be scrutinized even less than otherwise.

(f) The Interests of Donors[15]

In a section titled "Why Aid?", the Commission writes that the "simplest answer" to the question why the rich countries should help the poor is the moral one: "that it is only right for those who have to share with those who have not" (p. 8). There is, however, no valid connection between foreign aid and the moral duty of individuals to behave charitably towards the less fortunate or the weaker. The moral obligation to help weaker fellow men is on individuals who can voluntarily give up some of their resources to help others; it is not on such collectivities as the state which derive resources by taxation.

In any event, many taxpayers in the donor countries are poorer than many beneficiaries of aid in the recipient countries: in this respect the operation of aid differs significantly from private charity (and also from that of redistributive taxation). Foreign aid generally favours primarily better-off people in the recipient countries (especially politicians, civil servants, academics and businessmen) and the urban as against the rural population. These are among the persons and groups who tend to benefit directly from aid regardless of its effects on general living standards or on development. The poorest groups in the ldcs, such as the aborigines, the desert peoples and tribal societies, are hardly touched, if at all.

The Commission recognizes at times the inadequacy of the notion that moral obligation as normally understood can serve as an argument for aid. It notes that "moral obligations ... are usually felt with particular force inside national groups to which people belong and with which they identify" (p. 8). But "concern with the needs of other and poorer nations" (note the shift from "those who have not" to "poorer nations") is for the Commission "the expression of a new and fundamental aspect of the modern age—the awareness that we live in a village world, that we belong to a world community". "It is this [awareness, presumably] which makes the desire to help into more than a moral impulse felt by an individual; makes it into a political and social imperative for governments ..." (p. 8).

The attempt of the Commission to bridge the gap between moral obligation (of individuals) and social and political imperatives (for governments) does not succeed. If the awareness to which the Commission refers were widespread, there would be no need for governments to have foreign aid policies. It would be enough for them to help organize and direct, without recourse to taxation, the spontaneous reactions of their individual citizens who had this awareness (as is usual when natural catastrophes occur in foreign countries).

The Commission does not regard moral duty as the only or even the principal ground for aid. "There is also [and presumably mainly] the appeal of enlightened and constructive self-interest", which "is a respectable and valid basis for international action and policy" (p. 9). According to the Commission this enlightened self-interest is both economic and political.

Under the former heading, aid is said to benefit donor countries partly "through direct benefits from a bilateral aid relationship and also, more importantly, by the general increase in international trade which would follow international development" (p. 9). However, it is obvious from the Commission's discussion of its contention that the real volume of aid is often over-stated in the conventional statistics that there is nevertheless an appreciable transfer of resources, and thus a real cost and not a net benefit to the donors (pp. 139–41).

The other economic argument advanced by the Commission, that aid benefits the donors through the expansion of world trade as a result of international development, is invalid. It is invalid even if we were to accept as correct the views of the Commission that aid promotes development, that development increases international trade, and that the benefits to the donor countries are measured by the increase in international trade.

Even if foreign aid promoted development, it would not follow that the postulated increase in international trade would exceed that which would take place without aid. The resources represented by foreign aid have alternative uses; the implications of this consideration are neglected in the categorical assertion that foreign aid helps the donors by promoting international trade. In the absence of aid more resources would be invested in the donors' domestic economies, or in the economies of other developed countries, or in ldcs (including loans to their governments), according to the assessment of investors of the likely return. Capital is generally more productive in the donor countries than in the recipient countries. As foreign aid is by definition supplied gratis, or as heavily subsidised loans, foreign aid will retard overall world development through the diversion of investible resources.

These considerations are underlined by the presence in major donor countries of official restrictions on the export of capital and on private investment abroad outside the ldcs. Both in Britain and in the United States private investment in economies outside the underdeveloped world has now for some years been substantially restricted, and made subject to official scrutiny and approval. These restrictions have been justified by reference to balance-of-payments difficulties, which also have been invoked in support of restrictive financial and fiscal policies designed to restrict domestic expenditure. Substantial foreign aid has continued throughout the currency of these measures. These various policies and measures have retarded the material progress of the donors, investment in other developed countries, and thus, almost certainly the growth of world trade. This last result is an especially probable consequence of restrictions on private foreign investment abroad, a notably effective instrument for the promotion of international trade.

It is probable that in the absence of foreign aid the restrictions imposed in developed countries against exports from ldcs would have been opposed far more vigorously in both developed countries and ldcs than they have been. In this way, too, foreign aid may have affected adversely the growth of international trade. Similarly, the flow of aid has almost certainly strengthened the position and resolve of governments of ldcs which restrict the inflow of foreign private capital and enterprise.

Thus the argument that foreign aid serves the economic interests of the donor countries is untenable. The remaining argument based on the self-interest of the donors suggests that foreign aid promotes their international political interests, especially their security; and this is also untenable.

Briefly, the argument is that accelerated development of ldcs makes the world a safer place for the donors. To quote from the Report, "the thing to remember is that the process [development], global in scope, and international in nature, must succeed if there is finally to be peace, security, and stability in the world" (p. 11).

It is doubtful whether the Commission wishes this argument to be taken seriously. It says that "aid for development does not usually buy dependable friends" (p. 9). And it notes that development is not "an assurance of peaceful and responsible international behavior". It is "not a guarantee of political stability or an antidote to violence". History "holds too many cases of highly developed or rapidly developing nations which have behaved both aggressively and irresponsibly towards their neighbours" (p. 7).

Indeed, foreign aid is hardly an effective instrument for the promotion of the security of the donors. Aid reduces their resources, and to that extent weakens their position and influence in times of conflict.[16] Moreover, it is only materially developed countries which can imperil the security of the donors. With the exception of mainland China, a country not considered in the Report, the military, technical and economic resources of ldcs are far too small to support aggression which can endanger the security of the donors. It is only if and when they progress far beyond their present levels of economic attainment that they can possibly become aggressors of sufficient stature to affect the world scene or the security of the donors. Thus while in their present condition the recipients of aid are militarily ineffective and therefore necessarily harmless to the donor countries, they might conceivably become dangerous if they became materially much more advanced. Thus if foreign aid had the effects on the material progress of the recipients attributed to it by the Commission, it could endanger the security of the donors rather than promote it.[17]

The necessity for aid to reduce a wide and widening gap in incomes and living standards between rich and poor countries has become a staple of discussions on aid. According to the opening sentence of the Report, "the widening gap between the developed and developing countries has become a central issue of our time" (p. 3). The widening gap reinforces the duty and interest of donors to give aid. Aid must be continued and expanded "to reduce disparities . . . and to help the poorer countries to move forward . . . into the industrial and technological age so that the world will not become more and more starkly divided between the haves and the have-nots . . ." (pp. 7-8).

Foreign aid, by definition, removes resources from the donors. But it does not follow that it thereby reduces international income differences in any other way, because it does not necessarily promote the development of the recipients and often retards it. In some instances aid will affect adversely the rate of growth and possibly even the level of the per capita incomes in recipient countries, thus widening international differences in income. In other instances it will not affect the situation substantially. In yet others it might have a favourable effect, that is in countries where the general conditions necessary for economic progress are present, and where government policies are appropriate and not affected adversely by the flow of aid.

Thus the need to reduce international income differences does not provide a valid argument for aid, even if this objective is accepted and it is thought that its pursuit is an appropriate ground for the expenditure of taxpayers' money.

The Commission's reference to the widening gap in any case defies analysis because it is not stated to what period and groupings of countries the statement relates, nor whether the reference is to a difference in absolute magnitudes or to the ratio between them. The Report shows no recognition of the misleading nature of the word "gap". The per capita incomes of countries show a more or less continuous gradation with no clear discontinuity between one half and the remainder: it follows that the difference in per capita incomes of two groups depends on where the line is drawn, which is arbitrary especially in the absence of a clear discontinuity. Moreover, the array of per capita incomes does not remain constant, so that the distinction is not only arbitrary but also fluid.[18]

II THE DEVELOPMENT SETTING

(a) Differences in Economic Performance

In various parts of the Report, the Commission observes that the ldcs differ greatly among themselves, and that the economic prospects of some are better than those of others. No serious attempt is made, however, to explain differences in economic performance and promise. Yet some idea of the reasons for these differences is relevant to the assessment of the likely effects of foreign aid.

It is notable that, although its Report ranges widely, the Commission nevertheless was not more curious about the circumstances and processes of economic change, whether of growth or of decline (the latter an aspect of economic history not mentioned in the Report). Serious consideration and discussion of these complex and imperfectly understood matters might, of course, have looked odd in a Report which is heroic both in the simplicity of its major recommended instrumentality for growth and in the reasoning underlying its recommendation, and also in the universal scope of its recommended application.

Societies, ethnic groups and the populations of countries differ greatly in their cultural heritage, customs, sets of values, attitudes and motivations; the prospects of economic growth—in such matters as rate of change, extent of stress and dislocation associated with change, continuity of growth, and likely level of long-run achievement—are significantly affected by such influences. It is possible also that human faculties, including those appropriate for economic growth, may not be equally distributed among all peoples or groups. Not much is known about the operation of these various influences and their interactions at any particular time. Moreover, understanding of changes over time of these factors and influences and of their mutual interactions is far from complete.[19]

The Report does not include any discussion of such differences among people and societies. The only differences it appears to regard as having relevance for its concerns are differences in wealth and income among societies and among persons.

One can sympathize to some extent with the Commission's remark that "the growth process is still mysterious" (p. 52). But its apparent lack of awareness of the complexities of development further undermines the acceptability of its Report and its main prescriptions.

(b) The Historical Setting

The treatment in the Report of certain aspects of economic history deserves some examination, since it indirectly reflects the Commission's views on economic development.

On the first page of the Report it is said that " economic growth in many of the developing countries has proceeded [in the last two decades] at faster rates than the industrialized countries ever enjoyed at a similar stage in their own history" (p. 3). Later it becomes clear that the dates of the so-called similar stage in the history of the now-advanced countries include 1790 to 1820 for the United Kingdom (p. 27). The preceding centuries of economic change and growth in the United Kingdom are ignored in this comparison, and the material progress and the slow development of a material culture over these centuries are implicitly written off as irrelevant. The Commission's comparison of the present ldcs with England of the 1820s ignores the historical fact of the low level of general economic attainment of these countries when they were drawn into the international economy as recently as the late nineteenth century. It is neither sensible nor fair to the inhabitants of the ldcs to compare their historical, social and institutional backgrounds and their economic prospects with those of Western Europe at the beginning of the nineteenth century.[20] By adopting the approach that investment expenditure is all, the Commission here has fallen into the error, against which it warns elsewhere, of a belief in instant development (to use its words).[21]

While in the Commission's view the ldcs today generally are at what it calls the same stage of economic development as Britain or Germany in the early nineteenth century, it notes that economic development has but recently begun in much of the underdeveloped world. This is stated most explicitly with reference to Africa in Annex I ("The Development Situation") to the Report: "Compared to the rest of the developing world, Africa has been a late starter in economic development" (p. 262). There can be no quarrel with this generalisation. But when it is then stated that the date of the start coincides with the granting of independence to former colonial territories, this version of economic history is obvious nonsense.

It is not clear whether the Commission accepts this interpretation. On one occasion the Commission appears to do so by referring to a "backlog of deep poverty" with which these territories "entered political independence" (p. 25). However, in the preceding paragraph of the Report reference is made to the fact that "some other Asian [i.e. other than Japan], Latin American, and African countries made significant economic progress between 1880 and 1913, caused primarily by the rapid expansion of world trade and free capital movement during that period" (p. 25). The conflict between the Annex and the body of the Report cannot be resolved by the subsequent observation in the latter that "basic change in their economic and social structure was limited" (p. 25). For, in fact, in several of the affected colonies the most acute social and economic strains and problems were not associated with stagnation but those stemming from the differential impact of rapid economic change on attitudes, institutions and economic sectors. These problems have been noted by many writers, including critics of colonial administration. They are not referred to in the Annex, which does, on the contrary, allege that the colonial powers were responsible for the material backwardness of their former colonies, particularly in Africa. Once again, it is not clear whether the Commission accepts these particular views expressed in the Annex. Possibly it does not accept them. It observes that some of the ldcs "have had an independent existence for centuries" while "others have only emerged from colonial status in the last decades" (p. 25); and it (correctly) does not assert or imply that this difference is causally connected with differences in economic performance. However, neither the Annex nor the Report itself mentions the fact that the two countries in sub-saharan Africa not colonized by European powers, Ethiopia (except for a short period in the 1930s) and Liberia, are more backward in economic and general material achievement than most of the former colonies. The colonial administrations in fact provided their territories with significantly more trained and educated manpower than emerged in the independent African states. Yet the scarcity of trained manpower in the former colonies is in the Annex attributed "in large measure" to the "past failings of colonial administration" (p. 262). Our observations are not intended as support for the colonial system. Similarly, it is not said as an argument in favour of the general policies of the governments of South Africa and Rhodesia that the African populations in these countries are more highly trained and educated than in many African countries, including Ethiopia and Liberia.[22]

(c) *The Contemporary Political Setting*
The Commission's approach to contemporary history implies that aid operates in a political vacuum.

Throughout the life of the Commission a major war raged in Nigeria, the most populous country in Africa. There was large-scale expulsion of Asians from East Africa. Following severe and bloody communal disturbances in Malaysia, the restrictions on the activities of the Chinese were reinforced and extended. These various events and policies followed earlier but recent expulsion of Indians from Burma and Ceylon, of Asians from Africa, and of Chinese from Indonesia, large-scale massacres in Nigeria and Indonesia, and wars in the Sudan and Uganda. These events are not mentioned in the Report or in the Annex on the development situation.[23] Their disregard lends an air of unreality to the Report.[24]

These events throw into relief a more pervasive phenomenon, namely the presence in the ldcs of distinct ethnic, religious or tribal groups and of conflicts of interest among them.[25] Recognition of this political and social situation is directly relevant to the Commission's main arguments and proposals.

The development prospects of an ldc are plainly affected much more by the presence of such divisions and conflicts than by investment expenditures. Thus the expectations from aid should not be considered in a political vacuum. The extent and intensity of internal divisions, moreover, are affected by government policy. And as we have seen government policy, in turn, is directly affected by aid. The inflow of aid necessarily adds resources to the political authority relatively to economic decision-makers in the rest of the economy. This effect increases the prizes of political power, because the government's economic patronage is inevitably enlarged regardless of its political complexion or ideology. It becomes more important for contending groups to attempt to gain political control. Participation in political life and government administration becomes more attractive (or even necessary), compared to participation in economic activity. These effects are much enhanced when governments pursue policies of close and extensive state control of the economy by whatever name such a policy may be called: in particular, political tensions among distinct racial, religious, or tribal groups are exacerbated. Access to aid resources facilitates the pursuit of such policies. And in practice some major donors have favoured the pursuit of such policies and have allocated aid accordingly. Thus aid does not operate in a political vacuum, is not politically neutral, and is not neutral in its repercussions on some of the major factors influencing economic development.

The political and social heterogeneity within the typical 1dc, which reinforces the divergence of interest between governments and governed, bears on many of the issues in the Report. Thus in the context of the financing of investment expenditure from domestic sources, the Report includes the statement that "the ability of governments to tax is important because it reflects a growing sense of national community" (pp. 30–1). The ability of a government to tax or to increase taxation depends upon many factors; and governments have been able to increase taxation in countries experiencing regional or ethnic tensions and conflicts, the expulsion of categories of citizens, and unpopular tyrannical rule. Again, the Commission discusses technical assistance at length. It succeeds in doing so without noting in the context that in several ldcs large numbers of people with proven technical, administrative and entrepreneurial ability, and whose roots in these countries go back several generations or decades, have been expelled or denied the opportunity of exercising their talents and using their knowledge and experience of the local economy. Examples include people of all colours, the vast majority having been non-white.

The practice of treating countries as if they were persons and of generalizing on a world-wide basis leads the Commission into statements which are obviously at variance with reality. A clear example is the statement that "the poorer countries of the world have made their choice for development. It is part of their unfinished revolution. They are determined to achieve a better life for themselves [the countries?] and their children" (p. 10). The Commission itself contradicts this statement by writing subsequently that the governments of some ldcs "proclaim the primacy of traditional and nonmaterial values" (p. 24), and that some ldcs have shown "lack of commitment to economic development" (p. 29). Indeed, these are under-statements of the situation in certain ldcs. Quite apart from the expulsion or restriction of minorities which we have already noted,[26] the commitment to development is hard to reconcile with such legislation as that introduced in India in the 1950s prohibiting the slaughter of cattle.

(d) The Private Sector

The Report does not include any systematic discussion of the economic policies which the Commission favours for adoption by ldcs. However, it does contain frequent references to particular policy measures and policy attitudes; and in the remainder of this part of our review we consider some of the recommended policies. The Report enters a strong plea for the private sector in ldcs. Experience, the Commission states, "shows that a strong and vigorous private sector is an important element in the achievement of rapid growth"; and it regrets that it is still unusual in the ldcs "to regard private enterprise as a suitable instrument of economic growth, or to create conditions which actively favor the emergence of new firms" (p. 64). The promotion of domestic private enterprise is not advocated for its own contribution alone, but also because a "strong domestic private sector also serves to attract direct investment from abroad which can greatly stimulate the development process" (p. 64). The Report encourages the flow of resources to the ldcs in the form of direct investment by foreign firms and of government borrowing in the capital markets of the developed countries.

The Report, further, observes how economic policies in a variety of ways have frequently brought about a waste of resources. In the non-farming sector "one of the reasons why extensive development efforts have failed to create adequate employment opportunities has undoubtedly been the overstimulation of capital-intensive and labor-saving technology by artificial distortion of factor prices" (p. 59). State-fostered industrialization in many cases has meant that "new industries have been so extensively supported that they have become a burden rather than a benefit to the economy" (p. 37); and in many countries "import substitution has taken place almost regardless of price or quality" (pp. 63–4).

The Commission believes that there is "increasing recognition of the importance of price incentives and market discipline for both public and private producers" (p. 38). It supports this tendency. It notes how the provision of price incentives—or, rather, the removal of price disincentives (p. 29)—has worked wonders in agriculture in several countries: "As controls over production were relaxed and prices for farm products were made remunerative, farmers proved willing to adopt a new technology with amazing rapidity" (p. 33). In West Pakistan, it was assumed that "massive public programs" would be required to achieve the sinking of tubewells for irrigation: in the event "individual farmers adopted this innovation spontaneously" because of its productivity (p. 34). The responsiveness of peasant farmers to changes in costs and prices is also noted, and it is commented that the "lessons of this experience for development policy extend beyond the sphere of agriculture" (p. 35).

However, the Commission does not discuss the effect of aid programmes in facilitating the pursuit of economic policies which the Commission itself regards as wasteful or undesirable. The absence of discussion of this issue reflects its apparent attitude that aid leaves unaffected the economic position, weight and policies of the recipient governments. Moreover, in spite of its insistence on the importance of incentives, the Commission does not examine the adverse implications of taxation designed to mobilise domestic resources for development, a policy which it applauds.

(e) Egalitarianism

According to the Commission ldcs "have only recently begun to recognize that measures to make income distribution more equitable not only serve a social objective, but are also necessary for a sustained development effort" (p. 29). The Commission subsequently urges that "policies which serve to distribute income more equitably must ... become as important as those designed to accelerate growth"; on this occasion, however, it is recognized that "the objective of rapid growth and equitable distribution of income appear in conflict", and recourse is had to an undefined notion of "stable development" (p. 54).

The Commission does not say what it means by an equitable distribution of income; but it seems that what is meant is less inequality in the distribution of incomes, although the extent of the desired reduction in inequality is not indicated. Similarly, there is virtually no discussion of the recommended methods by which the desired change in income distribution is to be achieved. The Commission does observe that "restrictions on social mobility and individual opportunity created by class and caste will have to be broken and social systems will need to reward merit" (p. 54). This formulation obscures the central problem. The achievement of equality of opportunity at times means the reduction of incomes of persons or groups who had enjoyed protected economic positions.[27] However, in its turn greater equality of opportunity is bound to lead to wide differences in income and wealth. Even in a culturally homogeneous society people differ greatly in their economic abilities, attitudes and motivations. These differences are much more pronounced in economies which are moving progressively from subsistence activity to production for the market or which are otherwise undergoing rapid economic change. The differences become wider still when people of different cultures live within the same country, as do, for instance, Chinese, Indians and Malays in South East Asia. The presence of such personal and cultural differences prevents any simple reconciliation between equality of incomes and equality of opportunity.

In general terms, there is no reason to expect that the promotion of material progress would require policies designed substantially to reduce differences in personal incomes.[28] The opposite seems to be the case. Throughout the underdeveloped world, notably in South East Asia and in Africa, the prospect of material success induced countless people to work hard, save, invest, incur risks, and establish and develop enterprises, often far from home. In these conditions the disincentive effect of egalitarian policies is likely to be pronounced. There are also other ways in which policies designed greatly to reduce differences in incomes obstruct material progress, including the economic improvement of the position and prospects of the poorest groups. Such policies are bound to induce people to conceal their wealth, to remove it abroad, and to eschew investment and economic activity in directions where the results are readily discernible. They divert energy from productive economic activity. Many alert people are likely to emigrate or to transfer their activities from economic life to political life or to administration where the social and economic rewards relative to cost and risk become much greater in these conditions.

Policies designed to reduce differences in personal incomes are almost certain to involve increased centralization and hence to increase the inequality of power between rulers and subjects. This, in turn, is likely to lead to the creation of new positions of privilege and power, and to work against the "greater degree of participation in political and economic life" (p. 54) which the Commission hopes will accompany the attainment of a more equitable distribution of income.[29]

The Report emphasizes the need for land reform as an important egalitarian measure necessary for material progress. Such reform "must be undertaken", it is said, "to provide incentives for future investment in agriculture and for increased production" (p. 54). Moreover, it "will be needed in many developing countries not only to accelerate technological change and stimulate production in the long run, but also to generate rural employment" (p. 62).

Land reform is an elastic term which can be made to stretch from the official encouragement of the voluntary consolidation (by exchange or purchase) of fragmented holdings to the confiscation of land and its distribution to favoured categories of persons (such as former tenants or farm workers). It is obvious that the effects of land reform depend crucially on what is done in its name. The Commission does not specify what it means by the term; hence no worthwhile discussion is possible of the merits of its recommendation (referred to three times in the Report). It does not explain how it would achieve the desired consequences.

The most usual interpretation of land reform involves partial or total confiscation of land-owners (and in some instances detailed regulation of tenancy arrangements). If the purpose of such measures is a reduction in differences in income and wealth, it is not clear why ownership of land, rather than total income and wealth, should be taken as their basis. In many ldcs a large proportion of land-owners are less well-off than large sections of the urban population. (The Commission does not observe that in many parts of the less developed world, indeed probably in most of it including the poorest areas, there are no substantial land-owners.) If, on the other hand, the aim of land reform is to increase agricultural productivity, the effect is likely to be the opposite of that intended. Land reform measures engender a feeling of insecurity, discourage investment in land and its improvement, and inhibit the achievement of the most productive division of functions in the supply of capital, entrepreneurship and labour in the rural sector.

(f) Population Growth

In the Commission's view "no other phenomenon casts a darker shadow over the prospects of international development [the latter a synonym in the Report for the development of ldcs] than the staggering growth of population. It is evident that it is a major cause of the large discrepancy between rates of economic improvement in rich and poor countries" (p. 55). Consequently the Commission urges that the ldcs should be put under pressure in aid negotiations "for adequate analysis of population problems and of the bearing of these problems on development programs" (p. 195), and that the aid-giving countries should devote more resources to the study of population problems (as well as put their own houses in order in respect of population policies).

The Commission thinks it desirable that the people of the ldcs should be made aware of methods of birth control. We share its view because we believe that the basic case for economic development is not that it increases happiness but that it increases the range of choice. Birth control widens this range of choice in a literally vital aspect of human life. Various arguments of wide moral and political significance can be adduced for and against this position and its application in this context, which we need not pursue here. But even if one accepts the Commission's argument that information on this subject should be made available to the people of the underdeveloped world, it is debatable whether it should be financed or subsidized by the taxpayers of the donor countries, many of whom object to birth control.

The Commission is on much weaker ground in its discussion of the more narrowly economic benefits to be expected from an intensive campaign in favour of birth control. To begin with, it is doubtful whether a significant proportion of the population of the ldcs would avail itself of birth control facilities. The Commission is ambivalent on this point. It recognizes that over much of the under-developed world any response is likely to be limited and substantially delayed because children are so often an economic asset when they work on the farm and also when much of the cost of maintaining them is not borne by parents. The Commission thinks, however, that with economic progress the proportion of parents who wish to limit their families would increase appreciably. This last judgment is highly speculative: the occurrence of material progress and people's response to it are conjectural. It is doubtful whether even intense campaigns for birth control will significantly affect fertility rates in South Asia and Africa over the next decade or two.

The Commission is cautious in its assessment of what can be achieved by population policies: "the likelihood of a rapid slowing down of population growth is not great, although some countries are in a far more favorable position than others in this respect" (p. 55). This caution is appropriate, especially since the year 2000 marks the furthest time-horizon referred to in the Report. However, the Commission's discussion tends to exaggerate the benefits in terms of increased incomes per head to be expected from a reduction in the rate of growth of population.

The Commission's analysis is largely in terms of physical resources, notably land and capital per head, as the determinant of economic development. As we have noted earlier, there is a virtually complete neglect of the more important determinants of development such as human capacities and motivations and social institutions and values.

Many of the most backward areas of the underdeveloped world are very sparsely populated, including areas which are not particularly infertile. Conversely, both in ldcs and developed countries (including many countries classified as ldcs until recently but no longer so regarded) there is very high population density. Poverty in material resources and high population densities and rates of growth did not prevent rapid progress in Hong Kong and Japan. Possibly per capita incomes in these countries would have risen even faster had the population grown less rapidly. But their experience makes it clear that even in countries notoriously deficient in natural resources, high population density and a rapid population growth do not present formidable barriers to material progress if the required faculties, motivations and institutions are present. And capital formation is better viewed as an accompaniment—a symptom concomitant—of economic progress rather than as the crucial causal variable.

It is true, of course, that in both developed and less developed countries acceleration of economic progress has often been accompanied by a substantial reduction in population growth. But this does not mean that the former was caused by the latter. Indeed, a reduction in population growth cannot possibly affect levels of income over a short period of years or even a decade or two, because one is dealing here with the effects of *changes in rates of change* of numbers on the *levels* of income. Even if per capita incomes were determined primarily by the volume of physical resources per head (which is not the case), changes in rates of population growth could not affect significantly the per capita volume of resources immediately or over a short period. This consideration nullifies any expectation of a rise in per capita incomes within a generation or two as a result of a reduction in population growth. A more plausible explanation of the historical experience of a simultaneous fall in birth rate and acceleration of material progress is that both reflect changes in attitudes and motivation.

III THE AID CONSENSUS

The Commission stresses the novelty of its approach together with improved knowledge since the 1950s as basis of support for its far-reaching proposals. In fact the main ideas, method of approach and policy proposals of the Report are conventional and show clear continuity with the most influential literature of the 1950s.[30]

This continuity is evident in the treatment of a number of major topics: the allegedly decisive role of investment expenditure, and the inadequacy of domestic saving, especially voluntary saving; the emphasis on the volume of investment expenditure rather than on the methods of its collection and deployment or on the conditions for its productivity; the significance of external constraints which issue in balance-of-payments difficulties; the disregard of differences among persons and groups except those in income and wealth; the disregard of the interaction between the conventional variables of economics and the determinants of development (which are appropriately treated parametrically in standard economic analysis but inappropriately so in the study of development); and uncritical acceptance of the idea of self-sustaining growth. And inevitably the main policy proposal is the same as that of the 1950s: large-scale expansion of foreign aid.[31]

On many topics pertinent to the Commission's proposals more is known now than in the 1950s, chiefly in that the development experience of the last two decades has confirmed what should have been recognized before. Examples include recognition of the diversity, especially ethnic and cultural diversity, of ldcs and the implications of this diversity for economic development; the significance of personal and group abilities, attitudes and motivations as determinants of economic performance; the effects of close state economic controls in exacerbating political tension; the comparative ineffectiveness of foreign aid in promoting economic improvement; and the wide margins of bias in the interpretation of national income statistics. As in earlier discussions of the subject, these matters are virtually ignored in the Report.

In political and public discussion support for foreign aid is now practically unanimous. The case for aid has come to be regarded as *chose jugée*. This indeed is the approach of the Pearson Report. However, this consensus is based on assertion, not on systematic reasoning or historical experience.

NOTES

1 Cheap consumer goods serve as significant incentives to emergence from subsistence production to production for sale, an obvious condition of material progress, and one which often involves and promotes far-reaching changes in attitudes. Further, the arbitrary nature of the distinction between investment and consumption is especially pronounced in poor countries: apart from the role of consumer goods as incentive goods, there are many commodities usually classed as consumer goods (and whose purchase is not treated as investment expenditure) which directly increase productivity by improving the health and efficiency of people and of domestic animals, and by preserving stocks of commodities, especially of food. Familiar examples include insecticides, pesticides, bicycles, torches, and other hardware.

2 There are only two instances which lend some superficial support to the notion that appreciable depression of consumption is necessary for economic advance: the industrial revolution in England, and Soviet experience since about 1928. But neither example stands up to close examination.

It is unlikely that per capita consumption in England declined substantially for any length of time during the industrial revolution in view of the great improvement in the production and transport of consumer goods in the closing decades of the eighteenth century. (It is even less likely that living standards declined: the increase in life expectation suggests the opposite.) Even if it did occur, it would not have been necessitated by diversion of resources from consumption to investment because the demands made on resources by capital formation during the industrial revolution were modest; they were certainly not on the scale which would have required a reduction in real consumption at a time of considerable technical improvement.

The hardships experienced at times during the industrial revolution in England reflected various factors such as the labour-saving character of certain forms of technical change; certain results of the enclosure movement; large-scale migration to the cities where the administrative machinery was not ready for it; large-scale immigration from Ireland; and a heavy fall in mortality, especially infant mortality, which, while obviously evidence of an improvement in people's conditions, aggravated the social and administrative problems facing the cities.

The severe hardships of the population of the Soviet Union were the results of the pursuit of political objectives unrelated to capital formation required for a prospective rise in living standards.

3   The argument is developed at much greater length in P. T. Bauer, *Dissent on Development: Studies and Debates in Development Economics,* Weidenfeld and Nicolson, London, 1972.

4   Repeated or persistent payments difficulties bring about important repercussions apart from their financial effects. They serve as genuine or spurious justification for a wide range of specific controls as well as for the establishment of state enterprises and monopolies. These measures and policies in turn set up a series of consequences adverse to economic development: obstruction of the progress of low-cost producers and traders; preoccupation both in business and in government with the administration and circumvention of controls; restriction of geographical and occupational mobility and of the range and variety of external contacts; diversion of ability and energy from economic activity to political life; and the promotion and exacerbation of political tension.

5   The views of the Commission on the productivity of foreign private capital are worth noting: "There can be no doubt about the contribution which private capital can render to economic development. Indeed, dollar for dollar, it may be more effective than official aid both because it is more closely linked to the management and technology which industrial ventures require, and because those who risk their own money may be expected to be particularly interested in its efficient use" (p. 122).

6   There is an extensive discussion in the Report on the need to provide aid to enable ldcs to service the indebtness resulting in large part from post-war aid arrangements. The Commission fails to note that the advocacy of aid for debt relief implies either that aid has not served to raise productivity even to the modest extent required for the servicing of soft loans, or that it has been accompanied by domestic policies resulting in an inability or unwillingness to service them.

7   It is conceivable that in exceptional circumstances the government of an ldc may be unable to raise funds abroad on commercial terms because of extraordinary external political uncertainties, for example on the creation of a new state. Taiwan and Israel may be thought of as possible instances of such highly exceptional circumstances.

A government considered worthy of credit on commercial terms can borrow on the strength of its current and prospective revenues. It can therefore finance from the proceeds of borrowing (whether external or domestic) even highly risky projects of a kind which have to be in the public sector because their main expected benefits are indiscriminate. In other words, high commercial risk alone does not prevent recourse to external borrowing.

8 The Commission recognizes that this figure represents a large increase, but regards such an increase as necessary to secure the basis for an international community. The Commission may have realized that so large an increase was unlikely to be accepted by some of the major donors, but may have considered its proposal as a bargaining figure which even if it is not accepted would still bring about a larger flow than a more modest suggestion.

9 The same point is developed at some length in the review of the Turkish experience in the Annex to the Report.

10 H. Myint, "Dualism and the Internal Integration of the Underdeveloped Economies", *Banca Nazionale del Lavoro Quarterly Review*, No. 93, June 1970, pp. 28, 30.

11 Myint explains how many of these distortions are the result of economic policies.

12 The second sentence quoted in the text is not altogether clear; in the context, however, it should read ". . . be expected to promote (achieve) progress towards self-sustaining growth".

13 It is not the unreliability of national income in the statistical sense which presents the principal difficulty in this field. Much more serious and intractable are the problems of interpretation of the statistics, especially in inter-temporal and inter-country comparisons, where economic interpretation may be subject to errors of the order of several hundred per cent. Those problems are analysed and illustrated in D. Usher, *The Price Mechanism and the Meaning of National Income Statistics*, Oxford, 1968. Yet the Commission links its argument and major proposals to changes in growth rates of 1 per cent per annum.

14 The Commission urges that the aid relationship in multilateral programmes "focused upon long-term development" "should enjoy a presumption that it will survive changes in government, short of extreme tyranny or financial irresponsibility" (p. 128).

15 The views of the Commission examined in this section naturally assume that aid promotes development. We have no further observations on this issue, which is, indeed, not relevant to the points we make here.

16 In addition, the international political conduct and influence of the donors are adversely affected by some of the usual arguments used in the advocacy of aid, which allege that the Western countries have caused the poverty of the ldcs to which they now owe restitution. (The text of the Report does not include such arguments.)

17 Conflicts originated by a weak or small country or within such a country have often served as convenient starting points or pretexts for aggressive action by more powerful countries. Such a situation can arise at any level of economic development. Its possibility does not affect what is said in the text above.

18 There are other major ambiguities in the concept of the widening gap besides those noted above. And even if all these ambiguities were cleared up, a so-called gap could not serve as a basis for policy or even for sensible discussion without reference to the conduct of the governments and populations under review.

19 On this subject, the Italian economic historian, Carlo Cipolla, is worth

quoting: "We are in complete ignorance of the interaction between cultural and biological development and, unfortunately, not enough scholars dare to venture into this essential field for fear of being accused of racialism, nazism, or some other kind of unpleasant mental disposition". "Editor's Introduction", Carlo M. Cipolla (ed.), *The Economic Decline of Empires*, 1970, p. 12.

20   The observations of Professor Peter Mathias can serve as an effective critique of the attitude towards economic development apparent in the Report:

... The economists' perspectives of past economic change have too often been circumscribed by assumptions which have led them to prescribe the Industrial Revolution in Britain as the first case history relevant to students interested in the problems of backwardness and growth in more recent times. This surely is perverse and misleading. To the extent that historical case studies have any relevance at all—not by exact parallel but by analogy, by widening the range of awareness about problems and inter-relationships—it could be argued that, in the extent of backwardness, in levels of wealth, in the degree of "monetization" or subsistence, in the general nature of problems of political unity and administrative efficiency, many countries today face situations more comparable with those in early-modern or medieval Europe than in mid-eighteenth-century Britain. Moreover, case histories of economic decline, relative if not absolute, can prove as illuminating as those of growth. Generalizing on the basis of a handful of success stories can give a very foreshortened perspective.

Preface by Peter Mathias, in Brian Pullan (ed.), *Crisis and Change in the Venetian Economy in the Sixteenth and Seventeenth Centuries*, 1968.

21   An example of such a warning is its observation that "many considered political independence and economic development synonymous, unaware of the long and slow process by which the power and affluence of the industrialized countries had been reached" (p. 26). Indeed, on the theme of the time-horizon appropriate to the consideration of economic growth, different parts of the Report appear to have been written by different hands. A less charitable interpretation would be that the Commission wanted to have the best of both worlds: on the one hand, development is attainable within a relatively short time, and within a lifetime aid will become largely unnecessary; on the other hand, disappointment with the results of past aid should not lead to aid-weariness, because development is a long process. An example of this internal inconsistency is to be found in the first chapter. The "spirit of disenchantment" with aid said to be evident in some donor countries is explained in part in terms of earlier "misconceptions and unrealistic expectations of 'instant development' when we should have known that development was a long-term process" (p. 4). A few pages later the Report says: "We live at a time when the ability to transform the world is only limited by faintness of heart or narrowness of vision. We can now set ourselves goals that would have seemed chimerical a few decades ago and, working together, we can reach them" (p. 11).

22   South Africa, Rhodesia, Angola and Mozambique are excluded from

the review of Africa presented in the Annex. "Further south lie Portuguese Angola and Mozambique and white-governed Rhodesia, South, and South-West Africa. This latter group is not treated here" (p. 261). As these countries have large indigenous populations and do not receive foreign aid, an examination of their development experience might have been instructive.

23 In the Annex there is an indirect reference to one of these events. It is stated that most of the Chinese in Indonesia "were excluded from rural retail trade and many left Indonesia altogether. Their departure has left Indonesia with a serious shortage of entrepreneurs" (p. 341).

24 The sense of unreality also comes through in the references in the Report to the world community and to the community of developing nations. Specifically, there is no community of developing nations. There exists a large number of independent states in the under-developed world, with competing or even conflicting interests (for example in respect of the allocation of aid). Moreover, several of these states are openly hostile to each other (as at one point is noted in the Report), maintain large defence forces against each other and have engaged in large-scale expulsion of each other's nationals and even of groups of their own subjects suspected of having real or alleged ties with other ldcs.

25 The weak cohesion within many African states is a feature noted by many students of independent Africa. Thus Professor M. Gluckman has written: "There may be much consensus arising from the national struggle for independence, despite tribal divisions. But there is re-latively little cohesion." And Professor Lucy Mair refers to the "crucial political fact of the new African states, that . . . it is only in the small ethnic groups, defined by the recognition of hereditary authority, that established political institutions actually exist". Victor Turner (ed.), *Profiles of Change, Colonialism in Africa 1870–1960*, vol. 3, Cambridge, 1971, pp. 157–8 and 191.

26 When the restrictions on the activities on non-Burmese gathered momentum in Burma in the 1960s, an executive of a large expatriate company discussed this policy with a cabinet minister whom he knew personally. The minister said he well realized that the policy would retard material progress, but he said he did not mind this very much: what was important was to rid the country of aliens.

Annex I of the Report notes that in many African countries, "par-ticularly in East and Central Africa, the need to combine rapid 'Africanization' with satisfactory growth has raised very difficult problems" (p. 264)

27 Even substantial differences in incomes and wealth in ldcs do not usually (much less generally) reflect protected positions or privilege in the accepted sense of the terms. In these countries, as elsewhere, the higher incomes of the richest usually reflect the possession of such economic faculties and attitudes as ability to perceive and exploit opportunities, readiness to undertake risk, or to save and to take a long view. For instance, these are the faculties which have enabled the poor Chinese migrants of South East Asia to out-distance both the indigenous people and other migrant groups. Their material suc-cess owes nothing to official favours or privilege; indeed, they have had to overcome much official hostility, opposition and legislation and regulations explicitly discriminating against them.

28 Some differences in personal incomes are reduced in the course of economic development when the scarcity value of the resources owned by the better-off is reduced relatively to that of the resources owned by the poorest. The results of this process are quite different, however, from those to be expected from policies designed deliberately to reduce directly substantial differences in income.

29 Apparently associated with the desirability or necessity of policies to produce a greater equality in incomes is the Commission's diagnosis that there is a "vital need to bring about mass participation in development" (p. 5; also p. 54). Again, it is not all clear what mass participation is intended to mean. One can imagine at least two quite different meanings. It can mean that a large proportion of the population is interested in personal economic improvement and is engaged in productive economic activity and dispersed economic decision-making. Or, it may refer to mass participation in state-sponsored community projects and the mass display of support for government policy. Mass participation in the former sense is a major aspect of economic development. Mass participation in the second sense has never played a part in economic development, and there is no reason why it should do so. In practice it has been an aspect or instrument of the politicization of economic life and is likely to retard material advance.

30 For instance, the 1951 United Nations Report, *Measures for the Economic Development of Underdeveloped Countries*, and the numerous publications emanating from the Center for International Studies of the Massachusetts Institute of Technology.

Indeed, in several directions the Report goes even further than most of the literature of the 1950s. Thus the neglect in the Report of the differences among societies is carried to lengths unusual even by the broad-brush techniques and wide aggregation usual in the development literature: "The phase of economic history in which we live began to accelerate in England. In the nineteenth century it spread to Europe and North America" (p. 25). Who are the "we"? There are enormous differences in the material culture and its background of the many different societies living in the world today. The industrialised societies of North America and Western Europe, the tribal societies of Africa, the aborigines and the desert peoples, the Chinese of South East Asia, are all present in the twentieth century, but as far as material culture and its background are concerned they are not contemporaneous.

31 Indeed, the continuity extends even to matters of detail and to the implications of the proposals. For instance, the Commission envisages an increase in the annual rate of growth of GNP from the current average rate of 5 per cent to at least 6 per cent as evidence of the achievement of self-sustaining growth. Professors Millikan and Rostow in their book, *A Proposal*, New York, 1957, suggested a somewhat similar criterion, namely a 1 per cent rise in per capita incomes over five years. Again, we have shown that the Pearson proposals imply an open-ended commitment by the donors; so did Professors Millikan and Rostow's proposal that the United States should underwrite the total capital requirements of the ldcs which can use capital productively.

3

THE WHITE MAN'S BURDEN IN A NEO-COLONIAL SETTING

by

T. J. Byres

*School of Oriental and African Studies,
University of London*

THE WHITE MAN'S BURDEN IN A
NEO-COLONIAL SETTING

*Men say that it is not good for a servant to eat plums with
his lord; and to the poor, it is not good to have partage and
division with him which is rich and mighty; whereof Aesop
rehearseth such a fable.*

*The Cow, the Goat and the Sheep went once a-hunting in
the chase with a Lion, and they took a Hart. And when they
came to have their part and share in it, the Lion said to
them—*

*"My lords, I let you wit that the first part is mine, because
I am your lord; the second because I am stronger than ye be;
the third because I ran more swift than ye did; and whosoever
toucheth the fourth part, he shall be my mortal enemy!"*

*And thus the Lion took for himself alone the Hart. And
therefore this fable teacheth to all folk that the poor ought
not to hold fellowship with the mighty. For the mighty man
is never faithful to the poor.*

(Aesop)

I A GRAND ASSIZE AND ITS ASSUMPTIONS

In October, 1967, the President of the World Bank, George
Woods, suggested a "grand assize" to

> study the consequences of twenty years of development assistance,
> assess the results, clarify the errors and propose the policies which
> will work better in the future (p. vii of the Report).

In August, 1968, Lester Pearson, former Prime Minister of Canada,
accepted an invitation from Robert McNamara, successor to Mr
Woods, to set up a Commission to undertake such a study. Mr
Pearson duly instituted the "grand assize", and the whole operation was financed by the World Bank. The cost must have been
considerable. As well as Mr Pearson the Commission had seven
members. The eight wise commissioners, in their turn, were served
by an executive secretary, a deputy staff director, and thirteen
"experts"; the Chairman, Mr Pearson, had a personal staff of
two; there were ten research assistants; and the Commission made
use of twenty-three high-powered consultants. Even Gunnar Myrdal
did not match this. The development jetset do not give up their
time for peanuts, though one can only guess at the sums involved.
The Commission worked with speed. The Report was submitted

on 15 September, 1969, after eleven months of work: in the hands of the Bank, the Commission's patron, for the annual meeting of the Board of Governors of October, 1969. It was published with great *brouhaha* by Praegers in late 1969, and distributed by the World Bank with lavish generosity.[1]

In 1966 Teresa Hayter, then of the Overseas Development Institute Ltd., was commissioned to write a study of the World Bank's activities in Latin America. This was the second commission in an ODI series, financed by the World Bank,

supposed to evaluate and publicize the Bank's activities.[2]

Teresa Hayter had already written a study on French Aid, which accorded well with ODI principles. ODI duly published it.[3] Her background seemed in every respect impeccable. She proceeded to Latin America in 1967, and by June 1968 she had produced the first draft of a study entitled *Leverage: The World Bank, the International Monetary Fund and the United States Agency for International Development in Latin America*. Before the draft appeared attempts were made by the Bank to "persuade" her out of any consideration of "leverage". She did not yield. Her draft described unsavoury truths about pressure on recipient countries. The emperor, it was unequivocally stated, wears no clothes. Further attempts were made by the World Bank and at ODI to get Teresa Hayter to play the game and re-clothe the emperor. They were unsuccessful. ODI refused to publish. Penguins have since done so.[4]

The contrast between the experience of the Pearson Report and that of Teresa Hayter's manuscript—both commissioned by the World Bank—is marked. The one published with great despatch and much attendant publicity, the other suppressed (though in the end published by a private publisher and attracting almost as much publicity). Now, the comparison between the mighty Pearson Commission and a mere slip of a girl may seem to some histrionic. It is not. The contrast is instructive. The unsavoury truths recorded by Teresa Hayter are not new. We have known of "leverage", of pressure upon recipients by donors, of the dubious motivation behind the giving of aid, and so on, since the 1950s, though most writers on aid simply ignore these facts. Teresa Hayter does not tell us anything that is substantially new. She does, however, set out *in extenso* and systematically truths about the nature of foreign aid which are essential to any understanding of its logic and its true effects. One of the central weaknesses of the Pearson Report is its ignoring of the issues which Teresa Hayter highlighted. It is a "grand assize" which has turned out to be something less than grand. I shall return to the matter of "leverage" below.

Indeed, the Report is far less than a "grand assize" in several important respects. It is, I think, an important document, since it represents the essence of an influential approach to "development"—that of the decent, compassionate, reasonable and well-intentioned Western liberal[5]—and allows us to see that approach in its naked form, without the technicalities which are the beauty aids and false limbs of the academic economist. But it is no "grand assize". It reads like a plan document (and should, perhaps, be judged as such): bland, presenting a united front to its audience,[6] providing exhortation, oversimplifying and evading really difficult issues. We shall illustrate these features as we proceed. From a "grand assize" one expects considerably more: something in the tradition of a Royal Commission, with bulky Report, voluminous supporting (and conflicting) evidence, and dissenting memoranda from members of the Commission. Future scholars will find the Pearson Report useful as a *general statement*, as a piece of special pleading, but not as a quarry of information which cannot be found elsewhere.

A substantial omission from the deliberations of a supposed "grand assize" is any consideration of socialist countries either as aid donors or as aid recipients. The Commission acknowledges its sin of omission, but quite unrepentantly:

> The Commission is conscious of the fact that it has not had the benefit of contact with, and information from, communist countries. This omission, together with the absence of detailed published information from those countries, means that their programmes of development co-operation and aid—nearly all of which are bilateral— are not dealt with in the Report (p. ix).

The Commission exaggerates the lack of information.[7] Even limited information, however, is better than none. To ignore socialist aid-givers (most notably the Soviet Union) is to omit an important part of the reality with which a "grand assize" should have been concerned. The total system includes socialist countries and cannot be understood without reference to them. Similarly, the experience of socialist aid-recipients is important. Yet, China, Cuba, North Vietnam and North Korea might not exist. It is difficult, however, to exclude the largest country in the world completely from one's thoughts, and the Commission is forced on to the defensive:

> A word is necessary about the omission of Mainland China from this concentration. Both as a political phenomenon and as a case study in development, Mainland China is clearly of central interest and significance. It is not practicable at the moment, however, to

obtain the detailed social and economic information about the country which is available for most of the others. Therefore, attention will be directed elsewhere (Annex 1, p. 330).

This is, to say the least, disingenuous. Information is not so scarce. There is a thriving journal in *The China Quarterly* which publishes articles, reviews and general information on China. There is also a steady stream of books, monographs and articles published elsewhere.[8] There is certainly enough, for example, to provide a far more comprehensive and convincing picture than is done for Indonesia.[9] The Commission openly stresses the dearth of information on Indonesia. It has its reasons for examining it, however.

There are several interwoven strands in the Report and a number of implicit assumptions, which together constitute a particular view of reality. There are, to be sure, qualifications scattered about its pages. Granted these, certain features do recur in striking fashion. The predominant note is one of *optimism*, summed up in the sentence:

The seeds of dynamic change have been planted (p. 44)[10].

This is, significantly, a "Green Revolution" metaphor, though used at the end of a section on "Economic Management". The Commission, indeed, assumes that the "Green Revolution" has arrived in poor countries.[11] The optimism is tempered by the consideration that more aid on better terms is necessary if the dynamic changes are to continue unabated. But pessimism and any possible dark side to the picture are not allowed to obtrude. A central, underlying premiss is that *harmony* prevails in relations between rich and poor nations. The "invisible hand" is not mentioned. It is, however, pervasive. There is little indication that the interests of rich and poor may not ultimately be congruent or that conflict and contradiction are important. Just as harmony is assumed to exist (or to be possible) so it is supposed that the ultimate aim of aid is (or can be) the *well-being* (whatever this means) of the underdeveloped world. That the relationship between rich and poor may essentially be one of exploiter and exploited is not hinted at. Moreover, the Commission operates in a universe more or less devoid of politics (though there is the odd reference to or brief section on politics), in which there is an undifferentiated "society", peopled by "reasonable" men.

Such are the bare bones of an approach whose adherents are men of high purpose, with a genuine desire to see an end to the barbarities of poverty and deprivation in the underdeveloped world. My argument shall be that the vision is false, and, further, that we will not comprehend it fully unless we look at its *ideological* role.

II THE WHITE MAN'S BURDEN: MYTH AND IDEOLOGY

When Kipling wrote his famous poem in 1898 he was, among other things, articulating in powerful fashion a part of the ideology of imperialism. When published in the London *Times* of 4 February, 1899 it touched a responsive chord in the spirit of the British bourgeosie. It gave justification to actions already taken, to behaviour then current, to attitudes of racial superiority[12] and to pride in imperial might. If repressed guilt needed a solvent here it was. But it also proved remarkably prophetic. It appeared in the New York *Sun* and *Tribune* of 5 February, 1889. It was written as a call to the USA to share the burden borne by Britain—the White Man's Burden, the civilizing mission—at the time when the USA had conquered Cuba and the Philippines and seemed, for a moment, to falter in her resolve. Kipling need not have worried, for, on 6 February, 1889

the American Senate voted by a sufficient majority to take over the administration of the Philippines.[13]

Theodore Roosevelt, just elected Governor of New York State, had received from Kipling a prior copy of the poem. He wrote to H. Cabot Lodge:

I send you an advance copy of a poem by Kipling which is rather poor poetry, but good sense from the expansionist standpoint.[14]

The USA, too, had acquired an ideologue.

British imperialism found in Kipling the distiller of a heady potion. His work was an important part of the ideology of British imperialism. Its power rested upon Kipling's deep understanding of "British India": not the real India of flesh-and-blood Indians, which few Englishmen acknowledged, let alone understood, but of the "British in India". He gave expression to their yearnings and legitimacy to their activities (at least in their own eyes). He provided a moral basis for their actions—an ideology.[15] That he ignored the evils of imperialism, that he was probably not even conscious of them, was an integral part of his role.

The relations which have developed between rich and poor nations since the early 1950s can most accurately be described as neo-colonial (of which more anon), despite the obloquy which attaches to that term in certain quarters. Neo-colonialism has acquired no bard. Nor is it likely to. It has about it none of the panoply and pageant which lent a romantic air to Empire. A conclave of aid donors is no parallel to an imperial durbar. It has, however, acquired an ideology. Thus to view the Pearson Report is to see it in its proper light. It is an ideological statement in two connected senses. Firstly, inasmuch as it seeks to provide a moral basis for action (more aid, better terms, multilateral channels etc) it is openly ideological. Thus:

> why should the rich countries seek to help other nations when even the richest of them are saddled with heavy social and economic problems within their own borders?
> The simplest answer to the question is the moral one: that it is only right for those who have to share with those who have not (p. 8).

Secondly, and more importantly, to the extent that the action is part of a system whose true nature is not perceived, serves interests which are not acknowledged, and has effects very different from those stated, it is ideological in the classic Marxist sense that it represents "false consciousness".[16]

It is illuminating, in this respect, to press the comparison with Kipling a little further. Significantly, the myth of the White Man's Burden remains. As Kipling had it:

> Take up the White Man's burden—
> Send forth the best ye breed—
> Go bind your sons to exile
> To serve your captives' need.

The White Man's Burden is now aid and the sons bound to exile droves of "experts". Both of these elements are important ideologically. It is worth examining them a little more closely.

Early in the Report we read:

> But development will not normally create, nor should it be expected to create, immediate economic windfalls for a donor country (p. 9).

Later, in a section entitled "The Burden of Foreign Aid" (pp. 139–41) the qualifications which are entered begin to undermine the generalization. The Commission stresses that

> the real burden of aid ... clearly runs far below the dollar value of all resources transferred. The fact deserves to be more widely known (p. 141).

We are reminded that foreign investment is not "aid", but is done for profit and is no different from similar flows between industrialized countries; that actual grants have declined as a proportion of total aid; that the concessional element in loans has diminished considerably; that most aid is given on a bilateral basis; that when aid takes the form of goods which would have otherwise gone to waste (for example, food) the burden on donors is slight; that aid-tying reduces the real burden to the donor by promoting exports and production in the donor economy; that aid has given rise to a heavy debt problem; that military aid cannot be regarded as a burden on the donor (pp. 14–22, 92, 96, 139–41, Chapters 8 and 9). But all that this amounts to, for the Commission, is that aid is less of a burden than is popularly supposed. The Commissioners stick tenaciously to the position that *there is a burden*. It is deeply embedded in their collective psyche. Aid is a burden, though one that should be increased. Put thus the image is one of a dis-interested group of rich nations being implored to act selflessly and help their less-fortunate brethren. One can almost detect the medieval injunction against the taking of interest:

> Mutuum date nihil inde sperantes
> (Lend hoping for nothing again)[17]

The Roman Catholic Church found great difficulty in implementing its laws against usury, especially when the mighty were involved.[18] The Pearson Commission, with no coercive power at its disposal, has even less chance of being listened to.

The undesirable features of aid identified by the Commission can be taken far further than the Commission takes them. Aid-tying is considerably more pernicious than the Report allows and merits more detailed treatment[19]; the burden of debt repayment has more sombre implications than those suggested;[20] and so on. This is to restrict the argument to the Commission's chosen terms. Even in so confining the argument we can almost reverse the position with regard to where the burden falls. As Paul Streeten has put it, evocatively:

> The Kings of Siam are said to have ruined obnoxious countries by presenting them with white elephants that had to be maintained at vast expense. In the modern setting this can be achieved best by tying a high-interest loan, called "aid", to projects and to donors' exports and to confine it to the import content (or better still, some part of it) of the project. But even untied aid on soft terms can be used to promote exports of a white elephantine nature, because capital grants do not cover the subsequent recurrent expenditure which the elephant inflicts on its owners. Receiving aid is not just like receiving an elephant but like making love to an elephant. There is no pleasure in it, you run the risk of being crushed and it takes years before you see the results.[21]

But even Streeten's more extreme statement remains partial. That it is quite improper to represent aid as a burden upon the donors, that the true burden is carried by the recipients (just as in Kipling's time it was borne by the "captives"), can be perceived adequately only with a wider vision. The Commission portrays the contrary by fragmenting reality. In the Report there is never a hint that aid is part of a *general system*—neo-colonialism—whose net effect is to secure the exploitation of the underdeveloped by the developed world, or that aid is only one of several interlocking economic mechanisms at work (the other important ones being international trade and private foreign investment).[22] The objective role that aid plays cannot be appreciated in isolation from the other mechanisms of neo-colonialism. To this I shall return.

Kipling's "sons bound to exile" have their analogues, in the Report, in the shape of "experts". Some prominence is given to their contribution to "development" (pp. 50–1, 179–85). For example:

> But the contribution of aid cannot be expressed in purely financial terms. Aid has financed the work of large numbers of personnel and very extensive training programmes in the developing countries. It has thus contributed to the transfer of technology and ideas. In 1968 alone, there were over 100,000 experts and volunteers working in the developing countries ... To these must be added the consultants, engineers, and analysts engaged in preparing and implementing capital projects as well as those experts and trainees supported by private organizations; these are nearly equal in numbers to officially financed personnel. This two-way flow of people has powerfully stimulated change, introduced new management skills, raised educational standards, and helped to create much infrastructure and expanded industry (pp. 50–51).

And so the panegyric continues. At two points inadequacies are admitted. One relates to the limited supply of competent people and the increasing dissatisfaction, in developing countries, with the quality of technical personnel (p. 184). The other is in relation to education and comes with an uncharacteristic flash of acerbity:

> On the whole, however, it must be said that aid from abroad has served mainly to buttress classical methods, applied by unquestioning teachers, both local and foreign, trained in a mold cast over a hundred years ago (p. 200).

The criticisms are, however, miniscule when set against the praise. It should be the other way round.

There are, no doubt, many worthy men among the legions of "experts" who throng in foreign climes. There are different kinds of "expert" (economists in abundance, engineers, agronomists, edu-

cationists, political scientists, etc., etc., etc.). on assignments of varying nature, scope and duration, with a wide range of motives for
being there. Generalization is, perhaps, hazardous, though the Commission was not deterred from firm pronouncement. The hazards
are *a fortiori* great because of the dearth of any worthwhile treatment in the literature (which is, after all, written by "experts" who
are no more self-questioning than any other group of human beings). In fiction, William J. Lederer's and Eugene Burdick's novel,
The Ugly American, despite its own naïve chauvinism, reveals a
little of the reality.[23] Among economists Dudley Seers has given
some thought to the issues involved.[24] And unique in his attempt
at self-analysis is Adam Curle, in a study which is at once honest,
amusing, and instructive.[25]

One can be conscious of diversity and of the possibility of being
very unfair to some, yet put with confidence a case very different
to the one in the Report (which is unfair in the other direction).
Thus, all too often the "experts" are men of second-rate ability
(especially those on longer assignments), sometimes less qualified
than the "natives" they are advising (in a country like India, for
example), eager to succeed but unable to do so at home, and "anti-
native" because of their own inadequacies. Even when their abilities are not in doubt they are frequently unsuited to life abroad.
With their large salaries—out of all keeping with their "contribution"—their duty-free alcohol and their air-conditioning existence they cause justified ill-feeling. They come from a huge variety
of organizations, public and private, and are sometimes chosen by
appointing boards singularly unsuited to make the choice. They
have little understanding of the societies they are meant to be helping and little sympathy for them. They may resent having to be
there at all. They arrive with ethnocentric biases, which become
more pronounced the longer they stay. It is worth looking a little
more closely at Curle. His few pages are far more revealing than the
turgid prose of the Report. He is a most unusual "expert", con-
forming to few of the preceding stereotypes. His insights have to
them a universal ring.

Curle describes his expectations as an adviser in a passage which
is no less psychologically valid for being couched in terms of
fantasy:

> When anticipating my first advisory assignment I had imagined that
> on arrival in the country where I was to serve I would be ushered
> deferentially into the office of the minister, who would rise eagerly,
> saying, "We have been waiting for your help: we can't see our way
> through this problem and rely entirely on your advice." I would
> reply gravely in such clichéd terms as I would do my best to

justify his faith in my abilities. Then, after a few weeks during which the most secret files were open to me, a private helicopter was put at my disposal, and I had dined alone with the prime minister's old mother, I would present my report. The president (for I had been going steadily up in the world) would shake me by the hand. "You have solved our problem", he would say, conferring an exotic order on me. At the next cabinet meeting, copies of my report would be circulated to all members. "This must be implemented in full, gentlemen, and at once."[26]

The *hubris* of Kipling's "civilizing mission" is not there (though it may well be with other "experts"), but there is an unmistakeable sense of superiority. Inevitably, disappointment and frustration follow, as the welcome received is less than fulsome, as confusion and uncertainty grow, as quick results simply do not come.[27] Curle next identifies two basic reactions to the confusion, self-doubt, worry and depression: the schizoid and the depressive. The *schizoid* reacts to self-doubt by attributing his failure to the stupidity, chicanery, irresponsibility and laziness of the natives. He (or she) will tend to be dogmatic: to have a simple view of development, which can be secured by the proper use of a single factor (be it deficit finance, fertilizers, birth control or what have you).[28] The *depressive*, on the other hand, is all too conscious of his inadequacy. This was Curle's own condition, and he is a trifle reticent about it. He himself recovered, after a few months, from his "miserable sense of uselessness".[29] The schizoid, I think, predominates among "experts" (some depressives will simply be crushed by the experience), his hostility towards the "natives" an echo of another of Kipling's verses:

> And when your goal is nearest
> The end for others sought
> Watch Sloth and heathen Folly
> Bring all your hope to nought

But no suggestion of the existence of such attitudes among "experts" appears in the Report.

The Report rejects firmly the neo-Kiplingesque view that "Sloth and heathen Folly" interfere seriously with the effective utilization of aid:

It is not our impression, from the evidence we have received, that an excessive amount of aid has been dissipated through abnormal waste, mismanagement, or corruption (pp. 168–9).

The auditing of bilateral aid programmes done by countries like the United States, Britain, Japan, France and Germany is quoted in evidence (p. 169). One can, perhaps, detect an underlying fear that there may be a germ of truth in the allegation, but a liberal stand is taken. It is important, ideologically, for the Commission to posit that the aims and standards of the *donor* countries are being met. This is necessary if one is to argue convincingly that aid has contributed significantly to growth, that more aid on better terms is essential if gains are to be consolidated, and, as we shall see, that the aid relationship can be truly one of "partnership". The question of whether the aims and standards of donor countries are the appropriate ones is, of course, never raised. It is possible to conceive of growth according to different aims and standards—those of socialist countries. No such possibility is acknowledged and the experience of socialist countries is ignored. It is also possible to conceive of little or no growth. On this the Commission faces a moral dilemma. I have already pointed out that an unequivocal moral stand is taken, and now morality faces a test. The Commission is at pains to identify criteria whereby the "performance" of aid-receivers may be judged. Growth of GNP is not enough. A move towards "financial independence" is the important aim and this can be assessed by reference to the domestic savings rate and the ratio of exports to imports (pp. 138–43). Suppose, however, that a country does not perform well according to these criteria. Should starving, hopelessly poor people be allowed to rot because of the ineptitude of their governments, or because of their very backwardness? Is this something which the conscience of the affluent can tolerate? Is the principle of "nothing succeeds like success" the only one? The chapter "Partners in Development" concludes as follows:

> It is our view that a world-wide co-operative campaign to set the developing countries on a path of rapid growth towards economic independence is a task within our range of accomplishment. It is a noble goal to which mankind is called in the last third of the twentieth century (p. 135).

Is it "noble" to ignore the slow-runners, the deprived, hungry, and obstinately backward? Or does nobility respond only to a successful push towards capitalism? The Commission seems unaware of the conflict between "morality" and its notion of efficiency.

I have argued that the Report has an ideological function. This is not to say that the Commissioners set out deliberately and wilfully to mislead. Certainly not. It is, however, to argue that objectively the Report's role is to conceal the true nature of aid in the process of providing a moral basis for the system of which aid is an integral part. Further strands in the ideological fabric of the Report will become obvious as we proceed. Here, however, we can ask: Ideology for whom? To persuade whom? To what basic ends? Is it to provide a rationale for action already taken? Or to bring about action of a radical kind? Again intention and objective function may diverge. The Report may be seen as setting out to reach three broad audiences: firstly, the doubting Thomases in the developed world—for the most part governments and politicians and the interests they represent—who need to be persuaded that aid should be sustained, or, better, increased; secondly, recipient governments who need some encouragement, especially to be enthusiastic hosts to private foreign investment (see below); and thirdly the advocates of aid, who are provided with ammunition. It fails, I think, to generate a set of arguments which will move the first and second groups. I very much doubt whether a sceptic— even a mild one—will be converted by what he reads. The third audience has already reacted favourably,[30] but this is unlikely to bring action. The Report has only a *post hoc*, a rationalizing function. It sets the seal on the *status quo*. So, too, did Kipling.

Action will not be forthcoming, because of the nature of the interests involved. These the Commission misrepresents. In the next section I shall examine the manner of this unwitting misrepresentation.

III NEO-COLONIALISM, ECONOMIC INTERESTS AND REALPOLITIK

The Commission does refer occasionally to *colonialism*. Colonialism happened and it was regrettable[31] (though occasionally the regret is tinged with a little nostalgia for the past).[32] Memories of colonial experience produce attitudes of suspicion and distrust among underdeveloped countries, especially with regard to foreign investment (pp. 99–100). These are quite unjustified. Exploitation— an ungracious term not actually used by the Commission—there may have been in the past, but those days have long gone. Foreign investment now confers great benefits upon underdeveloped countries (indeed, the Report never says explicitly that it did anything else in colonial times).[33] Moreover, in the *post-colonial* situation *ex-colonial* powers have been motivated by a sense of responsibility to give handsome amounts of aid to former colonies. Thus:

> France and Britain became major aid-givers in the 1950s, mainly to help provide an economic base for the independence of their former colonies (p. 138).

And even the apparently undesirable turns out to be virtuous:

There are many reasons for the continued preference for bilateral channels. Above all, responsibilities towards former colonial territories and other historic ties have led several aid-givers into bilateral relationships, and have undoubtedly made them provide far more aid than they would have done within a more internationalized aid system (p. 209).

The transition from subjection to independence has thereby been rendered smooth. Neo-colonialism does not exist. It is never mentioned, even to reject it. That in itself is suspicious.

The picture painted in the Report bears little resemblance to reality. We shall start with private foreign investment. We are told magisterially that

political sensitivity . . . explains why much discussion of the economic impact of foreign investment has been couched in emotional language and has been clouded by many misunderstandings (p. 100).

We are then taken through the supposed misconceptions and receive the final judgment:

. . . available facts do suggest that direct foreign investment has added substantially to the real national income of developing countries. In so doing it has also enhanced their capacity to finance their future development (p. 104).

The only supporting evidence is a brief reference to the oil producing countries and an even briefer one to the exporters of mineral products (p. 104). Even if one accepts the Commission's position on these countries (which is by no means certain[34]) it is hardly a basis upon which to generalize for the whole underdeveloped world. The Report does stress the absence of any detailed empirical work (pp. 103–4) but seems blissfully unaware of a substantial piece of work on India by Michael Kidron, which was certainly available to the Commission.[35] Kidron's conclusions are very different from the Commission's. Let us examine the supposed "misconceptions" and the Commission's treatment of them (especially in relation to Kidron's meticulously documented findings).

The first major misconception, apparently, is to

measure the balance-of-payments impact of foreign investment by comparing "new capital inflow" with the total profits of the accumulated foreign investment in the country (p. 100).

One wonders who of the misconceiving the Commission has in mind. For even the most unsophisticated of critics of foreign investment identify *remittance* of profits as the mechanism of drain, there being a well-established tradition stretching back to the Indian nationalist writer, Dadabhai Naoroji.[36] When the Commission tells us, therefore, that

> such a comparison neglects to take into account the re-investment of profits by foreign investors in the host country (pp. 100–101),

it is tilting at a windmill. With this windmill out of the way we can concentrate on the non-ephemeral.

The Report goes on to argue that a simple comparison of profit remittance with capital inflow does considerably less than justice to foreign investment's contribution. It

> fails to note the impact of foreign investment on export promotion and import saving (p. 101).

Indeed, all direct and indirect effects must be taken into account in the context of the economy as a whole. Here we have an interesting use of words. Apparently, "effects" are synonymous with "benefits", for no disadvantages are considered. It is a major misconception to ignore foreign investment's role in transferring advanced technology, which would be difficult and costly to acquire in the absence of foreign investment; in generating external economies, in the shape of "notable improvements in infrastructure and social overhead facilities"; in stimulating local entrepreneurs via "increased demand, demonstration effects, and access to foreign technology and business methods". Moreover, high profits simply imply that foreign investment "is particularly efficient". If, perchance, these profits are the result of monopoly or distorted prices, the answer is simple: reduce tariffs, legislate against "specific monopoly practices" and re-negotiate concession agreements. Under no circumstances must you think ill of foreign investment. It must be given every encouragement (pp. 101–4). Such is the essence of the case.

Remittance of profits, to start off with, can be grossly understated. There are many ways of concealing the amount of surplus which actually leaves the host country. Thus, the prices of goods, materials and services supplied as investment in kind may be marked up considerably, with branches and subsidiaries of the large international company charged prices far higher than world prices for components, intermediate goods, etc. Or profits may be concealed as royalties (say on patent rights) or fees (for drawings, technical assistance etc.).[37] The commissars of monopoly capital are capable of immense ingenuity. Secondly, *export promotion* no doubt follows upon foreign investment in oil production or mineral extraction. It is by no means certain, however, when investment is in modern manufacturing industry (industries like chemicals, pharmaceuticals, cigarettes, electrical goods). Here, foreign-controlled firms look essentially to domestic markets.[38] Why should the representatives of monopoly capital want to export to countries in which they already have a stake? *Import-saving*, thirdly, can also be illusory. Foreign investment may involve some import-substitution, but if it is in industries producing non-essential goods (like soft drinks, ink, ball-point pens, tooth paste, tooth brushes, razor blades, domestic refrigerators[39]), which would not anyway have been imported, there is no saving on imports. Imports may even be added to if these industries use foreign machinery, and, at a further remove, if they make demands upon domestic resources like steel and cement, which have an import content. On the fourth issue, the *transfer of advanced technology*, there are many examples of inappropriate technology being used. Advanced technology is essential in underdeveloped economies in certain sectors and industries: in, for example, producer good industries. Indiscriminate use can, however, be harmful, especially in consumer goods. Costs may be unnecessarily raised and employment jeopardized. The foreign investor's interests compel him in the direction of advanced technology: in a joint venture he controls technical operations, he has a direct interest in supplying equipment, he is reluctant to transfer skills, he does not know local conditions, and he does not want to supply equipment which can be easily copied.[40] These are not the interests of the host economy. The supposed *external economies*, next, are difficult to locate. Are we merely hearing one of the ritual incantations of our time? The Report provides no concrete examples. Finally, *local entrepreneurs* may be stimulated by demand and demonstration effects into producing non-essential goods (say, cosmetics and air-conditioners, as well as those already noted), which absorb scarce resources needed elsewhere in the economy.

The foregoing underlines foreign investment's distinctly neocolonial nature. The interests of foreign capital are served to the marked disadvantage of underdeveloped host economies. Advanced capitalist economies no longer have formal political dominion, backed up by a force (though military intervention is certainly resorted to on occasions[41]), but underdeveloped economies are economically dependent upon them and have become increasingly so. Moreover, it is precisely because advanced capitalism is *not* critically dependent upon underdeveloped economies (or any one underdeveloped economy) for its continued growth that the influence is strong.[42] Foreign firms hold key positions in a number of industries,[43] but the activities of these international firms in any single underdeveloped country represent a very small proportion of their total turnover.[44] To withdraw from any one underdeveloped economy (even a large one like India) will not involve major losses, and there may be threats to do so. These threats moderate the treatment accorded to foreign capital and allow it to retain its privileges. The relationship involves substantial elements of exploitation,[45] of non-equivalent exchange, as the evidence presented in the previous paragraph shows. Certainly, price-rigging, for example, is a powerful force shifting the international terms of trade against the underdeveloped world.[46] Thus one of the mechanisms of neo-colonialism—*foreign investment*—is closely connected with a second one—*the international trade network*. The relationship inherent in the operation of private foreign investment, further, is powerfully reinforced by the operation of *foreign aid* —the third of the neo-colonial mechanisms—which has made dependence upon the developed world excessive. The complementary nature of these mechanisms is to be stressed. Heavy economic dependence brings political interference and this in its turn allows influence upon the manner of economic change, who shall direct it and who shall benefit from it. Before turning to these crucial considerations—which do not appear in the Report—examination of the motives for giving foreign aid is revealing.

The very central propositions of the Report are that aid has been crucial to the development so far achieved in underdeveloped countries and that future development will be prevented unless more aid on better terms is forthcoming. These I shall subject to critical scrutiny in the next and concluding section. At this juncture I would like to establish the *motives* for giving aid. There can be no doubt about the broad reasons for private foreign investment (whatever the precise weight we attach to any one reason). They are the search for high profits, growing markets and an assured supply of raw materials.[47] We can argue about the results of this for the host country, but few would deny the intrinsic motivation. Aid's *raison d'être* is a more contentious issue. I have already indicated the sense of responsibility attributed by the Commission to ex-colonial powers like Britain and France. These countries, we are asked to believe, have given aid to former colonies out of an altruistic desire to see independence firmly rooted in a secure economic base. I have also drawn attention to the Report's strong moral stand. Such a stand is predicated upon an assumption that selflessness has lain behind aid in the past and can give rise to substantially more aid in the future. The Commission does, on occasion, appeal to enlightened self-interest (a growing world economy benefits all—p. 9) and does, once or twice, suggest selfish reasons for giving aid (the promotion of donor's exports, political and strategic advantage—pp. 4, 172, 178, 188). But these are not the primary motives attributed by the Commission to donors. In this the Commission goes woefully astray. Thus Britain and France have surely seen their bilateral agreements and tied aid essentially as serving their own political and economic interests: as means of retaining power and influence in regions traditionally under their control and of maintaining markets and privileged access to raw materials in countries which were important to them economically.[48] Other powers with a colonial past are similarly motivated, while those without one are equally certainly in search of political benefits and economic gain. The largest donor of all (in absolute terms), the USA, makes no secret—when defending the aid programme before an American audience—of aid's being a tool of foreign policy, used to bring political and economic advantage to herself.[49]

We can now turn to the range of problems the discussion of which, in the context of Latin America, brought the wrath of the World Bank upon Teresa Hayter's head: in her terminology, "leverage", in mine, political interference and influence upon the manner of economic change, who shall direct it and who shall benefit from it. We have noted that foreign investment, foreign aid and the international trade network are the *economic* mechanisms of neo-colonialism. These do not operate blindly and inexorably in a political vacuum. They are supported and abetted by the *political* mechanisms of neo-colonialism.[50] The Commission fails to analyse these or to specify the political environment in which the "grand assize" proceeds. It is this failure, along with the reluctance to acknowledge the basic motives for giving aid (which is part of the more general misrepresentation of the nature of the relationship between developed and underdeveloped countries), which lends such an air of unreality to almost all of the Report's recommendations. I have already suggested the phenomenon of "false consciousness" and its ideological role. Let us now examine the unreality of the substantive proposals. These are set out in detail in Chapters 6 to 11 inclusive (pp. 124–230) and from them emerge, I think, two overarching themes. The first is that the relationship between donor and recipient must be and can be one of genuine "partnership", and the second that considerably more aid on better terms is necessary and possible.

The chapter entitled "Partners in Development" (pp. 124–35) (to be read along with the final chapter, "An International Framework for Development" (pp. 208–30), which is its natural extension) is a very important one. It is the chapter which provides the Report's title and this underlines its ideological significance. The Commission returns again and again to the proposition that "partnership" is essential. Donors and recipients must work *together*, on a basis of *equality* and *mutuality*. This is firmly assumed to be possible. The Commission walks a tightrope in its reasoning. Thus it is perfectly proper that

> aid should be linked to performance...

and that donors should be

> interested in whether recipients make sincere efforts to help themselves, or whether the resources put at their disposal are wasted.

On the other hand, however,

> this interest, unless carefully limited and institutionalized, creates opportunities for friction, waste of energy, and mutual irritation. Any such relationship must involve advice, consultation, and persuasion, but there must be clear and accepted channels for this and an equally clear distinction between the responsibilities of the partners. The formation and execution of development policies must ultimately be the responsibility of the recipient alone, but the donors have a right to be heard and to be informed of major events and decisions (p. 127).

Again the assumption that we are dealing with reasonable men of equal status (and echoes here of another liberal attempt to suggest decent procedures: John White's proposed democratic role for donors of Her Majesty's "loyal opposition").[51] Thus true partnership can be achieved if aid-giving is done on a multilateral basis. Multilateral processes can be truly mutual, with criticism and advice flowing both ways (i.e. donors as well as recipients would be open to criticism—pp. 129–30) with international organizations acting as honest brokers, and with "overtones of charity or interventionism" eliminated for ever (pp. 213–14).

As a matter of urgency, it is recommended, new multilateral groupings must be formed, with the World Bank and the regional development banks taking the lead in achieving this end, and the World Bank "or another appropriate existing agency" providing the reporting services for such groups (i.e. doing the monitoring of the performance of recipients and the behaviour of donors—pp. 131, 135).[52] An account is provided of the important landmarks in the evolution of multilateral processes. The World Bank, though subjected to a little mild criticism (p. 219), is a more or less exemplary organization (pp. 208, 218–27). In particular, the World Bank's affiliate, the International Development Association (IDA), established in 1960 to provide aid on highly concessional terms, is singled out for attention: with its "proven record" and "committed leadership" it shows how successful both multilateral organization and concessional finance can be (pp. 211, 222–7). The three regional development banks are "highly promising" institutions (p. 217). The Aid India Consortium (founded 1956), the European Development Fund (1958) and the Alliance for Progress (1961) are held up for praise (pp. 128–31). The Alliance for Progress is mentioned as an especially splendid example of the success of multilateral action (pp. 128–9; Annex 1, pp. 244–7). There are several recommendations as to how existing multilateral machinery might be improved (pp. 215–27). These include the strengthening of the regional development banks (pp. 218), closer co-operation between the World Bank and IMF (p. 220), a committing of at least half of the interest due on bilateral loans to allow the World Bank to subsidize interest rates on Bank lending (p. 222), an increase in the flow of capital into IDA and a more certain basis to that flow (p. 224), and a very much larger scale of operations for IDA (p. 227).

There are two distinct issues involved here. The first and most important is whether the implementation of the Commission's recommendations would really lead to a change in the relationship between rich and poor. Can equality be institutionalized without any shift in the underlying power structure? The second is whether a significant increase in multilateralism is likely. Will the stage ever be reached when we can test the first proposition?

On the first issue, the Commission's belief in the possibility of genuine "partnership" smacks of liberal utopianism. One is struck by the political naiveté: by the evasion of fundamental political issues. The central fallacy is the notion of equality. There is no equality. There are dominating partners, most notably the USA. Partnership can never be more than unequal because of the motives and the interests of the donors. The dominating partner, supplying large amounts of aid, will do so only and exclusively if it sees its own interests—however perceived—served. The next fallacy, stemming from the first and basic one, is to assume that the establishing of a complicated network of multilateral institutions will guarantee mutuality. No matter what forms, structures and institutions are created the dominating interest will have a preponderant influence. More bluntly, US interests will be served. If not, the US will withdraw. This is not changed by a switch from bilateral to multilateral relationships. Individual countries, and especially the larger donors, are reluctant to agree to this change because it becomes rather more difficult to interfere and to influence. But he who pays the piper still calls the tune.

We do well to recall Keynes' speech in 1946, at Savannah, at the first meeting of the IMF and IBRD.[53] Keynes, nearing the end of his remarkable life, and with that understanding of reality and that prescience so rare among academic economists, was only too well aware of the dangers latent in any possible multilateral institution. Having the week before attended the opening night of the Sleeping Beauty—Diaghilev's Sleeping Princess[54]—he chose the following, very appropriate, imagery:

Hidden behind veils or beards of Spanish moss I do not doubt that the usual fairies will be putting in an appearance at the christening, carrying appropriate gifts. What gifts and blessings are likely to be most serviceable to the twins, whom (rightly or wrongly) we have decided to call Master Fund and Miss Bank?

The first fairy should bring, I suggest, a Joseph's coat, a many coloured raiment to be worn by these children as a perpetual reminder that they belong to the whole world and that their sole allegiance is to the general good, without fear or favour to any particular interest. Pious words exceedingly difficult to fulfil. There is scarcely any enduring successful experience yet of an international body which has fulfilled the hopes of its progenitors. Either an institution has become diverted to be the instrument of a limited group, or it has been a puppet of sawdust through which the breath of life does not blow. Every incident and adjunct of our new-born institutions must be best calculated to emphasize and maintain their truly international character and purpose.

The second fairy, being up to date, will bring perhaps a box of mixed vitamins, A, B, C, D and all the rest of the alphabet. The children may faithfully wear their many-coloured raiment, yet themselves show pale delicate faces. Energy and a fearless spirit, which does not shelve and avoid difficult issues, but welcomes them and is determined to solve them, is what we must demand from our nurslings.

The third fairy, perhaps much older and not nearly so up to date may, like the Pope with his cardinals, close the lips of our children with her hand and then open them again, invoking a spirit of wisdom, patience and grave discretion, so that, as they grow up, they will be the respected and safe recipients of confidences, of troubles and of perplexities, a reliable and prudent support to those who need them in all times of difficulty. If these institutions are to win the full confidence of the suspicious world, it must not only be, but appear, that their approach to every problem is absolutely objective and oecumenical, without prejudice or favour.

I am asking and hoping, you will see, a great deal.

I hope that Mr Kelchner has not made any mistake and that there is no malicious fairy, no Carabosse whom he has overlooked and forgotten to ask to the party. For if so, the curses which that bad fairy will pronounce will, I feel sure, run as follows:—"You two brats shall grow up politicians; your every thought and act shall have an *arriére-pensée*; everything you determine shall not be for its own sake or on its own merits but because of something else."

If this should happen then the best that could befall—and that is how it might turn out—would be for the children to fall into an eternal slumber, never to waken or be heard of again in the courts or markets of mankind.

The Commission might with profit have considered these eloquent words. Alas, Keynes' fears have proved only too justified. The influence of Carabosse has prevailed over that of the good fairies.

The World Bank has been a persistent advocate of private foreign investment in recipient countries and has brought considerable pressure to bear in support of foreign capital. It will not lend to countries whose treatment of private foreign investment is deemed unsatisfactory.[55] Recipients do not have an inviolable right to protect their sovereignty and guard their interests as they see fit. But ideological influence is not restricted to obtaining privileged treatment for foreign capital. Indigenous private enterprise is championed, too, and the growth of national bourgeoisies encouraged. In 1956, when India seemed to be "swinging left", Eugene Black, George Wood's predecessor as President of the World Bank,[56] wrote as follows to T. T. Krishnamachari, India's Minister of Finance, delivering a World Bank ultimatum:

> In making my own comments, I should like first to emphasize once again that India's interest lies in giving private enterprise, both Indian and foreign, every encouragement to make its maximum contribution to the development of the economy particularly in the industrial field. While I recognize that the Government of India itself must play an important role in India's economic development I have the distinct impression that the potentialities of private enterprise are subjected to unnecessary restrictions there.[57]

Such "advice", with the attendant threat (explicit or implicit) that assistance may be cut or even stopped unless action is taken, and complemented by similar advice and threats from bilateral donors (especially the USA) has been given abundantly to the World Bank's customers in the underdeveloped world.[58] So much for the first fairy's "Joseph's coat". And so much for equality, mutuality and partnership.

The Indian case is of particular interest. Of all underdeveloped countries which seek and receive foreign aid India has seemed most favourably placed to resist interference: she is large, relatively powerful as poor countries go, has attempted in the past to follow a policy of non-alignment, and has been courted by both communist and non-communist blocs. Yet this has not brought anything which resembles genuine "partnership" and immunity from "leverage".

Until the early 1960s interference, though by no means non-existent, was not substantial. An anonymous but remarkably well-informed observer wrote in 1964, *à propos* of the World Bank:

> We were hitherto at the milder end of the advice-scale. We are moving, one fears, rapidly to the other end ... Whatever the cause, the fact seems to be that the ratio of advice to aid is increasingly being weighted in favour of advice even as we adjust more and more our policy to such advice ... Truly, advice feeds on its acceptance ... What is at stake is the Indianness of our Plans.[59]

How right he was. As Nehru's power waned in his last years, as his lieutenants struck out on their own (most notably T. T. Krishnamachari[60]), as the "neutrality" image became tarnished, and as the private sector grew in self-confidence and strength,[61] so did India's vulnerability increase.

Our anonymous contributor noted the attack upon price and production controls mounted in the Bank's 1963 Report on India, the remarkable similarity of language on these issues in that Report and in the Finance Minister's Budget Speech of 1964 (he quotes passages which are very alike) and the revision of coal prices and relaxing of steel control. He expressed apprehension at "ominous reports" of an even greater offensive being staged by Bank officials. The apprehension was not misplaced. Since then basic policy decisions have been taken in response to Bank pressure in association with pressure from the USA. Thus the Indian devaluation of 1966 was almost certainly "forced" by the USA via the World Bank.[62] The Bank, indeed, has sought to invade the whole decision-making process and participate actively in Indian planning. India's so-called New Economic Policy—which started with devaluation and which includes liberalisation of import and industrial licensing and a shift of interest towards agriculture—was heralded by the earlier Bank-induced decontrol measures and "actively promoted" by the Bank and other donors.[63] Whatever the rights and wrongs of these policy shifts—and I would argue that they are damaging to India[64] —they represent capitulation to foreign interference and make further interference likely. Significantly they have been accompanied by World Bank pressure to accept on liberal terms private foreign investment in fertilizer plants, with the very obvious implication "that such a 'sensible' policy would make it easier to have the required aid programme approved by the Consortium".[65] Clearly, the World Bank operates very effectively as one of the political mechanisms of neo-colonialism, bringing pressure to bear upon the poor nations to serve the interests of advanced capitalism and to take their own first steps along the capitalist path.[66]

None of the foregoing suggests that the multilateralism beloved of the Commission is likely to produce true partnership. Nor do the operation and activities of other multilateral institutions identified and praised in the Report. The IDA continues to be a branch of the World Bank and only recently it was made clear that continued support of it by the USA was dependent upon its customers treating foreign (i.e. American and Canadian) firms in the proper manner.[67] Those "highly promising" institutions, the three regional development banks have simply not achieved the "non-political" status once hoped for. They have remained firmly in the grip of the rich countries and have served their ends.[68] The Alliance for Progress, that model for multilateral action, which was in its origins an attempt to prevent revolution in Latin America,[69] has written into its character (on the insistence of the American delegates at Punta del Este) a clause committing the signatories to promoting "conditions that will encourage the flow of foreign investment".[70] Alliance for Progress "program loans" are paid in instalments and payment may be suspended if receiving governments do not act in an appropriate manner.[71] When the Inter-American Committee for the Alliance for Progress (CIAP) was set up in 1963 the United States insisted on retaining the power to *decide* on aid allocation, and threaten to withdraw if the Latin Americans demanded any other right than to advise.[72]

Multilateral institutions, then, are far from being synonymous with "partnership". But what chance, anyway, of the Commission's recommendations being implemented? The evidence would appear to suggest that the world's largest donor, the USA, is most unlikely to move any further towards multilateralism.[73] The second largest of donors, France, remains intransigently bilateral in her approach.[74] Quite simply, any substantial movement towards multilateral procedures, while it would not bring genuine "partnership", would be contrary to the economic and political interests of the large donors. Their freedom of manoeuvre would be less and their control impaired somewhat. Smaller donors, on the other hand, might gain. In these circumstances the possibility of the Report's proposals finding practical embodiment is remote.

We can now turn to the Commission's second overarching theme: that more aid on better terms is necessary and possible. This is developed at some length in three chapters: "How Much aid", "Development Debts", and "More Effective Aid". It is proposed that all industrialized countries should increase their "resource transfers" (i.e. aid plus private flows) to underdeveloped countries to at least 1 per cent of GNP by 1975 at the latest (p. 147). This was running at an average of 0.77 per cent in 1968 (with the figure for

the United States, who contributed exactly half of the total "resource transfer", at 0.65 per cent) (p. 145). Official aid, more importantly, should rise from an average of 0.39 per cent of GNP to
a figure for net disbursements of 0.70 per cent by 1975 if possible
and by 1980 at the very latest (the American figure in 1968 was
0.42 per cent) (pp. 148–9). Debt relief should be a legitimate form
of aid, the inflexibility of debt-servicing obligations reduced, and
the terms of official assistance considerably "softened" (lower
interest rates, longer maturity and longer grace-periods (pp. 160–7).
Continuity should be introduced into aid-giving so that the un-
predictability of future aid may be minimized (p. 111). Very important, aid-tying should be halted, or at least reduced (pp. 172–6).
Project aid should be reformed and there should be less of it; there
should be more programme aid (pp. 176–9). And so on.

Two basic questions arise. Firstly: what chances of success are
there for these proposals? Secondly: if they were implemented,
would they lead to growth or development (in some sense) of a
desirable kind? The answer to the first question is that the recommendations have an even bleaker prospect than those on multilateralism. Thus, the American coolness towards multilateralism is
part of a more general disenchantment with aid in that country.
Aid is one of the mechanisms of neo-colonialism, to be sure, but
America's massive neo-colonial commitment in Vietnam represents
a considerable drain of resources. Moreover, it is not clear that
American capitalism would gain significantly from any rise in aid
disbursements (through more hospitable hosts to foreign investment,
larger markets or more privileged access to raw materials), or that
the ideological harvest would be great. For these reasons present
aid levels may be maintained, or cut somewhat, but are unlikely to
be increased (unless, of course, there were a Russian aid offensive
or a dramatic resurgence of the cold war—which are not among
the reasons given or envisaged by the Commission for a rise in the
quantity of aid). Similarly, there is little evidence that other aid
donors are likely to raise the amount of aid which they give. A
portent may be seen in the recent report that the IDA, one of the
Commission's favourites, "has run out of funds".[75] This augurs ill
for both multilateralism and any possibility of a rise in aid.
America's leading role can be seen here. Eighteen other countries
are ready to put up $1,400 million as their part of the replenish-
ment agreement but the agreement cannot come into effect until
the American contribution of $960 million is forthcoming.[76] It is
most unlikely, also, that the terms upon which aid is given will improve to any marked extent. If favoured régimes seemed on the
point of collapse and political instability threatened then, indeed,

debt obligations, for example, might be treated charitably. But debt repayment, aid tying, project aid, etc., are of the very essence of neo-colonial relationships. They may be moderated temporarily for compelling political reasons. They will not disappear.

Even if aid increased and terms improved, however, aid would still operate as a "lever". It would not cease to be a mechanism of neo-colonialism. It is one of the central weaknesses of the Report of the Pearson Commission that this is simply ignored. Though re-furbished and streamlined aid would continue to shore up particular kinds of régime, to support certain classes (most notably the national bourgeoisie and rich peasants), to prevent far-reaching social and political change, to encourage the capitalist-free enter-prise route towards modernisation (though not too quickly), to insist upon the operation of the "market", to allow invasion of the decision-making process in underdeveloped countries, to influence priorities, and so on. This raises one final question, to which I would like to address myself in the next and concluding section. How valid is the Commission's all-pervading assumption that aid has contributed significantly to "development" in the past and that gains will not be consolidated or future "development" secured unless far more aid is forthcoming? More provocatively: is aid really necessary? Thus to pose the question, in its extreme form, is to be, so far as the liberal view is concerned, openly sacrilegious. But let us not hesitate to pin the *Theses* to the door of the church at Wittenberg.

IV IS AID REALLY NECESSARY?

Until fairly recently only a very few economists, of extreme *laissez-faire* views, questioned the desirability, the necessity or the positive contribution to growth and development of foreign aid. These were, most notably, P. T. Bauer, Milton Friedman and B. R. Shenoy.[77] They did so rigorously (within their own assump-tions), consistently and in the face of unpopularity. Their position is represented forcefully elsewhere in this volume, in the essay by P. T. Bauer and B. S. Yamey. Of late, aid's role as a development-inducing force has been called into doubt from a standpoint at the opposite end of the ideological spectrum, by economists like Keith Griffin, R. B. Sutcliffe and Ashok Rudra.[78] It is from this latter position that I would question the Commission's assumption, for reasons very different from those adduced by the *laissez-faire* econo-mists. Keith Griffin does so, too, in his paper.

I have already discussed the motives for giving aid and argued that aid is a neo-colonial mechanism. This is not, of course, inconsistent with "change", "growth" and "development" of a kind. Exploitation may at one and the same time perpetuate (or increase) inequality and give rise to all round absolute increases. We must scrutinise the nature of the "change", growth" and "development" in terms of immediate results (which may be misleading), longer-run implications (which may be uncertain), and possible alternatives (from history or from contemporary poor economies which appear to grow and develop without heavy dependence on foreign aid). We can do this in the process of examining the reasoning employed in the Report to justify its argument that aid's contribution is large and essential.

The reasoning in the Report is not clothed in technical language, nor is it rigorously formulated (the two are not, of course, the same). We should not criticize it on these grounds. An excessively technical presentation or too much rigour (the *rigour mortis*, which, I believe, Nicholas Kaldor has referred to) would have rendered it unintelligible to the wide audience for which it is meant. It does, however, employ recognizably orthodox arguments which are more usually presented in the jargon of economists. Thus, the initial step in the demonstration that aid contributes significantly to growth amounts to the familiar proposition that aid eases both a domestic savings constraint and a foreign exchange constraint (the so-called two-gap approach used, for example, in the models of Chenery, Strout, McKinnon and others[79]). Of the two constraints the latter receives by far the greater attention and is assumed to be the more important (pp. 48–9, 69–79, 131–2, 143). It is further assumed that the two are quite independent of one another. In fact, this latter assumption is a piece of mystification. It conceals one of aid's most significant effects, which has long—as well as short—run repercussions.

The distinction is an essentially false one.[80] The foreign exchange constraint *can* be alleviated, in principle, by a higher savings rate: i.e. by *domestic* action. This is true both on the import and the export side. Thus, much foreign aid makes possible imports of capital goods and this seems fine inasmuch as future capacity is being created. If, however, the capital equipment is used to manufacture "non-essential" consumer goods, or to manufacture intermediate goods which are then so used, aid is simply financing part of the consumption of the upper classes.[81] It is performing a political function in allowing governments to avoid difficult measures (such as taxing the upper classes more heavily). Moreover, by allowing such classes (the national bourgeoisie, landlords and rich peasants) to grow in strength aid does not merely postpone effective action. It makes it considerably more difficult to take it in future. Similarly, domestic action might yield rather more export earnings than have been forthcoming. There are, to be sure, market difficulties. But there is also a supply problem, which could be alleviated if domestic consumption (especially upper-class consumption) were reduced.[82]

We should at this point recall the Commission's performance criteria, noted above: success in raising the domestic savings rate and the ratio of exports to imports.[83] We observe that these are unlikely to be invoked simply because to invoke them would be at variance with donors' interests: politically because it might undermine favoured régimes, and economically because competition from exporters in underdeveloped economies is not desirable.

The second major step in the Commission's justification of aid relates to the contribution of "experts". The Commission places great emphasis upon it. I have already discussed this at some length in relation to the myth of the "white man's burden" and concluded that the burden lay, rather, upon the recipients.[84] The net effect of experts is, I think, an unhealthy one. It hardly convinces one of the necessity for aid.

As we proceed so we become more vague. The third step is to attribute to aid the properties of the philosopher's stone, which we achieve in these scientific days by stressing its catalytic role.

The role of foreign aid ... has not been merely to supplement domestic resources ... Aid has to a large extent been a catalyst ... It has been of first importance in the psychology of development. Economic policy aimed at growth requires a certain boldness, a willingness to experiment ... A cushion of foreign resources makes it possible to pursue bolder policies and take steps to accelerate development that might otherwise not be possible. The provision of aid, and the mutual examination of problems which this entails, has made possible basic reforms in most of the major developing countries which otherwise would not have occurred ... Aid, increasingly focused on the imperatives of long-term development has helped to make possible a good record of development in the past two decades (pp. 51–2; see also Annex 1, 236).

According to this logic aid has been associated with all that is most progressive.

To my mind this is the exact opposite of what has really happened. At the very least it is open to considerable doubt. Far from aid having induced boldness and an experimenting spirit it has bred timidity and a propensity to walk well-trodden paths. The World Bank and the USA prefer "small" to "large" plans, balanced budgets to deficit finance, the development of agriculture to industrialization, light industry to heavy industry and so on.

It is with the latter rather than the former that I would associate boldness and experimentation. And what of "basic reforms"? The only ones mentioned—"bold policy changes"—are "devaluation and liberalization of restriction on imports" (p. 236). One can only express surprise. If these are reforms they are reforms which benefit donor countries. Aid, on the contrary, has served to distract attention from and obviate the need for truly basic reforms: in taxation, distribution of income, land tenure, etc. (the Alliance for Progress notwithstanding). These can come only from radical political and social change, and aid has helped prevent that. The Commission does not reveal what exactly the "imperatives of long-term development" are. If, among other things, they include a significantly increased capacity to mobilize domestic resources and an ability to lift the foreign exchange constraint by internal effort (both of which are stressed elsewhere in the Report) then aid has not so succeeded. Underdeveloped economies have become increasingly dependent upon aid and progressively more enmeshed in repayment obligations.[85] These are the "imperatives of long-term vulnerability".

Intrinsic to all of the Commission's thinking and a key part of its ideological function is acceptance of given social and political structures. If aid is necessary it is necessary in the context of these structures (and in order to maintain them). If we accept these as fixed, immutable and, indeed, desirable then, no doubt, aid does make possible a certain growth of GNP. It is only in this sense that it is "necessary". If, contrariwise, one argues that existing social and political structures constitute the tap-root of "backwardness" and prevent a satisfactory undertaking of the "tasks of development" then aid, because it supports these structures, is positively harmful. If one further recalls that aid is part of a neo-colonial system which successfully exploits the underdeveloped world and which ensures that part of any surplus created accrues to rich countries we see that it is doubly harmful.

There is only one slight hint in the whole Report that there may be an *alternative* to aid (which almost, but not quite, suggests that the savings and foreign exchange constraints may not, after all, be independent): that social and political structures are not immutable:

Of course, some developing countries could achieve and maintain a 6 per cent growth rate without foreign aid if they and the international community were prepared to accept the consequences, human and political, associated with abrupt and enforced increases in savings and tax ratios (p. 126).

That is all. The alternative is rejected with indecent haste, without any consideration. There is no mention of the immense hardship, deprivation and squalor which policies of *festina lente* allow to persist.[86] I pointed out above the Commission's exclusion of communist countries from its deliberations and the spurious justification given for this by an avowed "grand assize".[87] In so proceeding the Commission avoided the uncomfortable possibility that large and increasing amounts of aid may not, after all, be a *sine qua non* for growth. Such is the moral of China's path. The Commission might also have noted that Japan, the only Asian country so far to join the ranks of advanced capitalism, proceeded in her early years of industrialization (in the late nineteenth and early twentieth centuries) with very little foreign resources. Draconian domestic action made this possible.[88] Can one really say that the human consequences of Chinese policy or of the measures taken in Meiji Japan are any harsher than the realities of Indian life? Poverty in India continues to be massive and to show little sign of diminution.[89]

In conclusion, a brief glance at the Chinese experience and a few comparisons between China and India are instructive.[90] China received assistance from the Soviet Union between 1950 and 1960 (mainly in the form of industrial machinery, plant and technical assistance),[91] which has been estimated as accounting for 3.6 per cent of fixed capital formation and 3 per cent of total net investment for the years 1952–7.[92] Indeed, China's aid to other underdeveloped countries between 1953 and 1960 was only marginally less than the financial assistance which she herself received from the Soviet Union.[93] After 1960 China received no foreign assistance at all and, moreover, cleared her debts to the Soviet Union with remarkable speed (probably by 1964).[94] India, by contrast, has increased her dependence on foreign aid from 5.8 per cent of total planned investment during the first Plan, 21.1 per cent in the Second, 19.9 per cent in the Third and a targeted figure of 28.8 per cent in the Fourth.[95] Net aid, meanwhile, has fallen from 80 per cent of gross aid in the Third to 66 per cent in the Fourth[96] and will continue to fall. China has had no interference with her domestic policies, while, as we have seen, interference with Indian policy—making and choice of priorities has increased from the early 1960s on (in my discussion I concentrated on interference via multilateral channels, but numerous examples of successful and attempted interference on the basis of purely bilateral relationships could have been given.[97]) China, moreover, has no repayment obligations, while India's are crushing and must constitute a brake on future growth. Agricultural production in the two economies has grown at roughly the same rate (at a trend rate of around 3 per cent per annum),[98] but China's rate of growth of industrial production has been substantially higher.[99] In the crucial "machine-tool sector", China approaches self-sufficiency while India is still heavily dependent on imports.[100] China's ability to generate greater industrial growth with a similar growth in agriculture and substantially less foreign aid derives, in part, from a far greater ability to mobilise an agricultural surplus and use it for the necessary capital formation.[101] Aid in the form of P.L.480 food has allowed India to avoid necessary action in the rural sector and so strengthen already powerful rural vested interests.[102] Future mobilization of an agricultural surplus on favourable terms is made more difficult.

One could continue in this vein. One could also stress the more positive aspects of Indian growth and development and emphasize, for example, the severe setbacks consequent upon China's "Cultural Revolution". What is clear, however, is that China is poised for far greater future growth than is India. Aid, in substantial quantities, is not necessary. There is an alternative.

NOTES

1 For the factual details in this paragraph see pp. iv, v, vi, vii, viii, x, 400 of the Report.
2 Teresa Hayter, *Aid As Imperialism* (London, 1971), p. 193. The first in the series was John White, *Pledged to Development* (London, 1967).
3 Teresa Hayter, *French Aid* (London, 1966).
4 The details of World Bank "persuasion" and of the manuscript's eventual rejection by ODI are given in calm and clinical fashion by Teresa Hayter in op. cit., Preface and Appendix. The Appendix, entitled "The Birth and Death of an ODI Study" is a fascinating account of how the sordid business unfolded.
5 That the Commissioners included Arthur Lewis and Saburo Okita and the Consultants representatives from underdeveloped countries does not in any way cast doubt on this point. It merely underlines that the approach is not confined to experts in Western countries.
6 There are two occasions when the united front is momentarily broken (see Report, pp. 104 and 164). At one point (p. 104) we are told that Professor Lewis and Sir Edward Boyle agree with a particular sentence (i.e. "But in our judgement, available facts do suggest that direct foreign investment has added substantially to the real national income of developing countries"), but not all the preceding theoretical arguments adduced. At another (p. 164) Mr Marjolin expressed disagreement with the Commission's recommendation on the softening of terms on official development assistance loans. Mr Marjolin wanted a less blanket recommendation.

7 Even if information cannot be obtained directly from countries like the Soviet Union it is possible to learn much about their activities as donors by looking at the aid which countries like India, for example, have received from them. Information on this *is* available. There is, anyway, a not insignificant literature on Soviet aid to China (some of which is listed below), while the Commission would surely have had access to studies such as James Richard Carter, *The Net Cost of Soviet Foreign Aid* (New York, 1971) which was being completed while the Commission deliberated.

8. These are too numerous to list here. One should, however, mention Joint Committee of the US Congress, *An Economic Profile of Mainland China* (Washington, 1967 and New York, 1968) and the associated document, *Mainland China in the World Economy. Hearings* (Washington, 1967); A. Eckstein, W. Galenson and T. C. Liu (eds.), *Economic Trends in Communist China* (Chicago, 1968), and Ping-ti Ho and Tang Tsou (eds.), *China in Crisis, 2 Vols.* (Chicago, 1968).

9 Indonesia is discussed in Annex 1, pp. 337–45 of the Report.

10 See also p. 43: "The record of development is encouraging. The achievements have been substantial, and they have shown that less developed societies can move forward."

11 See pp. 32–6 and 61–2 of the Report. It is, in fact, by no means certain that a "Green Revolution" has come to poor countries. The Commission is premature in its judgment.

12 An interesting account of the nature of racialist attitudes in British India may be seen in Francis G. Hutchins, *The Illusion of Permanence: British Imperialism in India* (Princeton, 1967), Chapters 2, 3 and 5.

13 Charles Carrington, *Rudyard Kipling. His Life and Work* (Pelican Books, 1970), p. 337. The factual details in this paragraph are drawn from Carrington, pp. 334–7. He would not, I think, have agreed with my interpretation of them.

14 Carrington, op. cit., p. 337.

15 David Apter, *The Politics of Modernization* (Chicago, 1965), p. 314, defines ideology in such terms. This is not, however, a sufficient definition of ideology. See below.

16 The analysis of ideology in these terms is to be seen, of course, in Karl Marx and Friedrich Engels, *The German Ideology*. For a useful non-Marxist account of the development of the concept of ideology see A. L. Macfie, "Economics—Science, Ideology, Philosophy?" *Scottish Journal of Political Economy*, Volume X, No. 2, June 1963, pp. 212–25.

17 The words are those of St. Luke vi, 35, as quoted from the Vilgate. See W. J. Ashley, *An Introduction to English Economic History and Theory, Volume 1, Part 1, The Middle Ages* (London, 1888), pp. 148 and 210. Mediaeval attitudes towards interest and usury are treated in Arthur Birnie, *An Economic History of the British Isles* (8th edition, London 1955), pp. 112–16; R. H. Tawney, *Religion and the Rise of Capitalism* (Pelican Books, 1948), pp. 43–67; Ashley, op. cit., pp. 148–63, and *Volume 1, Part II, The End of the Middle Ages* (London, 1925), pp. 377–488.

18 The extent to which such injunctions were ignored and the range of economic casuistry used to counter the Church's own sophistry are indicated in Birnie, loc. cit.; Tawney, op. cit., pp. 54–67; Ashley,

op. cit., Part I, pp. 154 and 196–203, and Part II, loc. cit. Today's donor countries are capable of being no less fertile in adducing arguments to justify their practices.

19 For the Report's treatment of aid-tying see pp. 92, 96, 154, 172–6. The Report points out that tying reduces the possibility of trade in capital goods between underdeveloped countries (pp. 92 and 96); that it involves over-pricing practices (pp. 154 and 172); that it has associated indirect costs—like imports and projects of low priority, administrative complications (p. 172); that it requires "extensive import and exchange controls" (p. 172). It is not, however, good enough for a grand assize to say, for example, that "over-pricing practices . . . are difficult to assess" (p. 154). An attempt should have been made. There was, after all, no shortage of man-power.

20 A report in *The Times* (of London), of 13 January 1969, noted: "Indian economists are beginning to fear that the country will face acute financial embarrassment in coming years when it might be preferable for the Government to renege on its massive aid debt and forgo further international economic assistance." The Indian Government has not yet reneged, but there is no doubting the seriousness of the situation.

21 Paul Streeten, "A Poor Nation's Guide to Getting Aid", *New Society*, 1 February 1968.

22 Significantly, the Report, when stressing the *positive and beneficial* role of capital and trade flows is at pains to observe that aid must be considered alongside international trade and private foreign investment. Indeed, it is pointed out (pp. 122–3) that aid, for investment in infrastructure, is a prerequisite for foreign investment. Even on the positive side, however, the three mechanisms are treated separately and not as part of a whole. Any possible complementarities of a negative kind are ignored. There is, perhaps, a very dim awareness (p. 107) when it is observed that "developed countries should, as far as possible, keep aid policy and disputes concerning foreign investment separate". That is as much as we get.

23 The novel appeared originally in 1958 and enjoyed some success, receiving the final accolade of being made into a film starring Marlon Brando. The paperback edition bears the splendid quotation, supposedly from the *New York Herald Tribune*: "If this were not a free country this book would be banned."

24 See, especially, Dudley Seers, "Why Visiting Economists Fail", *Journal of Political Economy*, Volume 70, No. 4, August 1962, pp. 325–38. Also his "The Limitations of the Special Case", *Bulletin of the Oxford Institute of Economics and Statistics*, Vol. 25, No. 2, May 1963, pp. 77–98, reprinted in Kurt Martin and John Knapp (eds.), *The Teaching of Development Economics* (London 1967), pp. 1–27.

25 Adam Curle, *Planning for Education in Pakistan. A Personal Case Study* (London, 1966), especially Chapter 1. At the time of publication Curle was Professor of Education and Development at Harvard.

26 Curle, op. cit., pp. 2–3.

27 Curle, op. cit., pp. 3–4.

28 Curle, op. cit., pp. 4–5.

29 Curle, op. cit., p. 5.

30 Analysis of the more-or-less liberal press in Britain and abroad reveals a general and enthusiastic acceptance of the Report's arguments and recommendations. See Fiona Wilson, "Press Comments on the Pearson Report", *Bulletin of the Institute of Development Studies*, Vol. 2, No. 2, December 1969, pp. 35–42. Academic members of the "aid lobby" are rather less enthusiastic since they are conscious of the Report's shortcomings. They have tended to accept the Commission's position as a base from which it is necessary to go forward. This is well exemplified in the contributions by Streeten and Lipton to this volume.

31 Pp. 232–4, 260, 262. It is noteworthy that these references are in the Annex to the Report. Any possible criticism is disarmed, rather, when we are told at the beginning of the lengthy Annex that it "is drawn from staff materials prepared in the course of the Commission's inquiry.... Views expressed or implied should not necessarily be attributed to the Commission" (p. 231). In fact, the line followed in the Annex is indistinguishable from the Commission's. One is sure that any offending material would not have appeared.

32 P. 341, for example. This is in a section on Indonesia, and is again in the Annex.

33 This is the central theme of Chapter 5, "Private Foreign Investment" (pp. 99–123). The theme is also pervasive in Annex 1 on "the Development Situation" (pp. 231–353).

34 We get a rather different view of the oil-producing countries in, for example, Michael Tanzer, *The Political Economy of International Oil and the Underdeveloped Countries* (Boston, 1969). See, especially, pp. 59–77 and 304–18. Despite the attacks on Tanzer by *inter alios* Edith T. Penrose (see her review in *Journal of Economic Literature*, Vol. VIII, No. 1, March 1970, pp. 95–7), his book is refreshing in the awkward questions it poses. On the exporters of mineral products see, for example, N. Girvan, *The Caribbean Bauxite Industry* (Jamaica, 1967).

35 Michael Kidron, *Foreign Investments in India* (London, 1965).

36 See Dadabhai Naoroji, *Poverty and Un-British Rule in India* (Delhi, 1962), and B. N. Ganguli, *Dadabhai Naoroji and the Drain Theory* (Bombay, 1965). Naoroji's book was first published in 1901 and is a collection of writings which started to appear in the 1870s. More recently we have Harry Magdoff, *The Age of Imperialism* (New York, 1966); Andre Gunder Frank, *Capitalism and Underdevelopment in Latin America* (New York, 1967), especially Chapter V.

37 The various devices are considered in Kidron, op. cit., pp. 226–8, 250–1, 266, 300–1. Kidron points out (p. 228) that foreign manufacturing firms often "prefer a high revenue from sales to their Indian branches and subsidiaries to profits made in India". At the time when he wrote royalties were taxed at a lower rate than profits and fees were tax-free.

38 Kidron, op. cit., pp. 245–6. "New-style" foreign investment in India is concentrated in a small number of technologically complex, patent-protected industries, which are international (as opposed to regional) in scope, whereas "old-style" capital was concentrated in extractive industries, processing for export, international trade and ancillary services, and was deployed by regional firms. (See Kidron, pp. 3–5, 32, 186–7, 222–3, 240–2.)

39 Kidron, op. cit., p. 300.

40 Kidron, op. cit., pp. 302 and 313–14.

41 We need only remind ourselves of the Suez adventure of 1956, various American sorties in Latin America (the Dominican Republic in 1965, for example), France's military interference in Gabon in 1964, and so on. And let us not forget South-East Asia, with the most prolonged and horrifying intervention of all.

42 It is possible to derive distinct advantage without being critically dependent. That is to say, advanced capitalism would not be brought to its knees by a sudden diminution in neo-colonial activity, though its growth might be curtailed somewhat.

43 Kidron, op. cit., p. 222.

44 Kidron, op. cit., pp. 240–2.

45 Exploitation is, perhaps, an over-used term. Its meaning here is, I think, clear from the context. For those who may have an emotional blockage I define exploitation as follows. Exploitation is a situation of *unequal exchange*. Some kind of exchange is, I think, necessary, even if it is something intangible like "good government" that is being exchanged. If there is no exchange of any kind then the process is one of "robbery" or "plunder". In the exploitative relationship the exploiter has superior power—organizational, economic, political, military—and by virtue of that superior power extracts advantage: extracts "surplus" of one kind or another. Some sort of surplus must be there before it can be extracted. It has to be generated. And the superior power may have to take steps to see that it *is* generated.

46 Kidron, op. cit., p. 312 emphasizes the importance of this.

47 Motivation may, of course, be complex, but that the stated motives are the primary ones emerges from authorities as different as Charles P. Kindleberger, *American Business Abroad* (New Haven and London, 1969), especially Lectures 1, 2 and 5, and Magdoff, *The Age of Imperialism*, especially Chapters 1, 2 and 5.

48 This is hinted at in G. Ohlin, "The Evolution of Aid Doctrine", pp. 40–50, as reprinted in Jagdish Bhagwati and Richard S. Eckaus (eds.), *Foreign Aid. Selected Readings* (Penguin, 1970), pp. 21–62. For a more explicit statement on the motives behind French aid see Pierre Jalée, *The Pillage of the Third World* (New York, 1968), pp. 61–5.

49 Another contributor to this volume, Keith Griffin, draws attention to very clear statements by Dean Rusk and H. B. Chenery. One could quote equally unequivocal statements by Presidents Johnson and Kennedy, and by other respected and "neutral" academic economists.

50 In his Introduction to Teresa Hayter's book R. B. Sutcliffe stresses the need for "searching and sensitive inquiry, supported by a sophisticated analysis of the political mechanisms at work" (op. cit., p. 6). This, indeed, is so.

51 John White, *Pledged to Development* (London, 1967), p. 184. This is a theme of a section entitled "The Function of Management", op. cit., pp. 180–96.

52 There are three regional development banks. The first, the Inter-American Development Bank, was established in 1958. The African and Asian Banks came later. See pp. 217–18 of the Report. They are discussed in John White, *Regional Development Banks* (London, 1971).

53 The speech is recorded in full by Keynes' biographer. See R. F. Harrod, *The Life of John Maynard Keynes* (London, 1951) pp. 631–2. It is of interest that a recent historian of IMF, while nothing Keynes' speech does not reproduce it in full. It was, perhaps, too prophetic to include in an official history. See J. Keith Horsefield, *The International Monetary Fund. Vol. 1. Chronicle* (Washington, 1969), p. 123.

54 Harrod, op. cit., pp. 622–33 and 631.

55 See Hayter, op. cit., pp. 31 and 49. She cites (p. 31) an internal Bank document called *Policy Memorandum 204* which states this quite clearly. See also Kidron, op. cit., pp. 153–5 on the Bank's "active espousal of private enterprise, particularly foreign private enterprise".

56 Black was the World Bank's first President and served from 1949 to 1962. He was succeeded by George Woods—who suggested the Pearson "grand assize"—and Woods was President from 1962 to 1968. The current President, Robert McNamara, has been in office since 1968. All three Presidents have been American, with interests in business or banking.

57 Quoted in Kidron, op. cit., p. 154. This was written after a Bank Mission to India had submitted its Report.

58 Hayter, op. cit., pp. 31 and 49.

59 See "Aid and Advice", *The Economic Weekly*, Vol. XVI, No. 14, 4 April 1964, pp. 630–1.

60 This is stressed in *The Economic Weekly* piece.

61 Kidron (op. cit., pp. 65–181) gives an excellent account of how the business community gradually grew in self-confidence from the mid-1950s onwards.. As it did so it became more responsive to the blandishments of foreign capital and began to act as a pressure-group in its favour.

62 See Jagdish N. Bhagwati and Padma Desai, *India. Planning for Industrialisation* (London, 1970), pp. 128, 182, 484, 487. It is interesting to note that much of the discussion of the implications of such pressure is conducted, very briefly, in footnotes. This makes many of the footnotes more useful than the text. The "footnote syndrome" perhaps indicates a sneaking awareness that these issues are far more important than the authors are willing to admit.

63 Bhagwati and Desai, op, cit., pp. 182, 484, 496.

64 There are very few prepared to argue that the devaluation of 1966 has brought India any economic benefit at all. The New Economic Policy is almost a confession of the failure of planning. If planning has not yet failed it will surely be weakened by the operation of these measures.

65 Bhagwati and Desai, op. cit., p. 227.

66 The World Bank has now more or less taken over "planning" (so-called) and its implementation in Indonesia. See Hayter, op. cit., p. 70.

67 See *The Times* (of London), 8 July 1971, article headed "World Bank development branch out of funds".

68 This is clearly shown in John White, *Regional Development Banks* (London, 1971). John White argues that this is not the result of any conscious policy of neo-colonialism. Whether there was conscious neo-colonial intent is, perhaps, irrelevant. The objective role has certainly been a neo-colonial one.

69 See, for example, Keith Griffin, *Underdevelopment in Spanish*

America (London, 1969), p. 137 (and passim); J. P. Morray, "The United States and Latin America", especially p. 108, in James Petras and Maurice Zeitlin (eds.), *Latin America. Reform or Revolution?* (New York, 1968), pp. 99–119.

70 Morray, op. cit., pp. 107–8.
71 Morray, op. cit., pp. 111–12.
72 Hayter, *Aid as Imperialism*, pp. 103 and 186.
73 See, for example, P. J. Eldridge, *The Politics of Foreign Aid in India* (London, 1969), pp. 46–7; Robert E. Asher, *Development Assistance in the Seventies. Alternatives for the United States* (Washington D.C., 1970), p. 227; and Willard E. Thorp, *The Reality of Foreign Aid* (New York, 1971), pp. 164–5.
74 See, for example, Ohlin, op. cit., pp. 49 et passim; and OECD, *Resources For the Developing World. The Flow of Financial Resources to less Developed Countries, 1962–1968* (Paris, 1970), p. 69.
75 See article in *The Times* noted above.
76 loc. cit.
77 See, for example, P. T. Bauer, *Indian Economic Policy and Development* (London, 1961), pp. 119–41; P. T. Bauer and J. B. Wood, "Foreign Aid—the Soft Option", *Banca Nazionale del Lavoro Quarterly Review*, December 1961, pp. 403–18; M. Friedman, "Foreign Economic Aid: Means and Objectives", *Yale Review*, Vol. 47, Summer 1958, pp. 244–38, reprinted in Bhagwati and Eckaus (eds.), *Foreign Aid. Selected Readings*, pp. 63–78; B. R. Shenoy, *Indian Planning and Economic Development* (Bombay, 1963), pp. 88–118 and *Indian Economic Policy* (Bombay, 1968), pp. 261–80.
78 K. B. Griffin and J. L. Enos, "Foreign Assistance: Objectives and Consequences", *Economic Development and Cultural Change*, Vol. 18, No. 3, April 1970, pp. 313–27; Keith Griffin, "Foreign Capital, Domestic Savings and Economic Development", *Bulletin of the Oxford University Institute of Economics and Statistics*, Vol. 32, No. 2, May 1970, pp. 99–112; R. B. Sutcliffe, Foreword to Hayter, *Aid As Imperialism* and review of Pearson Report in *Journal of Development Studies*, Vol. 8, No. 1, October 1971, pp. 145–6; Ashok Rudra, "New Urgency About Aid", *Economic and Political Weekly*, Vol. V, No. 32, 8 August 1970, pp. 1341–5.
79 See, for example, R. I. McKinnon, "Foreign Exchange Constraints in Economic Development and Efficient Aid Allocation", *Economic Journal*, Vol. LXXIV, No. 294, June 1964, pp. 388–409; and Hollis B. Chenery and Alan M. Strout, "Foreign Assistance and Economic Development", *American Economic Review*, Vol. 56, No. 4, September 1966, pp. 679–733.
80 This is argued in an interesting article by Vijay Joshi, "Saving and Foreign Exchange Constraints", in Paul Streeten (ed.), *Unfashionable Economics. Essays in Honour of Lord Balogh* (London, 1970), pp. 111–33. Joshi treats the issue theoretically and in terms of real situations. The theoretical treatment is original. That the distinction is false in the real world has, of course, been pointed out by students of the Chinese economy and by certain critics of the Indian planners (most notably K. N. Raj).
81 K. N. Raj has calculated that the foreign cost of such "non-essential" expenditure (direct and indirect) amounted to about one quarter

of India's export earnings in the mid-1960s. K. N. Raj, *India, Pakistan and China. Economic Growth and Outlook* (Bombay, 1967), pp. 32–3.

82 Joshi (op. cit., p. 123) makes this point.
83 See above, p. 89.
84 See above, pp. 86–8.
85 The Indian situation is a case in point. See below, p. 107.
86 This is one of the main themes in Barrington Moore Jr. *Social Origins of Dictatorship and Democracy* (London, 1967), pp. 314–410 (especially pp. 385–410), which relate to India. This is a most rewarding book.
87 See above, p. 81.
88 There is a large and growing literature on Meiji Japan. See, for example, M. Bronfenbrenner, "Some lessons of Japan's Economic Development, 1853–1938", *Pacific Affairs*, Vol XXXIV, No. 1, Spring 1961, pp. 7–27; K. Ohkawa and H. Rosovsky, "The Role of Agriculture in Modern Japanese Economic Development", *Economic Development and Cultural Exchange,* Vol. 9, part 2, October 1960, pp. 43–68, reprinted in C. K. Eicher and L. W. Witt, *Agriculture in Economic Development* (New York, 1964), pp. 45–69; David Landes, "Japan and Europe: Contrasts in Industrialisation" pp. 93–7, in William W. Lockwood (ed.), *The State and Economic Enterprise in Japan* (Princeton, 1965), pp. 93–182; James I Nakamura, *Agricultural Production and the Economic Development of Japan, 1873–1922* (Princeton, 1966), Chapter 7.
89 For a detailed empirical study see V. M. Dandekar and Nilakantha Rath, "Poverty in India—1. Dimensions and Trends", *Economic and Political Weekly*, Vol. VI, No. 1, 2 January 1971, pp. 25–48, and "Poverty in India—2. Policies and Programmes", *Economic and Political Weekly*, Vol. VI, No. 2, 9 January, pp. 106–46. This, the only comprehensive study of Indian poverty, is something of a *tour de Force.*
90 I am deeply indebted to my colleague Dr K. R. Walker for the enlightenment which he has provided on the Chinese economy. He would not accept all that I argue, nor, indeed, the general approach in this paper, and he bears absolutely no responsibility for any of the views expressed or errors perpetrated. Over the last three years we have prepared a great deal of comparative material for our M.Sc course, "Comparative Economic Systems: India and China", and this may some day be published. The generalizations in this paragraph are based, to a large extent, on the material and my interpretation of it.
91 Soviet aid to China is discussed by a variety of writers. See, for example, Choh-Ming Li, *Economic Development of Communist China* (Berkeley, 1959), p. 174 et passim; Chu-Yuan Cheng, *Economic Relations Between Peking and Moscow: 1949–63* (New York, 1964); Alexander Eckstein, *Communist China's Economic Growth and Foreign Trade* (New York, 1966), pp. 4–6, 135–82; Arthur J. Ashbrook Jr., "Main Lines of Chinese Communist Economic Policy", pp. 22–3, 31, in Joint Economic Committee of the US Congress, *An Economic Profile of Mainland China* (Washington, 1967 and New York, 1968), pp. 15–44; Robert L. Price, "International Trade of Communist China, 1950–1965", pp. 591–5, in *Profile,* pp. 579–608; Nai-Ruenn Chen and Walter Galenson, *The Chinese*

Economy Under Communism (Edinburgh, 1969), pp. 51–5, 58, 69, 70, 73, 75, 77, 78-9, 85, 86, 120, 137, 138, 157, 200, 206, 215, 221, 222, 225. These are only a few of the many.

92   Choh-Ming Li, op. cit., p. 174. Chu-Yuan Cheng (op. cit., p. 87) quotes figures which show Soviet loans as constituting 1.5 per cent of Chinese capital investments between 1953 and 1957, rising to a maximum of 3.5 per cent in 1957.

93   Chu-Yuan Cheng, op. cit., pp. 87–8.

94   Ashbrook, op. cit., p. 23.

95   Figures for the first three Plans are taken from Indian Economic Association, *Impact of Foreign Aid on Indian Economic Development* (Bombay, 1968), p. 53. The Fourth Plan figure is calculated from the first Draft Outline: Government of India, *Fourth Five Year Plan. A Draft Outline* (New Delhi, 1966), pp. 42 and 90–1.

96   Paul Streeten and Roger Hill, "Aid to India", p. 327, in Paul Streeten and Michael Lipton (eds.), *The Crisis of Indian Planning* (London, 1968), pp. 323–49.

97   One remarkable example is worthy of note. It is provided by Bhagwati and Desai (op. cit., pp. 209–10). In 1966 President Johnson announced the intention of starting an Indo-US Educational Foundation with the vast accumulation of PL480 funds. This would have meant an annual expenditure on education greater than that made by the Indian Government itself, "thus lending itself to the possibility of unprecedented ideological penetration of the educational system". This particular proposal was resisted.

98   This emerges from the comparative statistics which K. R. Walker and I have prepared for the years 1950 to 1965. There is no argument about the Indian figure. For a useful treatment see A. M. Khusro, "Economic Theory and Indian Agricultural Policy", in A. M. Khusro (ed.), *Readings in Agricultural Development* (Calcutta, 1968), pp. 1–54 (especially pp. 3–7). The Chinese figure is more contentious. Some observers would put it lower than 3 per cent.

99   This again is shown by the comparison made by Walker and myself. Chinese growth is very significantly higher in coal, steel, fertilizers and oil.

100   On this see K. N. Raj, "Role of the 'Machine-Tools Sector' in Economic Growth", pp. 219–23, in C. H. Feinstein (ed.), *Socialism, Capitalism and Economic Growth. Essays presented to Maurice Dobb* (London, 1967), pp. 217–26.

101   I have argued elsewhere the critical role of an "agricultural surplus" in the process of industrialization and the inefficacy of siphoning-off mechanisms in India. See T. J. Byres, "Industrialisation, the Peasantry and the Economic Debate in Post-Independence India", in A. V. Bhuleshkar (ed.), *Indian Economic Thought and Development. Jawarharlal Nehru Memorial*, Vol. II (Bombay, 1972). I must again record my gratitude to K. R. Walker for showing me just how effective Chinese mobilization policies have been.

102   I hope to examine this in detail in a forthcoming study. Many observers have noted the increased power of rich peasants in India.

4

PEARSON AND THE POLITICAL ECONOMY OF AID

by

Keith Griffin

Magdalen College, Oxford

PEARSON AND THE POLITICAL ECONOMY OF AID

I INTRODUCTION

It is widely believed that the purpose of foreign aid is to reduce world poverty. Alas, this is only partly true. The major purpose of aid is to further the economic and political interests of the aid giving nations; there is very little altruism in most aid programmes. This point is so obvious as to be trite, yet it is the inescapable point of departure for any assessment of the consequences of aid in practice.

Unfortunately, the Pearson Commission did not face this fact and as a result its report begins on the wrong foot. The Commissioners posed the right question but gave the wrong answer: "What, then, is the objective of co-operation for international development? . . . It is to help the poorer countries to move forward, in their own way, into the industrial and technological age so that the world will not become more and more starkly divided between the haves and the have-nots, the privileged and the less privileged" (pp. 7-8). In other words, the objectives are to reduce poverty, reduce international inequality and promote growth.

Many will agree that these *ought* to be the objectives of foreign aid, but it is highly doubtful that they have been. Consider, for example, the United States, the nation which accounts for more than half of what the OECD calls the "net flow of official development assistance to less-developed countries and multilateral agencies". Dean Rusk, Secretary of State under Presidents Kennedy and Johnson, has indicated very clearly what are the motives of the US aid programme:

"The foreign aid programme of the 1960s—as it was in the 1940s and 1950s—is planned and administered to serve the vital interests of the United States. It is a prime instrument of US foreign policy and our security would be in great jeopardy without the aid programme . . . US assistance fits into a carefully planned pattern based on a study of each country and an analysis of US interests."[1]

Some readers may feel that the above quotation is misleading, contending that Rusk was making a political statement for popular consumption in a country in which the man-in-the-street is hostile to aid. The government may act from generous motives but in order to get its programme accepted it is compelled to justify its actions in terms of self interest. Good deeds are disguised by

bad motives. In an age of double-think such behaviour by governments is plausible though unlikely. It is not even plausible, however,
that an economics don at Harvard would behave in a similar way.
Thus we can be reasonably confident that Professor Chenery is
accurate when he writes that "the main objective of foreign assistance, as of many other tools of foreign policy, is to produce the
kind of political and economic environment in the world in which
the United States can best pursue its own social goals".[2]

Professor Chenery and Mr Rusk do not specify what they mean
by "the vital interests of the United States", but it is evident that
this includes, among other things, first, the maintenance of the
political status quo and balance of international power and, second,
the promotion of prosperity in America. The latter is pursued in
many ways, one of which is by safeguarding and increasing US
overseas investments. Many documents testify to this. For instance,
the minority report of the Department of Commerce Committee
for the Alliance for Progress (subsequently endorsed by the
Chairman) argues that the "encouragement of private enterprise,
local and foreign, must become the main thrust of the Alliance".
The United States "should concentrate its economic aid programme
in countries that show the greatest inclination to adopt measures
to improve the investment climate, and withhold it from others
until satisfactory performance has been demonstrated". Similar
sentiments are expressed in the Rockefeller Report.[3] The Pearson
Report goes further and claims "there can be no doubt about the
contribution which private capital can render to economic development. Indeed, dollar for dollar, it may be more effective than
official aid . . ."[4]

This is an extraordinary claim by the Commission. First, not a
shred of empirical evidence is presented to show that what is
good for General Motors, Standard Oil or the United Fruit
Company is necessarily good for the underdeveloped nations.
Second, even if the contribution of private foreign capital to
development is positive, it is unlikely prima facie that a gift (aid)
would contribute less than a commercial loan or direct investment
of a similar amount. Third, no attempt is made by the Commission
to explain why investing countries have so often had to use force
to compel the underdeveloped countries to accept their capital.
If private foreign investment is as effective as the Commission
suggests, this should not be necessary.

Let us not deceive ourselves: force has been used with appalling
frequency to promote the interests of American business abroad.
The testimony of Major General Smedley from his autobiography
of 1935 illustrates the point. He writes as follows:

"I spent thirty-three years and four months in active service as a member of our country's most agile military force—the United States Marine Corps. I served in all commissioned ranks from a second lieutenant to major general. And during that period I spent most of my time being a high-class muscle man for Big Business, for Wall Street and for the bankers. In short I was a racketeer for capitalism.

"Thus I helped make Mexico and especially Tampico safe for American oil interests in 1914. I helped make Haiti and Cuba a decent place for the National City Bank boys to collect revenues in. I helped purify Nicaragua for American sugar interests in 1916. I helped make Honduras 'right' for American fruit companies in 1913. In China in 1927 I helped to see to it that Standard Oil went its way unmolested.

"During those years I had, as the boys in the back room would say, a swell racket. I was rewarded with honours, medals, promotions. Looking back on it, I feel I might have given Al Capone a few points. The best he could do was to operate his racket in three city districts. We Marines operated on three continents."[5]

The world has changed since Smedley wrote his life history, but not beyond recognition, as anyone who follows events in the Third World knows. Arms, aid and foreign business are closely associated. It is not just coincidence, for example, that the United States is the largest contributor of foreign aid, the biggest overseas investor and the nation with the most troops stationed abroad. Portugal supplies more public and private capital in relation to GNP than any other donor country. Virtually all of this goes to Angola and Mozambique, where guerilla warfare is rampant. France is second only to Portugal in the proportion of her national income devoted to foreign aid. Much of this goes to Algeria and other ex-colonies in Africa where French commercial interests are deeply entrenched. Some French troops are currently fighting in Chad.

We live in a world where it is still possible for one man to be in succession President of the Ford Motor Company, Secretary of Defence responsible for prosecuting the war in Indo-China, and President of the International Bank for Reconstruction and Development. In such a world it is hardly surprising that the connection between aid and development is tenuous. Aid is not intended to promote development and it has often failed to do so.

The Report recognizes that aid has often been used to further the interest of the donors. Early in the report it is stated that "a good deal of bilateral aid has indeed been dispensed in order to achieve short-term political favours, gain strategic advantages, or promote exports from the donor. Much foreign aid was granted in the 1950's to enable some countries to maintain large armed forces rather than to promote economic growth. In none of these cases was the promotion of long-term development a dominant objective of the aid given" (p. 4). It is a pity the Commissioners did not pursue this point more deeply. Had they done so they might have written an entirely different report.

II FOREIGN CAPITAL AND ECONOMIC GROWTH

The fact that, in general, aid has not been designed to promote growth does not necessarily imply that it has not done so. Growth, after all, could be a by-product of policies designed for other purposes. There may be a harmony of interests between the objectives of the donors and those of the recipients.

Several countries, notably Formosa, South Korea, Pakistan and Kenya, are repeatedly cited as examples of "aid that works".[6] This may indeed be true in these particular cases, although the evidence presented is far from conclusive. Moreover, politically, it is hard to think of four countries which have less appeal to those actively concerned with the development problems of poor nations. Three of the four were military dictatorships at the time the articles were written and, as the ODI acknowledges, "they are all authoritarian" and "all of them are fairly conservative in their politics, and Formosa is somewhere out on the far right end of the spectrum".[7] Chiang Kai-shek and Ayub Khan are hardly good advertisements for Western aid programmes.

The Report mentions that "the correlation between the amounts of aid received in the past decades and the growth performance is very weak" (p. 49). This is to put it mildly! A cross-section regression of twelve Latin American countries shows that the rate of growth of GNP is inversely related to the ratio of foreign capital imports to GNP. An examination of fifteen African and Asian countries showed that growth and capital imports were positively correlated but that the standard error of the regression co-efficient was very high.[8]

Mitchell Kellman has supplied additional evidence that foreign capital does not seem to have accelerated growth.[9] He measures aid dependence by the ratio of bilateral plus multilateral aid (A) to total imports (M), and finds that the rate of growth of income during 1960–1965 was inversely associated with (A/M) in both a forty-country sample and in a twelve-country sample of Latin American nations. Moreover, in a regression of the rate of growth of per capita income on (A/M), he obtained a negative association in Latin America and a barely positive association (0.01) in the forty-country sample. Thus, as far as one can determine on the basis of cross-section regression analysis, the hypothesis that aid promotes growth would appear to be untrue whether we look at Latin America alone or at the underdeveloped world as a whole, whether growth is measured net or gross of population increase, and whether dependence is measured as the ratio of aid to imports or as aid to income.

Incredible as it may seem, there is no statistical evidence that the $116,561 million of public and private capital that was transferred to the underdeveloped countries between 1956 and 1968 actually accelerated their growth. If anything, it may have retarded it. Yet the Pearson Commission makes no real attempt to explain why. Instead, rather pathetically, it merely asserts that aid "has been of first importance in the psychology of development" (pp. 51-2).

III CAPITAL IMPORTS AND DOMESTIC CONSUMPTION

The Commissioners, in common with most writers on foreign aid, assume that capital imports are (or should be) used entirely to increase investment in the recipient countries. In my opinion this is a false assumption: a large proportion of foreign capital is used to increase domestic consumption.

I have argued elsewhere, using indifferent curves and budget lines, that as long as households or governments place some value on additional present consumption one should expect capital imports to lead to a fall in the rate of saving.[10] A similar conclusion follows from the macroeconomic theory of consumption.

Economists are accustomed to thinking that aggregate consumption depends, among other things, upon national income. In a world in which capital transfers occur, however, it is reasonable to assume that consumption will be a positive function of total available resources, i.e. national income plus net capital imports. Especially when capital transfers are firmly expected, they will be treated as part of total income when expenditure decisions are made. Unanticipated capital transfers will be treated as transitory phenomena and may be largely saved, but in the case of anticipated capital transfers the normal marginal propensity to consume will apply. If this is accepted, it follows as surely as night follows day that—unless the marginal propensity to consume is zero—capital imports will raise total consumption and reduce domestic savings.

Assume a simple consumption function of the type

$$(1) \ C = \alpha \ (Y + A),$$

where C = total consumption, Y = national income and A = net capital imports. Since domestic savings (S) is equal to Y - C by definition, it follows that

$$\text{(2a)} \quad S = \beta Y - \alpha A$$

where $\beta = 1 - \alpha$. Equation (2a) tells us that given the level of national income, the larger the inflow of foreign capital the lower the level of domestic savings.

Of course foreign aid and private foreign investment may raise the level of national income and this, in turn, may lead to higher domestic savings. The important question, however, is whether a capital inflow tends to increase or decrease the *rate* of domestic savings, i.e., the ratio of savings to income. This question is easily answered by dividing through by Y in equation (2a):

$$\text{(2b)} \quad S/Y = \beta - \alpha A/Y$$

Evidently, the higher the ratio of aid to income the lower the rate of domestic savings.

A considerable amount of empirical evidence is accumulating which suggests that capital imports do affect domestic savings in the ways indicated in equations (2a) and (2b). For example, a group from the Organization of American States recently calculated a savings function for eighteen Latin American countries using data from around 1960. Their findings support the theory embodied in equation (2a):

$$S_t = 0.1716 \, Y_t - 0.6702 \, A_t; \; R^2 = 0.75$$
$$\quad (0.055) \qquad (0.204)$$

A regression of type (2b) of 32 underdeveloped countries from all regions of the world gave the following result:

$$S/Y = 11.2 - 0.73 \, A/Y; \; R^2 = 0.54$$
$$\qquad (0.11)$$

One can always object that results from cross-section analysis cannot be used to deduce the behaviour of a single country over time. If one is to have confidence in the hypothesis that aid leads to higher consumption (lower domestic savings), a large number of detailed country studies should be prepared. These do not yet exist. But there is some evidence from time-series regressions which tends to supports my hypothesis. For instance, in a study of Colombia in the period 1950-63, I smoothed out the bi-annual coffee cycle by using a two-year moving average and then regressed domestic savings on foreign capital. I obtained the following result[11]:

$$S/Y = 21.5 - 0.84\, A/Y;\ R^2 = 0.43$$
$$(0.29)$$

Thomas Weisskopf estimated savings functions of a type akin to equation (2a) from time series data for seventeen countries. "The values for all variables were compiled originally at current domestic prices and subsequently converted to constant prices by means of a single gross domestic product deflator for each country. The time series thus obtained were then converted into three-year moving averages for use in the regression analysis."[12] Weisskopf's savings function included three independent variables—income, capital imports and exports (E). His regression equation for Israel in the period 1953-1964, a major recipient of foreign capital, illustrates the sort of results obtained:

$$S = 88.3 + 0.125Y - 0.886\, A + 0.621E;\ R^2 = 0.999$$

Thus the cross-section and time-series studies are broadly consistent. They indicate that in most countries a very large fraction of all capital imports—say, between two-thirds and four-fifths—ultimately are used to supplement consumption rather than investment. If further research proves this to be correct, it follows that those who predict or assume that all resource transfers from abroad will be used to accelerate capital accumulation are likely to exaggerate the impact of capital imports on investment and growth.

In principle there is no need to deplore the fact that aid is used to increase consumption. Indeed, in so far as capital imports permit a more egalitarian distribution of consumption in the world they are to be welcomed. In practice, however, I doubt that capital imports have been used to reduce inequality. For example, in Pakistan, a major aid recipient, per capita income has been rising quite rapidly for about a decade. Moreover, between 1963/4 and 1969/70 the share of consumption in GNP increased by nearly two and a half per cent. At the same time, the per capita availability of food grains has remained roughly constant and the per capita availability of cotton cloth has declined by a considerable amount. In other words, the consumption of the poor declined, whereas that of the rich increased. Thus before one argues that foreign aid improves the distribution of consumption goods one needs to have much more evidence as to precisely whose consumption is increased by capital imports.

In some circumstances increased consumption may result in higher productivity of labour. It is a mistake to think that only investment contributes to growth. Certain types of expenditure on health, education, food and clothing may reduce illness, improve morale, raise levels of energy, increase receptiveness to change and so on. If the additional consumption which foreign aid permits were to be channelled in this direction, obviously it should be welcomed. Once again, however, there is little evidence that capital imports have financed an increase in consumption of those specific goods which would accelerate development. The most probable exception to this statement is the provision of food supplies under the American PL 480 programme. At its peak food aid accounted for nearly a third of all US official aid and almost a fifth of all bilateral aid. In theory this aid could lead to improved diets and higher productivity; in fact it seems often to have allowed governments to direct their attention to less urgent and less pro- ductive consumption activities. This point is accepted in the Report. Speaking of food aid they comment as follows: "It is nevertheless recognized that in the past it has sometimes also allowed some low-income countries to neglect agricultural policy over a long and critical period of accelerating population growth" (p. 175).

In addition to food aid, foreign assistance has been used to increase expenditure on education. If this additional expenditure were used to reform the educational system, spread knowledge more widely and increase the supply of relevant skills it could make a valuable contribution to the development process. Once again, however, it does not appear that aid has been used in this way. The Report states very firmly that "aid to education has mainly served to buttress traditional methods of teaching . . ." (p. 21). It has been "applied by unquestioning teachers, both local and foreign, trained in a mold cast over a hundred years ago. These traditional methods, with heavy emphasis on the humanities, do not adequately meet today's needs in the developing world" (p. 200).

Thus it does not appear that aid has been used systematically to increase productive consumption. It has almost certainly raised total consumption, but it has not thereby raised the pro- ductivity of labour. Generally speaking, it is unlikely that additional consumption will increase the productivity of labour unless the additional consumption is directed largely towards the poorest groups in the community. In other words, if the increased con- sumption which capital imports finance is to accelerate development, two conditions must be satisfied: first, aggregate consumption of specific items must increase (e.g. animal proteins) and, second, these items must be distributed to groups where their impact on productivity will be maximized. If capital imports enable the rich to drive more Mercedes, they will not accelerate growth; if they enable the poor to increase their skills, enjoy better health and have smaller families, they may make a significant contribution. The evidence from the Report is that the contribution has been negligible.

Even so, one might not worry if aid were given in the form of grants rather than loans. Foreign borrowing should be recommended only if the loans are used productively to increase investment and output, because it is only from additional output that the loans can be serviced. If loans are used to increase current consumption rather than earn or save foreign exchange, foreign loans—even on concessional terms—ultimately are likely to aggravate any balance of payments problems a country might have. One regrets, therefore, that the Commission was "persuaded that in the main the advantages of loans are overriding" (p. 163).

One of the important facts of the contemporary world economy is the growing number of underdeveloped countries that are unable to service their foreign debt. Many of the largest aid recipients, in fact, have had to renegotiate their debts, some more than once. Argentina and Indonesia have rescheduled their external debt three times; Turkey, Brazil and Ghana, twice; Chile, India and Peru, once (Table 20, pp. 383–4). Neither the Report nor the theoretical literature on foreign aid successfully accounts for this phenomenon, and the reason they don't is because it is assumed that capital imports are productively used and generate a surplus out of which the debt can be serviced. If this assumption were relaxed the facts could readily be explained.

Assume a country receives a net capital inflow of A and invests a certain fraction of it $(1 - \alpha)$. Ignoring the possible effects of increased consumption on the productivity of labour, and assuming an incremental output-capital ratio of "k", foreign capital will raise total output by $A (1 - \alpha) k$. Interest (r) must be paid on the entire loan, however, not just on that part which is invested. If

$$A (1 - \alpha) k < rA$$

the additional output generated by capital imports will be insufficient to service the debt.

Countries which are forced to borrow at relatively high rates of interest and yet have a strong tendency to consume a large proportion of their capital imports may well find that their repayment obligations exceed the value of the extra output produced. For example, if $\alpha = 0.8$ and $k = 0.3$, the balance of payments effects of foreign borrowing will be negative if $r > 0.06$.

The above illustration is unrealistic, however, because it is assumed that part of the capital import is consumed but all of the additional output can be saved. In practice, some fraction of the additional income will be consumed, say, α again. It is only out of the rest that debts can be serviced. In these circumstances, a country will encounter debt servicing problems even if the rate of interest is quite low. Specifically, the balance of payments effects will be unfavourable if

$$(1 - \alpha)^2 k < r$$

If α and k have the same values as assumed in the previous paragraph, repayment obligations will exceed additional savings unless the rate of interest is no higher than 1.2 per cent. The country will then appear to have a foreign exchange constraint, and some observers may attribute this to a "transformation problem", but in fact the difficulty is caused by a combination of excessive consumption and insufficiently productive investment.

IV AID AND THE EFFECTIVENESS OF INVESTMENT[13]

Our argument so far has been that most foreign aid is used to supplement consumption and thus it leads to only a small increase in total investment. If this were the end of the story one might conclude that the impact of aid in promoting growth has been exaggerated in the past but that nonetheless aid does have a small but positive contribution to make. This conclusion would be correct provided the slight rise in investment is not offset by a fall in the overall effectiveness of investment.

This is an important proviso, as there are indications that the output-capital ratio falls as aid increases. Unfortunately, this possibility was not investigated by the Commissioners, although in their report they did acknowledge that something was amiss: "The low correlation between aid and growth is also explained by the fact that much aid was given in ways which did not make it as efficient a contribution to development as it could have been" (p. 50).

Why does this occur? One reason is the motives of donors. At the very beginning of this chapter we argued that the objectives of the donors are largely political, not economic. In most instances the objectives can best be achieved by concentrating aid on large, dramatic, highly visible projects which stand as monuments to the generosity of the donors. The Tarbela dam in West Pakistan, which was financed by the IBRD, is a good example of a project with a low economic return which was expected to yield large political dividends.

Next, aid agencies have certain ideological biases against government ownership of directly productive activities. Since aid usually is channelled directly to the government of the recipient country, this ideological bias tends to alter the pattern of investment in favour of social overhead capital and economic infra-structure —transport facilities, electric energy, housing and schools. Road construction is encouraged; factory construction is discouraged. It is possible, of course, that in some countries infra-structure deserves priority, but a general bias against directly productive activities should tend to lower the aggregate output-capital ratio. This point can be put in another way: foreign aid tends to increase the size of the public sector, but it has done so by encouraging the expansion of relatively unproductive activities.

Furthermore, quite apart from motives and ideology, the administration of aid programmes may tend to lower the effectiveness of investment. The Commission has called attention to "the accumulation of rigid administrative rules and regulations" and to the fact that "many aid programs are afflicted by unnecessary administrative delays" (p. 169). There is also a problem of administrative economies of scale. If an agency is going to lend £50 million to a country it would normally prefer to finance one project costing £50 million than 25 projects costing £2 million each. By concentrating on a few large projects the agency can reduce the difficulties of supervising its projects and keep down its administrative costs. For this reason, aid programmes tend to sponsor large dams rather than small irrigation schemes, major highways rather than secondary roads, university buildings rather than village schools, etc. Again, there is no presumption that large projects have a higher rate of return than small projects. If anything, the opposite may be true, and any systematic tendency to alter the pattern of investment in favour of large schemes is likely to lower the output-capital ratio.

One of the great difficulties with project aid is that assistance normally can be used only to finance the foreign exchange costs of a project. This practice induces countries, first, to select projects which are intensive in foreign exchange and, second, to design any given project so as to maximize the foreign exchange component of total costs. The Commission recognizes that donor policy "encourages an uneconomic bias towards capital-intensive projects with a large foreign exchange component" (p. 177) and this bias too is likely to reduce the effectiveness of investment.

Finally, there is tied aid. From the recipient's point of view tied aid tends to lead, first, to a higher cost of imported goods—since the prices of goods imported under tied aid agreements will almost certainly be higher than world prices, and, second, to a continuing flow of high cost imports in the form of spare parts and ancillary equipment complementary to the aid financed imports. Thus a country may become "locked in" to a high cost source of supply via tied aid, and this might permanently reduce the productivity of its investments. The Commission evidently was concerned about the ill effects of tied aid and their warning is timely: "in a few cases direct costs alone seem to offset the concessionary value implied by the terms of aid loans. In many more instances, tying reduces the value of aid by far more than a small margin" (p. 172). It certainly is not obvious that a larger volume of aid that is tied is preferable to less aid that is untied. Indeed the practice of tying aid greatly increases the costs of investment to the underdeveloped countries, lowers the aggregate output-capital ratio and reduces the international competitiveness of aid financed activities.

In an earlier part of this chapter we showed that foreign capital imports do not result in a significant increase in the rate of investment. Next, we showed that an individual project financed by foreign aid is likely to have a lower output-capital ratio than the same project financed by domestic savings. Because of tied aid, political considerations and the preference of donors to finance only the foreign exchange costs of assisted projects, an aid financed scheme is likely to use resources less efficiently than a domestically financed scheme. The last and most important point we wish to make is that a country which relies heavily on foreign aid is likely to have a completely different set of investment projects from one which relies on domestic savings to finance development.

Whenever the preferences of donors for projects differ from those of recipients, foreign aid agencies may alter the pattern of investment without affecting the total very much. Suppose, for example, that in the absence of capital imports a country would undertake a £200 million investment programme consisting of a fertilizer plant, a series of small factories producing pumps for tubewells and a flour mill. Assume the capital-output ratio for these projects is 4, so that output rises by £50 million in the first instance. Alternatively, the country may be able to obtain £60 million of foreign aid tied, say, to investment in a large dam, an atomic energy station and a super-highway. As we have seen, consumption is likely to rise by approximately two-thirds of this aid, so that total investment is unlikely to rise to more than £220 million. If the capital-output ratio on this larger set of projects is higher that 4.4 the inflow of aid will cause a decline in the rate of growth of output.

In some cases foreign aid may finance the marginal project and leave all other projects unchanged. More frequently, however, the donors are able to preempt domestic resources and alter the entire investment programme, thereby substituting their preferences for those of the recipient government. When aid "leverage" is used in this way it is almost certain to affect adversely the overall effectiveness of investment. In some instances the decline in the effectiveness of investment will only partly offset the rise in capital formation. In other cases, however, the increase in investment seems to have been less than the decline in its effectiveness, and as a result the rate of growth declined. On balance, aid has probably neither retarded nor accelerated growth; its main contribution has been to increase total consumption fractionally. This is not a terribly exciting conclusion, and it certainly is one which most advocates of more aid would dispute, but I believe it is very close to the truth.

V AID AND INSTITUTIONAL REFORM

Obviously it is important to know what are the effects of aid in the recipient economy upon the volume and composition of consumption and investment and upon the rate of growth. But we want to know other things as well. In particular, what are the effects of foreign assistance upon a country's political system or institutional structure? Does foreign aid encourage or inhibit reforms which diminish inequality and accelerate expansion? These are difficult questions and the Pearson Commission made little attempt to answer them. There are, however, certain broad tendencies which can be identified and which merit additional research.

First, foreign aid largely accrues to governments and thereby tends to increase the relative size of the public sector. This, of course, is not inevitable, since the government could lend or give the resources to the private sector, but in practice the tendency seems clear enough. Second, the conditions under which aid is provided are such that the public sector is precluded from using it to invest in directly productive activities. In other words, donors have used their influence to ensure that the most profitable undertakings are reserved for the private sector. The US, for example, following the recommendations of the Clay Committee in 1963, has made it clear that American aid cannot be used for state investment in manufacturing industries. Third, several donors, notably AID and the World Bank, have exerted pressure on the underdeveloped countries in favour of private foreign investment. The Pearson Commission implicitly recognizes this in stating that "developed countries should, as far as possible, keep aid policy and disputes concerning foreign investment separate" (p. 107). The Commission itself has a highly favourable attitude to private foreign capital but believes that "improving the position of the private sector as a whole is the most important single step to improving the climate for foreign investment . . ." (p. 105).

Foreign aid, then, is biased in favour of private investment, domestic and foreign, yet paradoxically, it increases the size of the public sector. The outcome, contrary to the claims of some observers, is not socialism, but a strong state[14] at the service of private capital.

The governments of aid receiving countries more often than not have a vested interest in the preservaton of the *status quo*. They frequently are slow to innovate, anti-egalitarian, unresponsive to the wishes of the majority of the population, and hostile to institutional reform. India reached the verge of famine before the government decided to devote more attention to agriculture. Pakistan has reached the verge of national disintegration and still the government remains authoritarian. Latin America seems continually to be on the verge of revolution, yet reforms are painfully slow. Even when donors have attempted to encourage institutional change—such as during the early days of the Alliance for Progress —they have not succeeded. More often, governments which have become committed to radical reforms have encountered considerable opposition from aid giving countries and agencies. Peru, Cuba and Chile are countries where this has occurred.

The Report asserts that "the provision of aid, and the mutual examination of problems which this entails, has made possible basic reforms in most of the major developing countries which otherwise would not have occurred" (p. 52). If this statement were true, foreign aid programmes would deserve our applause. Unfortunately, it is false. Indeed, in my opinion, the Report contains nearly the opposite of the truth. The six largest aid recipients, in order, are India, Pakistan, South Vietnam, Brazil, South Korea and Turkey (Table 27, p. 392). Can anyone seriously maintain that "basic reforms" have been introduced in *any* of these countries as a result of aid? Surely the answer is "no"; neither donors nor recipients have wished to alter the *status quo*. Indeed, in some cases donors have taken active steps to ensure that it is maintained. The claim that aid has made possible basic reforms in the underdeveloped countries has virtually no foundation in fact, and it is mischievous of the Commission to suggest otherwise.

VI SUMMARY

The argument of the chapter is easily summarized:

1. The major purpose of foreign aid is to promote the interests of the donor nations, not to accelerate growth in the recipient countries.

2. There is no evidence that, in general, aid has resulted in a faster rate of growth. In some cases it seems to have retarded it.

3. In principle foreign assistance could be used to increase expenditure on investment, defence or consumption items. In practice it appears that most aid has been used to supplement consumption.

4. There is no evidence that, in general, the additional consumption financed by aid has been used to raise the material wellbeing of the poorest members of the population.

5. Nor is there evidence that the additional consumption has been channelled into productive activities which might ultimately raise the productivity of labour.

6. It is quite likely that foreign aid has been given in such a way that it leads to a lower output-capital ratio. On balance, the fall in the output-capital ratio offsets the positive effects of the somewhat higher level of investment which aid finances, so that the aggregate growth rate remains unaffected.

7. If aid is in the form of loans, and if these loans are used primarily to increase consumption, it is highly probable that the interest and repayment obligations will make the balance of payments position of the recipients worse rather than better.

8. Politically, foreign aid tends to create mixed economies dominated by private enterprise, domestic and foreign. Both donors and recipients regard aid as an instrument for maintaining the status quo.

9. The Pearson Report is an adequate statement of the conventional liberal view of the Western pro-aid lobby. The economics of this lobby is suspect, and the political objectives which lie behind aid programmes are unacceptable to those who advocate radical change.

NOTES

1 *Hearings* on House Resolution 10502, Committee on Foreign Affairs, US House of Representatives, 88th Congress, 2nd Session, 23 March 1964, p. 9.

2 H. B. Chenery, "Objectives and Criteria of Foreign Assistance", in G. Ranis (ed.), *The United States and the Developing Economies*, p. 81.

3 *Quality of Life in the Americas: Report of a US Presidential Mission for the Western Hemisphere*, Washington, 1969.

4 Pearson Report, p. 122.

134   FOREIGN RESOURCES AND ECONOMIC DEVELOPMENT

5   Quoted in F. F. Clairmonte, "Latin America: Meditations from Afar", mimeographed, Stockholm, 26 January 1970, p. 30.
6   See Overseas Development Institute, *Aid that Works*, a reprint of four articles that appeared in *The Economist* of 4 February, 11 February, 4 March and 11 March 1967.
7   Ibid., p. 11.
8   K. B. Griffin and J. L. Enos, "Foreign Assistance: Objectives and Consequences", *Economic Development and Cultural Change,* April 1970.
9   M. Kellman, "Foreign Assistance: Objectives and Consequences— Comment", *Economic Development and Cultural Change*, October 1971.
10   Keith Griffin, "Foreign Capital, Domestic Savings and Economic Development", *Bulletin* of the Oxford University Institute of Economics and Statistics, May 1970.
11   Keith Griffin, "Coffee and the Economic Development of Colombia", *Bulletin* of the Oxford University Institute of Economics and Statistics, May 1968.
12   Thomas E. Weisskopf, "The Impact of Foreign Capital Inflow on Domestic Savings in Underdeveloped Countries", a paper presented at the Second World Congress of the Econometric Society, Cambridge, England, September 1970, p. 7.
13   This section is based on Keith Griffin, "Foreign Capital, Domestic Savings and Economic Development", loc. cit., pp. 107–10.
14   Some aid is designed intentionally to strengthen the state, viz., military assistance. The interaction between foreign military assistance and domestic military dictatorship is a much neglected subject.

5

THE "CRISIS OF AID" AND THE PEARSON
REPORT*

by

Harry G. Johnson

*London School of Economics and Political Science
and
University of Chicago*

*This chapter is based on a lecture delivered by Professor Johnson at Edinburgh University on 6th March 1970, and appears here by kind permission of Edinburgh University Press.

THE "CRISIS OF AID" AND THE PEARSON REPORT

I DEVELOPMENT ASSISTANCE SINCE WORLD WAR TWO

One of the historically distinguishing characteristics of the period since the end of the Second World War has been the growth of concern in the advanced industrial countries over the widening gap in living standards between the rich and the poor countries, and the assumption of an obligation on their part to help promote the economic development of the poor countries through the contribution of substantial resources to development assistance. For some countries, such as France, and the United Kingdom, development aid has been envisaged largely as an obligation to former colonial territories; for other European countries, the motivation has varied between a sense of moral obligation and a sense of ultimate commercial advantage. The big impulse to development assistance, however, came from the leadership example and pressure of the United States, which initially approached development assistance in the spirit of the Marshall Plan for European Economic Recovery, and after successful completion of that Plan, under the visionary inspiration of President John F. Kennedy, turned its attention to the solution of the development problem of the poor two-thirds of the world's population. Development aid has become a major world endeavour, involving some $6½ billion of official aid disbursements and some $4½ billion of private investment and lending in recent years, and employing hundreds of thousands (perhaps even millions—I have no figures) of people as economists and administrators in national governments and international agencies, as technical advisers in all sorts of fields, and as trainees of various kinds.

The problem of European economic recovery, for which the Marshall Plan was developed, was however a quite different problem than the problem of promoting economic development in the poor countries. The war-ravaged European countries were established nation-states, culturally mature and economically advanced, lacking only an intensive but brief marginal injection of capital to restore their economies and set them on the path of "self-sustaining growth". The poor countries were in many cases newly-created states, lacking the political stability and cultural homogeneity of established nations; and their poverty reflected general backwardness in the industrial and agricultural arts and general paucity of productive resources, including social and human capital as well as the material means of production. Their development would necessarily be a relatively slow, painful, and wasteful process of "learning by doing" and of accumulating a complementary equipment of infra-structure, labour skills, material capital, and industrial knowledge, often while coping with the problems of achieving political stability and modernizing the society. In these circumstances, the Marshall Plan approach—the "crash programme" approach to setting nations on their economic feet and equipping them quickly for "self-sustaining" growth—was doomed to disappointment, with respect both to the degree of success achievable and the foreseeability of an early end to the need for the effort.

II THE "CRISIS OF AID" AND PEARSON

By the early 1960s, it was apparent that a "crisis of aid" was approaching. On the one hand, the need for development assistance, or at least the demand for it, was rising rapidly as the numbers of the developing countries, and the rate of economic growth to which they aspired, steadily increased. At the same time, the political stability and capacity to use aid of many of them was also increasing, as the early excesses of national "liberation" were recognized to be counter-productive. On the other hand, two of the three major aid donors, the United Kingdom and the United States, were in balance-of-payments difficulties that put pressure on their governments to limit their aid programmes; and public opinion in the United States was becoming both increasingly disillusioned with the apparent failures of US development assistance, and increasingly concerned about the domestic problems of race relations and poverty.

The emerging crisis of aid was symbolized by the First United Nations Conference on Trade and Development, held in Geneva in 1964 and largely inspired by the thinking of Dr Raul Prebisch. The main theme of the Conference was a demand by the developing countries for a "new trade policy for development"—largely the intellectual creation of Dr Prebisch—involving international commodity agreements to raise and stabilize the prices of the primary products on which these countries depended for the bulk of their export income, and preferences in the markets of the developed countries for the manufactures on which they planned to base their industrialization. This demand reflected the recognition that the halcyon days of competition in aid-giving between the West and the Soviet bloc had ended, that aid-givers were becoming decreasingly generous and increasingly choosy, and that any hope for important new sources of external resources for development lay in the field of trade rather than aid. Recognition of the increasing stringency of official aid-giving was also reflected in the concern of the developing countries to obtain redefinition of the target for developed country aid of 1 per cent of national income so as to increase the actual amount of aid it represented, and to obtain changes in the techniques of development lending—softening of financial terms, and untying of the aid—that would have the effect of increasing the real resource transfers actually involved.

As a consequence of the interest stirred up by the 1964 United Nations Conference on Trade and Development, and particularly of the shock to informed American opinion of the confrontation there of United States trade and aid policies with the demands of the developing countries, I was commissioned in 1965 by the Brookings Institution to make a study of the issues; similar studies by John Pincus and Theodore Geiger were commissioned by other sponsors. What emerged from these studies—reformulated in the light of hindsight, and stated very briefly— was, first, that none of the arguments from the self-interest of the advanced countries— political, military, and economic—that had been used from time to time in support of official aid-giving was at all persuasive; the prime case for aid had to be made in terms of the moral obligation of the rich to the poor, and was only as strong as that sense of moral obligation. Second, for a variety of economic reasons the official measurements of aid transfers grossly overstated the amount of real resources both transferred by the aid-donors to the aid-recipients, and received by the aid-recipients from the aid-donors— two magnitudes which are not necessarily even approximately the same. Third, while the developing countries could justifiably complain bitterly about the discrimination against their exports and thus their development implicit in the tariff and agricultural support policies of the developed countries and the rules governing commercial policy changes institutionalized in the General Agreement on Tariffs and Trade, the tariff preferences they were demanding would if implemented yield them negligible additional resources for development investment in the reasonably near term, while both experience and theoretical analysis showed that international commodity agreements of a substantially resource-transferring kind were very unlikely to be implementable—so that trade offered no real alternative as a substitute for additional aid. Finally, many of the exporting difficulties experienced by the developing countries were of their own making, the consequence on the one hand of heavy taxation of primary-producing export sectors and on the other of high-cost import-substitution policies, both of which impeded the growth of exports—so that even if expanded export opportunities were offered, they were likely to have little effect failing major changes in the developing countries' approach to development promotion.

It is relevant at this point to expand on the difference between the established official approach to development assistance and the approach of the economist, which underlies the last three of these points. The official approach, in this as in other areas of policy, is dominated by balance-of-payments considerations, and works in terms of flows of foreign exchange, i.e. financial flows. This approach suggests, quite wrongly, that additional export earnings are equivalent in benefit to additional loans or grants. It also lumps together in the aid total a heterogeneous collection of tied and untied official grants and loans on varying concessional terms, the domestic money value of food aid, and various kinds of private capital flows. And, further, it deducts the flow of servicing payments on past loans. This last practice, in turn, fosters the notion that debt service constitutes a "burden" on the economy, requiring "relief", which it should not be if the loans have been applied to good economic purpose. From the economic point of view, what matters is not the foreign exchange flows but the implicit transfer of real resources involved in any particular transaction. This involves, for official capital transfers, making deduction for any excess of the prices of the goods purchased with the aid over world market prices resulting from the tying of aid or the giving of aid in the form of surplus foodstuffs; and, for loans as contrasted with outright grants, reckoning the economic value at the value of the gift element involved in concessionary interest rates, grace periods, etc., and not at the much higher face value of the loan. On the same approach, the value of trade concessions to the recipient is not the resulting increase in the value of the trade concerned, unless that increase consists purely of an increase in prices, as with some forms of the proposed international commodity agreements. Otherwise, the value of a trade concession has to be reckoned in terms of the effect of additional export earnings in enabling a country to acquire importable goods more cheaply, in terms of resource cost, by exporting than it could obtain them by producing them domestically. As regards private capital transfers, which are included in the assistance totals, these being commercially profitable transactions presumably involve no cost to the citizens of the country from which they come, except to the extent that like other private capital exports they pay taxes to the country invested in which are lost to the home country under double taxation agreements, and these taxes exceed the costs of the social overhead expenditure the government of the home country would have had to incur if the capital had been invested at home.

These differences between the official and the economically scientific measurements of development assistance have undoubtedly played a significant part in the growing disillusionment with the effectiveness of development assistance, as has the fact that much so-called aid has been given for political and military purposes rather than the promotion of economic development, and may well indeed have been counter-productive in terms of promoting development. They have also helped to divert attention from recognition of the urgent importance of a larger volume of official aid in real terms, to schemes for extracting more real aid by subterfuge through the softening of aid terms, and to schemes for benefiting the developing countries by new trade arrangements and by linking aid to international monetary reform that hold either little promise of substantial benefit, or little promise of acceptance by the developed countries. As a result, the "crisis of aid" has been steadily deepening.

The United States Administration, Congress, and public, in particular, have become increasingly unwilling to go on providing development assistance at recent levels, let alone at the rising levels required to meet calculated needs for such assistance by the developing world. This reluctance has acted as a brake on the generosity of other advanced countries—a generosity otherwise stimulated in some cases by the moral shock of the Geneva UNCTAD Conference—since for balance-of-payments reasons other countries prefer not to get too far out of line with the scale of United States aid-giving. The growing relative scarcity of funds for development assistance has impinged most sharply on the International Bank for Reconstruction and Development (the "World Bank"), which is the United Nations institution most directly concerned with development finance and which, under its past President Mr George Woods and its current President Mr Robert McNamara, has been aggressively converting itself from a conservative semi-commercial bank into a development assistance agency.

In October 1967 Mr Woods suggested that a "grand assize" should be conducted by an international group of "stature and experience", to study the consequences and results of twenty years of development assistance and to make recommendations for the future. In August 1968 Mr McNamara followed up this suggestion by appointing the Right Honourable Lester B. Pearson, a Nobel Peace Prize winner for his part in settling the Suez crisis, and former Prime Minister of Canada, a rich but small North American country which has long played the role of intermediary between developed and developing countries but has only recently become coverted to belief in the importance of development assistance. Mr Pearson chose an appropriately distinguished group of colleagues: Sir Edward Boyle, a British politician and specialist in education; Roberto de Olivera Campos, a distinguished Brazilian economist, public servant, and banker; C. Douglas Dillon, American banker and recently distinguished Secretary of the US Treasury; Wilfred Guth, a German banker with experience at the International Monetary Fund; Sir Arthur Lewis, a pioneer in the academic field of economic development and in development advising; Robert Marjolin, French economic civil servant active in European economic integration; and Dr Saburo Okita, eminent Japanese public-service economist recently active in promoting Japanese involvement with the development of poor countries of the Pacific.

When the appointment of Mr Pearson was first announced, many academic economists like myself, concerned about the promotion of development but not involved in the official aid business, hoped that his Commission would initiate some of the fundamental scientific research into aid and its effects that the field so obviously needed. The announcement of the names of the other Commission members, however, made it clear that the Commission's work was to be a public relations exercise on behalf of increased aid, and especially of official and multilateral aid. And so it has proved to be. Mr Pearson set for his Commission, and achieved, the target of producing its report within a year. This target of quick reporting necessarily meant dependence on a staff of experts in the official economics of aid, whose function would be to assemble and organize material rather than to undertake fresh research. (Mr Pearson, incidentally, adopted the American practice of entrusting the staff with the preparation of the report, rather than the British practice according to which the Commission itself writes the report, a decision which, rumour has it, almost led to Sir Arthur Lewis refusing to sign the report.) The need for speed also meant that the Commissioners themselves consulted exclusively with the officials of governments and international institutions engaged in the aid business, and not at all with academic and political opponents of development assistance as currently practised. Consequently the Report of the Commission is a look at the aid business from the inside, so to speak: it queries no fundamental concepts used in aid analysis; it combines an excessively aggregative overall approach with an excessively ad hoc treatment of the myriad details; and its ultimate emphasis in its recommendations is on economic administration rather than economic analysis.

Given the public relations character of the Commission's assignment, and the circumstances in which it was appointed, one might have expected its Report to serve two functions. The first, and more important, would be to provide some fresh and appealing reasons for the giving of aid by the advanced countries, appealing especially to the aid-fatigued American public. The second, complementary to the first, would be to provide a rather optimistic but still plausibly sober review of past experience with development assistance, combined with a set of well-reasoned and sensible suggestions for the improvement of the efficiency of current methods of rendering and administering development assistance, both designed to give fresh hope to underpin the fresh motivation for aid-giving.

III NEW REASONS FOR GIVING AID: THE FAILURE OF PEARSON

In the event, the Report has succeeded reasonably well in the fulfilment of the second objective; its analysis and recommendations express the common-sense conclusions that would have been reached by most people asked to think about the contemporary aid-giving and aid-receiving process on the assumption that it was going to continue. But the second objective is subordinate to the first, and with respect to the first objective the Report can only be described as a dismal failure. It has provided no new and appealing reasons for the expansion of development assistance by the advanced countries, and has instead produced a series of pseudo-considerations whose hollowness and inconsistency with one another can only reinforce the arguments of the opponents of aid. The result is that both the ideological adherents and the ideological opponents of development assistance will be able to criticize the Report for the pusillanimous concessions it makes to the other side of the debate, while the open-minded average man will find the Report at once flabby and smug—if he bothers to read such a fat compendium of establishment wisdom at all.

The failure of the Report to provide a persuasive new reason for aid-giving is the inevitable result of the conflict between moral conception and the facts of reality that arises with any charitable operation such as development aid or the relief of poverty: the moral conception stresses the inherent dignity and worth of man as man, and hence leads to resentment on the one side and uneasiness on the other about the reality of economic difference, which is the occasion of the charity itself. This conflict is exacerbated when the participants in the charitable transfer are not individuals but nation-states jealous of their sovereignty. It can only be resolved by resort to the fiction on both sides of the charity transaction that the need for charity is temporary. Hence any effort to resolve the conflict within a general and consistent philosophy of sustained charity must prove self-defeating: charity can only be a continuing process if new reasons are continually being discovered as to why it will be temporary, and this precludes a general philosophy.

The failure of the Report with respect to its major function of re-motivating aid-giving is epitomized in its title: Partners in Development. This title attempts to assert for nation-states the equivalent of the oft-asserted equality of man. It is propoganda on behalf of the sovereignty of the developing nation-states, or a polite fiction to paper over the vast inequalities in resources between rich and poor nations. In either case, it is certain to evoke attitudes on both sides inimical to enlargement of the flow of development assistance. If nations are really equals, as the fiction asserts, what is the necessity or the purpose of aid? If they are not equals, as is the reality, why should rich nations transfer resources to poor nations that pretend to be equal but are not? On the other side, if nations should be equals but are visibly and indisputably not equals, why should aid transfers be regarded as charity rather than reparations for the injustice of the world? And why should the amount of charity be determined by the rich man's beneficence rather than the poor man's need? An alleged partnership formed out of the rich man's uneasy conscience and the poor man's resentful need is likely to disintegrate in mutual recrimination—as the aid relationship has indeed been doing.

The Report itself devotes a scant five pages to the crucial question, "Why Aid?" These five pages attempt to skate delicately over the major issues and to reconcile the irreconcilable with wise-sounding but empty platitudes. The argument begins negatively with the acknowledgment that aid will not buy a western ideology, political stability, or peaceful and internationally responsible behaviour from the recipients. In other words, aid serves no political self-interest of the aid-givers. Its objective instead is "to reduce disparities and remove inequalities . . . so that the world will not become more and more starkly divided between the haves and the have-nots." But if avoidance of such division has no implications for ideology, political stability, or peace, the argument for it must be moral. But the moral argument immediately raises, at least for an American audience, the conflict between the relief of domestic and the relief of foreign poverty. The Report asserts that "Both wars must be won". Why should rich nations help poor ones when they have pressing poverty problems of their own? The Report asserts that "The simplest answer to the question is the moral one:

that it is only right for those who have to share with those who
have not." But why should this moral obligation extend beyond the
bounds of sovereign states? The Commission appeals to "a new
and fundamental aspect of the modern age—the awareness that we
live in a village world, that we belong to a world community".
But awareness of the existence of others has only rarely and marginally been a reason powerful enough to motivate large-scale charity
towards them; and in any case the question is one of charity extended by the national government of a rich country to the national
government of a poor one, not from a rich individual to a poor
individual. Instead of arguing a moral case for intergovernmental
aid transfers, the Report abandons the subject by contradicting
itself: "the moral incentive for co-operation in international development . . . is not the basis on which support for international
development mainly rests".

"There is also the appeal of enlightened and constructive self-
interest." Economically, there is "the fullest possible utilization of
the world's resources, human and physical, which can be brought
about only by international co-operation" and which benefits the
rich countries through "direct benefits from a bilateral aid relationship" and through "the general increase in international trade
which would follow international development". But the Report
does not explain why aid, rather than other policies, presents the
best way of promoting fuller utilization of world resources; nor
does it examine whether the asserted economic benefits of aid-
giving are worth their resource cost; and it is careful to state that
donor countries should not expect development to create economic
windfalls for them. It is also concerned to assert that nothing
tangible in the way of political benefits should be expected.

Having in effect again disposed of self-interest as a motivation
for aid-giving, the Report then appeals to "the acceleration of
history" and the alleged consequential necessity to expand the concept of the national interest to embrace the common problems of
the world, and asserts that the emerging awareness of the world
community is "itself a major reason for international co-operation in
development". But that emerging awareness of the world community
is described as "an act of faith"; it does not by itself imply any
commitment to help poor nations to develop; and even if it is so
construed, it does not necessarily imply an expansion of development aid on present lines.

At this point, the Report refers to the fact that the developed
countries have accepted a commitment to help the poor nations (the
Report actually uses the question-begging phrase "impoverished
nations") to develop. The argument thus returns full circle to the

moral commitment which was earlier denied to be the main basis for support of development assistance. But it then asserts that "whatever is or is not done internationally, the poorer countries of the world have made their choice for development ... The only questions are: how fast, and by what means, and at what cost to themselves and to the world can development be achieved; and whether it has a clear and tangible goal." In other words, the Report abandons all pretence of discussing the justification for aid, and turns to the question—which assumes that such justification has been provided, though it clearly has not—of setting a target for aid.

"Our answer is that the goal of the international development effort is to put the less developed countries as soon as possible in a position where they can realize their aspirations with regard to economic progress without relying on foreign aid." The Report then asks, and answers affirmatively, the question "But can the majority of the developing countries achieve self-sustaining growth by the end of the century? For us the answer is clearly yes. In our view, the record of the past twenty years justifies that answer." And it adds: "The thing to remember is that the process, global in scope, and international in nature, must succeed if there is finally to be peace, security, and stability in the world."

It may be remarked that the developing countries could achieve self-sustaining growth at any moment, by abandoning their dependence on aid, though this might involve growing at a slower rate (not necessarily slower, because the Commission is unable to demonstrate that aid in the past has actually promoted growth). The question hinges on the rate of growth aspired to by the developing countries, a matter on which the Report is remarkably vague, presumably because of its acceptance of the principle of national sovereignty. It should also be noted that the thing the Commission wants us to remember is precisely what it has earlier been at pains to deny, that aid for development will buy peace, security, and stability in the developing world.

The chain of observations presented by the Report on the justification for development assistance is a set of pious but self-contradictory platitudes, designed to skate over the real issues while enabling the Commission to arrive at an ostensibly feasible compromise between the interests of the developed countries and the demands of the developing countries. That compromise consists, on the one hand, in adopting the view that if the average annual rate of growth of gross national product in the developing countries could be raised from the recent 5 per cent per annum to 6 per cent per annum by the end of the 1970s, these countries could by the

year 2000 finance their own growth and import requirements
without concessional loans. It consists, on the other hand, in assert-
ing that this change can be effected consistently with the already-
accepted commitment of the developed countries to channel 1 per
cent of their gross national products into development assistance,
provided that they implement that commitment and accept the
Commission's recommendations for increasing the element of real
as distinct from nominal aid involved, notably by increasing the
percentage of official aid from the 1968 percentage of 0.39 to 0.70
by 1975 or at latest 1980, and doubling the proportion in it of
multilateral aid to 20 per cent.

In effect, the Pearson Commission Report says that the political
demands of the developing countries for development assistance can
be satisfied if the developed countries will only live up to their
past moral commitments, while recommending various apparently
sensible changes in aid policies that will in fact increase the real
burden of those commitments substantially. At the same time
it holds out to the aid-givers the promise that, though the initial
crash-programme of development aid has not solved the development problem, it can still be solved within the time-span of a
generation, i.e. by the year 2000. Both the implication that no
further great effort is required, and the promise of a foreseeable
end to the need for charity, display a certain amount of political
sagacity. But the compromise is very unlikely to succeed in practical
political reality, and the offer of it is likely to provoke dissatisfaction
on both sides of the development assistance transaction. For the
developed countries, the Report fails to provide any cogent reason,
other than the doubtfully relevant aspirations of the developing
countries, why the developed countries should make the long jump
from present levels of official aid to the levels required to fulfil
its target for such aid: a past moral commitment to a target that
has not only not been fulfilled but whose fulfilment has steadily
been receding, proves neither that fulfilment of the target is
desirable, nor that it will be relatively painless. For the developing
countries and their sympathizers, an increase in the target minimum
rate of growth from 5 per cent to 6 per cent for the rest of the
century is a trivial *quid pro quo* indeed for the liquidation of the
assumed moral obligation on the rich countries to improve the lot
of the poor.

In my judgment, the failure of the Report to provide a new
motivation for more generous aid-giving is attributable funda-
mentally to the fact that the Commission has taken the sovereignty
of the nation-state as given, and has concerned itself with relations
between sovereign states that happen to be alternatively poor and

rich, instead of concerning itself with the fundamental units involved in the poverty problem, which units are people and not nations. In relations among sovereign nations, morality is an emotion without a cutting edge. In relations among people, however, the nation-state is an instrument of discrimination whose injustice and immorality can be demonstrated. The nation state discriminates economically in favour of its own citizens through its control of immigration; it discriminates further in their favour through its tariffs and other protective policies; and recently the richest nations have come to discriminate still further in favour of their own citizens (in their role as workers) through the imposition of restrictions on the outflow of capital. In this perspective, development assistance appears very much as conscience money paid by the rich to the poor to ease the conscience of the one and bribe off the indignation of the other; and the problem of promoting development appears more as one of reducing the discriminations between people associated with the national state than as one of increasing the international flow of conscience money—though more conscience money would undoubtedly help. The Report might have been far more effective if it had attacked the discriminatory features of the national state directly, and insisted on the need either to reduce the discrimination or to increase the flow of conscience money, rather than attempting to wheedle more development assistance in the name of faith in the brotherhood of man.

As already mentioned, the Report is far more successful in achieving its second (and secondary) objective—a reasonably optimistic review of past experience with development assistance, leading to a sensible set of suggestions for further improvement— than in achieving its first and crucial objective. A full review of its analysis of the development problem and of past achievements with respect to it, and of its recommendations for changes in development policies and practices, would be inappropriate to the present purpose. Four general themes of the Report, however, deserve some comment.

IV FOUR GENERAL THEMES IN THE REPORT

The first theme is that, despite the widely-felt disillusionment about the process of promoting the economic development of the poor countries, much more development has occurred than has generally been realized; that more is to come as infra-structure investment finally bears its fruits; that various past errors in approach are in process of being corrected; and that much has been learned about how to promote development. All of this is true. But one would expect development to occur when people have at last decided that they want it, when they have the successful examples of the already developed countries before their eyes, and when the maintenance of high activity and the progressive liberalization of international trade by the developed countries is providing an unprecedented opportunity for growth by osmosis. One would also expect people to learn, albeit slowly, from their own errors. The real questions are whether development aid has promoted or retarded development, and if it has promoted it, how significant its influence has been. Many of the critics of aid believe that it has encouraged national governments in the developing countries to pursue counter-developmental policies and permitted them to preserve archaic social and political structures, and so has retarded rather than promoted the modernization process.

The Report is in fact unable to adduce any clear evidence that aid has promoted growth; this may be largely because it lacked the time, staff resources, and economic competence to investigate the question in a properly scientific manner. Instead, it falls back on the undisputed fact that much aid was given for other purposes than development (how much was intended to promote development, and did it actually do so?), emphasizes the importance of the transfer of technology and ideas associated with aid (was the transfer always appropriate, and could it have been effected in some cheaper way?), and stresses the contribution of aid in supporting a psychological climate favourable to experimentation (good experiments, or bad?). The usefulness of aid in promoting development remains an act of faith; yet the rest of the Report depends on the assumption of its usefulness.

The second theme is the seriousness of the population problem in the developing countries, and the need for priority for population control. The Commission is right to view this subject with the gravest of alarm, but it fails to consider its full implications. The responsiveness of population to economic opportunity in the developing countries is one of the major reasons why developed countries are both reluctant to allow immigration from such countries, and doubtful about the beneficial effects of assistance for economic development to these countries. Freer immigration into the advanced countries—which should be, but is not, currently considered a possible remedy for poverty in the developing countries —more aid, and freer trade, all run the risk of aggravating the problem of inequality by stimulating the breeding of more poor people at the expense of the less philoprogenitive rich. Family planning may well be not only more important than additional development assistance, but a prerequisite to the provision of increased assistance.

The third theme is an emphasis on education and on technical development as major means to economic development, together —though this is implicit in the detail of the Report—with emphasis on more efficient selection of investment projects aimed at giving priority to those with high yields. The latter emphasis is important for the future, given the likelihood of increasing stringency in the availability of aid funds; but there is some danger that the emerging popularity of "cost-benefit analysis" will lead to more and more scarce resources being devoted to the allocation of funds among projects and less and less being available for the projects themselves. It is a well-known characteristic of bureaucracies that, the less money they have to spend, the more time and effort they devote to deciding exactly how to spend it..

The fourth theme is the desirability of increasing both the proportion of official aid in the total financial flows of development assistance, and the proportion of multilateral—as contrasted with bilateral—aid in the total of official flows. From the economic point of view, both changes would significantly augment the real flow of resources from rich to poor countries. But it is important to recognize the direction in which these recommendations lead. Essentially, they point in the direction of world government, not explicitly in the form of political federalism but implicitly in the form of a redistribution of income between nations through the instrumentality of international institutions and specifically of the World Bank. This may be a desirable direction of evolution, and indeed the only feasible path of human progress. But it should be recognized and discussed for what it is, and not disguised as an obvious and sensible step towards increased efficiency in the administration of development assistance. Presentation in that guise—which is essentially a proposal to increase the taxation of the rich countries for the benefit of the poor while depriving them of control over the spending of their own money—is likely to prove unacceptable to the citizens of the rich countries. Again, in this connection, the failure of the Pearson Commission to consider the consequences of the organization of mankind into nations is a crucial weakness in its argument.

V IMPLICATIONS OF THE FAILURE TO PROVIDE A NEW MOTIVATION FOR AID

The Report has, in my judgment, failed in its main purpose, a purpose crucial to its many sensible suggestions for reform, that of providing a new motivation for the giving of development assistance. Especially, it has failed to provide any arguments likely to appeal to the aid-weary and domestically-preoccupied American public. What are likely to be the consequences?

One major unfortunate consequence is likely to be that those who favour increased development aid will become increasingly shrill in their demands for increased aid, and increasingly intellectually dishonest in the arguments they present. This tendency is in fact already apparent. As one example, there is strong support in pro-development-assistance circles for the proposal to link international monetary reform to development finance by monetizing the new Special Drawing Rights at the International Monetary Fund, and distributing a large part or all of them to the developing countries to be earned back by unrequited exports by the developed countries. This is essentially a proposal to provide development assistance by inflationary world monetary expansion, based on the naive assumption that the governments of the advanced countries can be tricked by exploitation of the mysteries of money —which they can understand at least as well as the proponents of the scheme—into accepting a larger volume of aid commitments than they would be willing to provide by democratic budgetary vote. Another instance is the campaign currently being mounted in the United Kingdom to persuade the public to sanction additional aid allocations on the grounds that "trade follows aid", i.e. that the present sacrifice of aid resources will be economically justified by the gain of markets. If this proposition were true, which it is not, it would scarcely be necessary to advertise it. A third instance, evident at the recent Columbia University Conference on International Development, is the propensity of those who favour more aid for whatever reason to sign any document that recommends more aid, regardless of how silly or impracticable the specific proposals for giving more aid contained in it may be.

Another consequence is that the process of disillusionment of the American public with aid, and of American disengagement in the aid process, will continue. This is in spite of the fact that a presidential task force, reporting in March 1970, and clearly influenced by the Pearson Report, has recommended that the level of American assistance for economic development should be increased. Without powerful support from public opinion, such a recommendation is likely to perish in the Congress. And failing a powerful lead from the United States, other countries are unlikely to increase their development assistance contributions substantially.

The prospective decline of official aid obviously bodes ill for those who have made a career in the aid business, either as administrators or as advisors, or as outside, presumably independent, missionaries on behalf of aid to their fellow men. The world of official aid is in fact already showing many of the signs of a declining industry or community, and in particular showing a belated urgent concern about its own administrative efficiency. But will the decline in official aid actually seriously impair the process of economic development, to the detriment of the poor countries of the world?

I am inclined, perhaps optimistically, to return a negative answer to this question. The decline of official development aid that I foresee will mean an increased dependence on the private market mechanisms of economic development, as contrasted with governmental planning and control of the development process. These mechanisms are, internally, the forces of competition and the desire to improve one's individual welfare by increasing one's earning power. Externally, the most important are competition in international trade, on the one hand, and the international operations of the multinational corporation, on the other. I have considerable faith in the long-run powers of international competition to transform societies that have a latent urge to be transformed, though these powers may long be held in check by the use of political power to resist change and to attempt to capture the benefits of development for the politically powerful from the economically productive. I also believe that the liberalization of world trade that has already been accomplished through the General Agreement on Tariffs and Trade provides ample opportunities for the poor countries to develop through trade, though there is considerable scope for further widening of those opportunities. It is true, as already mentioned, that trade provides far fewer resources per dollar for development than does aid; but we are considering a process of development extending to the end of the century, and in that time trade opportunities should have full scope to do their work.

As regards the international corporation, this is a powerful agency for the transmission of technological progress, and the reallocation of capital resources, from the rich to the poor countries, which has already in the past two decades done much in its own way to diffuse the process of economic development around the globe. Too much should not be expected of the international corporation. It is a profit-seeking enterprise, which will diffuse development only to the extent that such diffusion is in its own interests. It is not a government, able to levy taxes on some people in order to invest in what it thinks will contribute to the economic development of others. But there is a considerable overlap of interests between the two. In particular, the corporation often finds it in its own interests, when operating in developing countries, both to invest in the training of local labour—both operative and managerial—and to invest in teaching modern efficient methods of production both to its supplier enterprises and to its customers. Where the interests of corporation and government conflict, it is not always obvious that government rather than the corporation has the better judgment of what is in the social interest.

To conclude, the Pearson Report may well represent the end, rather than the beginning, of a novel phase in world economic development—the end of a phase in which the powers of government to promote development by the use of its legal powers of control and planning and its economic powers of taxation of its citizens were grossly exaggerated, and the powers of free competition to promote growth were unduly discounted, rather than the beginning of a concerted move towards nations becoming "partners in development" and moving towards world government. The Pearson Report, in short, may be a tombstone rather than a milestone in the evolution of a developing world economy.

6

AID ALLOCATION WHEN AID IS INADEQUATE

Problems of the Non-Implementation of the Pearson Report

by

Michael Lipton

Institute of Development Studies at the University of Sussex

AID ALLOCATION WHEN AID IS INADEQUATE: PROBLEMS OF THE NON-IMPLEMENTATION OF THE PEARSON REPORT

I INTRODUCTION

The Pearson Commission, unlike some of its critics, rightly refused to "pick any targets one likes from the air".[1] Its "net aid" target of 0.7 per cent of donors' GNP by 1975[2] is aligned with (a) the requirements estimated by the UN Committee for the Second Development Decade (the Tinbergen Committee) for a 6 per cent yearly growth of national income in poor countries, a rate which they considered otherwise feasible; and (b) the recommendations agreed by less developed and developed countries at the second UN Conference on Trade and Development at New Delhi in 1968.[3] Unfortunately, no amount of agreement upon, and consistency among, non-binding targets by non-governmental meetings can secure the implementation of those targets. Although the Pearson goals represent the bare minima that could give even unreformed aid a chance to accelerate development significantly throughout the Third World, it was perfectly clear while the Report was being written that such minima would not be attained, and it has become clearer since. Therefore certain questions about the usefulness of aid to development, its concentration among countries and projects, and its role in helping the recipient towards self-reliance become crucial.[4]

II THE WORLD DECLINE OF AID

Commissioner Lewis points out that the 1 per cent target for flow of public and private resources by 1975 would represent "a drastic reversal of trends"[5] but expects that "all but two (OECD) countries will be able to report concrete measures (to the World Bank meeting in September) 1971, thus putting the pressure of the entire world community on these two".[6] It is essential to resist the emphasis on the 1 per cent total flow target, because total world flows of private resources are little affected by one donor's acts. If there is less British private investment in Guyana, then more US private investment may *ipso facto* become profitable. For this and other reasons, private flow targets (unlike aid targets) make little sense, because taxation and even exchange-control policies by developed countries exercise little, if any, impact on the *net* flow of private capital to less developed countries. Moreover, by aggregating private flows into aid targets, we conceal the fact that private flows contain no grant element; indeed, since investment is thought to be riskier in poor countries, the investor habitually requires a higher rate of return there.[7] Nor in many cases is there a net transfer of foreign exchange, because outflow of capital *plus profit repatriation* exceeds inflow of new capital.[8] Private foreign investment, in some sectors under some circumstances, can surely make a net contribution to development; but it is in no sense aid, nor is its volume effectively controlled by donor governments. It is therefore on the 0.7 per cent target for "net aid" that attention must be concentrated.[9]

The Pearson Report does not clearly tell us *how* drastic a reversal of trends is needed to achieve this modest goal. The OECD donors' net aid/GNP ratio fell steadily from a peak of 0.54 per cent in 1961 to 0.38 per cent in 1968, the last figure available to the Commissioners,[10] and fell further to 0.36 per cent in 1969 and 0.34 per cent in 1970[11]—less than half the target percentage for 1975. Even in absolute terms, the picture is bleak. OECD net aid rose 14 per cent in dollar terms from 1964 to 1970,[12] while export goods prices rose 11 per cent[13] and recipient populations by 15 per cent.[14] Since interest payments ate up a rising share of net aid,[15] the remaining net transfer—deflated to allow for rising prices of aid goods—fell by about $2\frac{1}{2}$ per cent per year, per recipient person, between 1964 and 1970.

The omens for the 1970s are terrible. In August 1971, one month before the meeting at which the Pearson Commission recommended the World Bank to call donors to account for progress towards its targets, Mr Nixon announced that the USA—already the world's most gravely defaulting donor—was to cut aid by 10 per cent to protect its foreign balance. The USA (and therefore other donors too) is mean and slow about replenishment of IDA.[16] As when the Report appeared (pp. 151–2), donors and recipients wish to phase out food aid, in 1967 totalling 18 per cent of all aid and £1,500 million of US aid alone; then as now, to "recognize that the political support for food aid is somewhat different from that for foreign assistance (but) that the United States should face this problem squarely" (p. 152) is hardly an adequate response to the issue. How is Congress to be persuaded to switch 40 per cent of US net aid from costless farm support[17] to real resource sacrifice for other countries?

Hence the cat of poverty is not going to be drowned in the cream of aid. It therefore becomes crucial to examine the relation between the small amounts of cream available in the past (and the future) and the sleekness or thrombosis of the recipients. By definition, *sufficient* aid induces growth; and one can identify a group of countries that received very large amounts of aid[18] in the 1950s and early 1960s and used it to generate self-sustaining growth, thereby cutting aid requirements in the late 1960s.[19] Chenery associates Israel, Taiwan, Jordan, Greece, Puerto Rico, South Korea and Panama with this "high-aid" strategy.[20] Indeed, if aid helps to finance "critical-minimum-effort"[21] rates of savings-and-growth below which self-sustained development is unlikely, one would expect it to show increasing returns: a miniscule dribble of aid is useless, a slightly bigger dribble is nearly useless, but a sub-stantial flow produces sustained results and can thus be turned off after a while without harm. That is probably an important reason why it is so hard to find relationships between past dribbles received[22] and the recipients' performance. Nevertheless, the understanding of such relationships is vital for a future in which aid will be increasingly scarce.

III AID AND GROWTH

Several linear regressions have been carried out to relate "aid" (or some more inclusive indicator of overseas capital inflows) with recipient "growth" (or with domestic saving, which is supposed to support such inflows in creating capital to produce growth). The secondary sources citing such regressions usually specify data and primary sources extremely incompletely, and often do not clearly define the countries, periods or variables for which the regression is being carried out. This means that quantitative results cannot be interpersonally falsified (the only criterion for their scientific validity); nor can one even form an estimate of likely biases in the basic data from which the results are obtained. Apart from this, the aid variable chosen—where it can be determined—is, as will be shown, seldom suited to testing the hypothesis under review. Nevertheless, the central importance of the aid-growth relationship (and the Commissioners' apparent insecurity about it[23]) perhaps make it worthwhile to set out the quantitative estimates that do exist. This is done in Table 1.

This table leaves a confused impression, partly because of conflicting results, but mainly because of conflicting methods, especially regarding treatment of causality and choices of variables and lags. One result stands out clearly: the current foreign deficit (imports less exports, visible and invisible) is inversely related to domestic saving in the same year. It is tempting, but as Mrs

Stewart has shown[24] wholly misleading, to rename the current foreign deficit "capital inflow" or "foreign saving" and to regard the regressions as saddling it with the blame for low domestic saving; the causation is exactly the other way round. If a country (a) produces for domestic consumption roughly as much as it consumes, but (b) saves less than it invests, then (c) the gap must be filled by an excess of imports over exports. If a country (d) consumes more than it produces for domestic consumption, then even if (e) it diverts enough spending from consumption to saving to pay for its total investment, (f) it still is not saving enough to avoid an import surplus. The causation runs from deficient domestic saving to a current-account deficit, not vice versa. There is every reason to expect current-account deficits and inadequate domestic savings to be linked—the latter as cause, the former as effect—and for them to be jointly associated as causes of slow growth, because of the often deflationary steps taken to correct the deficit, and also because of the need to divert potential economic surplus to paying foreigners high interest on the often short-term loans needed to cover the deficit. But it is misleading to blame genuine long-term foreign capital—especially aid—for the inadequate domestic saving that it remedies.

Low domestic saving induces an import surplus, which retards growth. But the longer the term, and the easier the terms, on which that surplus can be financed, the better for future saving and growth. Grants (or safe depletions of reserves) are best of all, then concessional loans, then long-term commercial loans, and worst of all are short-term loans, particularly export credits, which must be repaid too soon for the borrowing country to risk turning them into useful durable capital. Foreign deficits harm growth; given the foreign deficit, the larger the share that is financed by *true capital inflow*, ideally aid, the better. Investment helps growth; while a country is poor, it may need a temporary foreign deficit to support investment; insofar as poor countries can finance growth-generating investment only by growth-retarding deficits, those deficits had better be financed in a way that helps the recipient to minimise their ill-effects and to bring them to an end, *inter alia* by raising the yield of investment as a whole, but also by increasing domestic savings capacity.

So much for the one clear result of Table 1—the correlations numbered 7, 8, 9, 10, 11, 12, 14 and 17,[25] suggesting that a foreign deficit is linked to its root cause, low domestic saving. The correlations 5 and 6 try to establish a stronger conclusion in the opposite sense: that, presumably over a longer period, *being permitted* to run a big foreign deficit helps poor countries,

TABLE 1. AID-TYPE AND GROWTH-TYPE VARIABLES: QUANTITATIVE RELATIONSHIPS

"Dependent" variable	"Independent" variable	Sample	Quantitative results	Period	Source
		I. CROSS-SECTION			
1. Growth of GDP	Aid per head	51 LDCs[a]	"No significant correlation (coefficient: 0.16)" (?)[b]	1960–65	OECD
2. Growth of GNP	Aid/GNP ratio	15 countries, Africa and Asia	$Y = 4.8 + 0.18$ (0.26) A/Y $r^2 = 0.33$	1962–64	Griffin and Enos[c]
3. Growth of GNP	Aid/GNP ratio	12 countries Latin America	$Y = 42.97 - 6.78$ (?) A/Y $r^2 = 0.13$	1957–64	Griffin and Enos[d]
4. "Economic growth (of GDP)	Inflows of official capital and guaranteed export credits	40 LDCs	"No correlation"	1960–55	OECD[e]
5. "Growth"	Current foreign deficit	"Large" LDCs	"Marked positive link"	?	Chenery, citing S. Robinson[f]
6. "Growth"	Current foreign deficit	All available LDCs	Less marked, but significant greater than domestic saving	?	
7. Domestic saving/income	Current foreign deficit	32 LDCs	$S/Y = 11.2 - 0.73$ (0.11) (F/Y) $r^2 = 0.54$	1962–64	Griffin[g]
8. "	"	13 countries Asia & Mid-East	$S/Y = 16.1 - 0.82$ (0.52) (F/Y) $r^2 = 0.71$	1962–64	Griffin 1
9. "	"	ditto exc. Israel	$S/Y = 16.3 - 1.14$ (0.59) (F/Y) $r^2 = 0.90$	"	Griffin and Enos

"Dependent" variable	"Independent" variable	Sample	Quantitative results	Period	Source
10. Domestic saving	" "	18 countries Latin America	$S = 0.1716\,(0.005)\,Y - 0.06702\,(0.204)\,F$ $r^2 = 0.75$	About 1960	Griffin[h]
11. Net domestic saving/income	Current foreign deficit/income	33 countries (11 LDCs) various periods	1% rise in F/Y linked with 0.58% fall in saving ratio	Various 1880–1961	Clark[k]
II. TIME-SERIES					
12. Domestic saving/income	Current foreign deficit	14 years, Colombia	$S/Y = 21.5 - 0.84\,(0.29)\,(F/Y)$ $r^2 = 0.43$	1950–63	Griffin 1
13. Growth in GNP per person	Aid/GNP ratio *last year*	8 years, Turkey	$g = 12.5 - 0.047\,(0.011)\,(A/Y)\,(t-1)$ $r^2 = 0.62$	1957–64	Griffin and Enos
14. Domestic saving	Current foreign deficit	21 years, Brazil	$S = 1.78 + 0.15\,(0.02)\,Y\,(t-1) - 0.156\,(0.33)\,F$ $r^2 = 0.84$	1940–60	Leff
15. " "	" "	14 years, Brazil	$S = 3.16 + 0.16\,(0.02)\,Y\,(t-1) + 0.594\,(0.44)\,F$ $r^2 = 0.83$	1947–60	Leff
16. Gross investment	" "	21 years, Brazil	$I = 0.78 + 0.17\,(?)\,Y\,(t-1) + 0.849\,(?)\,F$ $r^2 = 0.90$	1947–60	Leff
17. Domestic saving	Capital inflow	?	Negative	?	Weisskopf, in Griffin 2

Sources: OECD is DAC 1968, pp. 126-8; K. B. Griffin and J. L. Enos, "Foreign Assistance: Objectives and Consequences", *Economic Development and Cultural Change*, April 1970, pp. 318-27; H. B. Chenery, in *WG*, p. 37., "Griffin 1" is in *Bulletin of the Oxford University Institute of Economics and Statistics*, May 1970, pp. 99-112 ("Foreign Capital, Domestic Savings and Economic Development") and "Griffin 2" is his "Reply" to comments in *ibid*, May 1971; C. Clark, *Population Growth and Land Use*, Macmillan, 1967, p. 268-70, cited in "Griffin 1" as is N. H. Leff, "Marginal Savings Rates in the Development Process: the Brazilian Experience", *Economic Journal*, September 1968, pp. 615-16.

Notes:

[a] Stated to contain over 80% of populations of all LDCs, (presumably) excluding China.

[b] Not stated if r, or r², or the coefficient in some regression equation. If, as one should presume, it is r², it *is* significant at 5 per cent.

[c] "Using United Nations data for the period 1962-64" (full reference).

[d] "We have used information collected by the US Agency for International Development."

[e] No further information is given in this citation from a restricted paper (IBRD, *Economic Growth, Trade and the Balance of Payments in the Developing Countries* 1960-65, Staff Paper of 15 March, 1968).

[f] Chenery says that "a number of studies" give "regression analyses [that] identify factors that are important to growth [but not necessarily] casual relationships". He cites one study as evidence of the aid-growth link, S. Robinson, "Aggregate Production Functions and Growth Models in Economic Development: a Cross-section Study", Ph.D. dissertation, Harvard University, 1969.

[g] The reference in Griffin 1 is "using United Nations data", but Griffin and Enos, *loc cit.*, refer us to *UN World Economic Survey, 1965* (full reference) for this and the next two results.

[h] Griffin 1 cites Inter-American Committee of the Alliance for Progress, Organization of American States, *La Brecha Externa de la America Latina*, 1968-1973, Washington, December, 1968, p. 30.

[k] Clark regresses net savings as a percentage of NNP at factor cost on (i) the logarithm of income per head in 1950 dollars, (ii) the decadal rate of population growth, (iii) war damage as a multiple of 1938 NNP at factor cost, (iv) a dummy variable, zero pre-1955 and 1 thereafter—variables which we must assume constant for our conclusion regarding (v) current foreign deficit/NNP at factor cost. He gives full primary data sources.

especially big ones, to grow. There is too little information in the
secondary source (the only one available to me) to assess this
evidence, but it gets some indirect support from correlation 16,
showing gross investment rising with the foreign deficit.

This result, in a particularly plausible version—that *concessionary*
means to run a foreign deficit promote growth—has recently come
under spirited attack, notably by Griffin.

The first blast was DAC 1968 (correlations 1 and 4) though
strictly speaking 1 does show a significant (at 5 per cent) and
positive aid-growth link for 51 ldcs while no details on 4 are
given. The Griffin–Enos results are based on 2, 3 and 13. Correlation 2 shows a *positive* aid-growth link for fifteen countries in Africa
and Asia, significant at 10 per cent, and suggesting, like correlation
1, that a 1 per cent rise in aid/income ratios is associated with about
0.2 per cent of extra yearly income growth.. Correlation 3 shows
a *negative* relationship for twelve countries in Latin America, but
is not significant even at 10 per cent, and suggests, not very
plausibly, that a Latin American country lucky enough to get no
aid in 1957–64 would have grown at 43 per cent per year, but that
each 1 per cent added to GNP by aid reduces the figure of 43 by 7.
Correlation 13 is not much more credible, as it means that
deprivation of aid would have produced $12\frac{1}{2}$ per cent yearly growth
of real income per head in Turkey from 1957 to 1964, a figure
never to my knowledge sustained anywhere. So we need not
perhaps take too tragically the implication—although the regression
coefficient is statistically significant at 0.5 per cent—that each 1 per
cent added to GNP by aid cuts that 12.5 by 0.047. In other words,
the only quantitative links remotely *credible* in respect of overall
growth indicated and *significant* statistically—equations 1 and 2
—do show a positive, though weak, association between growth
and aid. Given the small aid/GNP ratios of most poor countries,
the weakness of the indicators chosen for the regressions, and the
familiar deficiencies of the GNP data, the capacity of regressions
to suggest even this is rather surprising. Certainly one should not
assert that the whole aid ragbag—bribes, concealed military support, airports and hotels, export promotion and all—has made
nearly *enough* contributions to *development*. But, despite everything it seems to have made *some* contribution to *growth*.
Papanek's forthcoming papers(*Economic Journal*, 1972; *Journal
of Political Economy*, 1973) amply confirm this. Indeed the Indian
case renders it rather surprising that the reverse can be
suggested. It is in principle possible, as Griffin suggests, that aid
replaces almost as much domestic saving as it encourages (though
a long-period analysis would be needed to test this) and is especially

prone to support ventures with low returns; but he has come nowhere near proving that such dangers outweigh the basic common-sense of "more means more". Gifts of food might sometimes make people too lazy to hunt, or might raise their metabolic rate; but the general proposition that gifts of food reduce the growth rate of bodies is not very plausible, though it is true that food is generally given to people whose bodies have been growing slowly.

Before lots more regressions are run, it is worth asking just what relationship between aid and growth we are seeking to measure. Not one of the correlations linking "aid" to other things is accompanied by information about what exactly counts as aid, or even whether repayments of capital and/or interest have been deducted from gross flows. Aid is supposed to promote growth (*a*) by transferring resources to raise the recipient's economic surplus, thereby helping it to "invest more than it can save", or more generally to increase the resources for growth-inducing outlays, including some education and health expenditures and even some part of the extra food consumption of the *working* poor as well as most conventional investment; and (*b*) by enabling the recipient to "import more than it can export", insofar as it is impeded from building up a base for growth by lack of foreign exchange plus imperfect substitutability of domestic for foreign resources.

The supposed contribution of aid to growth, in its resource transfer role, can be measured only by the "grant element" of gross flows of aid—grants *plus* the discounted present value of the difference between concessional terms and "normal terms". The grant element is calculated for major *donors* by DAC each year—assuming 10 per cent interest with no grace period as "normal terms"—and is typically about 80 per cent of gross DAC aid, but this varies enormously among *recipients,* and considerably for the same recipient over time. If it were possible to estimate the effects of tying in raising the price of aid-financed exports *to each recipient* (or for different years to the same recipient), the proportion of gross (crude) aid comprising such overpricing should be further deducted from gross grant-element aid, before international or intertemporal comparison of true resource inflows are made. At present, however, while it is probably about right that world tying affects three-quarters of aid and raises the prices of tied goods by a fifth, no cross-national or intertemporal estimates of the volume of tied aid *by recipient* are available. The first step towards estimating the true aid resource inflow to each ldc would be for OECD (DAC) or the World Bank to estimate grant-equivalent aid, by years and recipients. Allowing for differences in tying would be a refinement.

12—FRAED * *

The contribution of aid to growth, as "import-enabler", is properly measured by net transfer (gross aid, minus capital repayments, minus interest repayments). Probably the correlations in Table 1 use the net *aid* figures (not net of interest repayments), which are far less difficult to come by on a recipient basis. A time-series of net aid (and even more of gross aid) will substantially overstate the "import-enabling" contribution in later years, as grace periods end and repayments of interest (and capital) build up. A cross-section will similarly overstate the relative amount of "import-enabling" done by aid in countries such as India, with a high ratio of loans to grants, and with aid programmes of fairly long standing, so that interest (and capital) payments on old aid loans loom large. In both cases any positive aid-growth link would be weakened. The first step towards estimating the true import-enabling aid inflow to each ldc would be for DAC or IBRD to estimate net transfer, by years and recipients. Once more, allowing for differences in tying—in this case by deducting the "overprice" component of each year's *gross* aid from that year's net transfer, which might well become negative—would be a welcome refinement. And measures of both "resource-transferring" and "import-enabling" aid should include aid from non-DAC sources.

Does one measure "aid", when relating it to growth, as a total or as a proportion of recipient income, imports, investment or population? Obviously a given total of aid will make a proportionately smaller contribution to growth of a relatively larger total base national product. Some sort of aid/income ratio, therefore, is indicated in measuring resource contribution from aid. As for import contribution, an aid/import ratio is a tempting mistake; it would make the donation of weighty aid to a small country statistically very difficult, because of its relatively high import needs. Aid is supposed to add *extra* import capacity, and once more it is relative to income that this contributes to income growth. Hence the use of aid/income ratios (though not of the aid measures) in correlations 2, 3 and 13 is justified, but it is hard to see why aid *per head* should be regressed on growth of *total* GDP in 1.

We thus need to regress "growth" on the ratio to output of (*a*) grant equivalent of gross aid, (*b*) net transfer, both preferably after deduction for tying.[26] "Growth" itself presents fewer problems than usual. Differential aid has unfortunately not been so used as to promote differential birth-rate reduction, and the choice of income-per-head rather than total output therefore has little to recommend it, as it will reduce the goodness of fit for quite spurious reasons. Nor is the choice of gross or net, factor cost or market price, likely to be *very* important in time-series or cross-section analysis. It can, however, be important to measure national rather than domestic product; in mid-1971 the IBRD rejected an application for aid from the Gabon on the grounds that most benefit would accrue to persons living in France.

Pricing raises a few problems. In measuring growth, output should of course be measured at constant prices for each country —preferably with a base-year near the middle of the period under test. If a time-series is being used, aid should be deflated to allow for changing dollar-import prices to the recipient country. If recipient countries overvalue their currencies to different degrees the true value of aid both in its "resource-transferring" and its "import-enabling" role is differentially understated among observations in a cross-section analysis; this may not be too serious because the value of all tradeables in GNP (i.e. most goods, as opposed to most services) is understated too, so that the effect on the aid/GNP ratio is proportionately much smaller than on aid alone.

The final problem, and perhaps the most interesting theoretically, is the length of time we should expect to elapse before aid promotes growth.[27] All the cross-sections reported in Table 1 correlate observations on a country's aid (or other deficit-supporting) receipts and its growth (or savings) performance in the same period. Apart from the point, made above, that inadequate saving—perhaps partly caused by low income and slow growth—*causes* the need for deficit support, including aid, it is hard to see why extra aid-financed investment (or imports) should be expected to produce instantaneous income, especially by those who believe, with much justice, that aid has been excessively concentrated on projects with very long gestation periods. This weakening of the measured aid-growth link by the failure to lag growth is especially serious if the period under review is very short, as in correlation 2. If we are testing whether aid (or in general capital inflow) "causes" domestic saving, then not only does failure to lag saving involve us in confusing the issue with that of inadequate saving as a cause of the current foreign deficit, but also a rather long lag is needed. The theoretical link of aid to savings is that (1) aid raises the economic surplus, including investment; (2) after a time, this raises income-per-head; (3) after more time, the share of income saved also goes up.

It is not clear what precise lags between aid (or even long-term capital inflow—though there is really no point in regarding the correlations that include short-term inflows too, such as 4–12 and 14–16, as tests of whether such inflows "cause" saving or growth) and growth or savings are appropriate. One year is probably too little even for growth—think of Durgapur!—and certainly for saving. Ideally some way of sorting out a whole series of different aid-growth lags, by distributed-lag or Fourier-series or spectral analysis, would be in order. It could be argued that "import-enabling" aid, i.e. net transfer, contributes to growth *sooner* than "resource-transferring" aid, i.e. grant-element of gross flows, and should thus be lagged by less.

Ultimately, then, testing for a causal link between aid and growth involves regressing the trend rate of growth of (say) GNP at constant prices, upon *two* proportions (both suitably lagged) of that dependent variable: aid, from all sources, as net transfer and as gross grant element.[28] Both time-series and cross-section analysis should be tried; the effect of excluding certain *a priori* notorious "aid" transfers, donors or recipients from the cross-sections should be attempted; and alternative lag structures should at least be tried. Linearity should not be assumed. The only remotely plausible evidence so far (correlations 1 and 2 only) does suggest some weak positive link—even measuring aid crudely, and lumping everything (from DAC sources) in, and not lagging—between aid, typically 10 per cent of recipient investment and growth. The real relationship between "good" aid and growth would perhaps be considerably stronger, but at present empirical statistics is silent on that relationship.

I recognize that it is irritating for statistical pioneers to be confronted with carping methodological criticism instead of counter-evidence. But a proper statistical test of the causal link between aid and growth would require several man-years of sustained effort. Merely to reiterate correlations, before the direction of causation or even the definition of variables has been clarified, is in this case to risk "falsisms". There is little difference between "Coffee puts you to sleep because (since one observes that it is taken when people feel sleepy) it has a *virtus dormitiva*" and "Foreign capital retards growth because, suitably defined, it flows in while saving and growth are low".

IV AID AND SELF-RELIANT GROWTH

Whatever the weaknesses of the correlations, one cannot deny that aid has done *too little* to promote growth, not (as the Commissioners rightly emphasize) because of any widespread graft and incompetence, but because of insufficient attention to what countries, sectors or projects should be supported with what types of aid. This is largely because the "theory of aid" as a path to self-reliant growth, admirably stated by Chenery and Strout,[29] has never been applied when deciding whether to accept or reject aid applications, let alone whether to make them. For example, suppose we take the "two-gap" approach;[30] if growth in a poor country is constrained by savings shortage it requires more gross grant-equivalent aid, if by foreign-exchange shortage more net transfer, and the steps to maximise extra recipient income from any allocation (subject to whatever unavoidable commercial, political and inertial limitations may exist) need to allow for this. But the failure to apply aid-allocation theory to practical aid decisions is far more fundamental.

How is aid supposed to promote self-reliant growth? The argument runs as follows. The recipient cannot finance gross savings of more than about 10 per cent of GNP, owing to poverty. Depreciation eats up at least 3 per cent of GNP. If population is growing at $2\frac{1}{3}$ per cent per year, and 3 units of new capital are needed to produce each extra unit of output, this leaves no room at all for increased income-per-head unless there is some aid. Each extra 3 per cent of GNP supplied to the recipient as aid will permit an extra 1 per cent of growth if the domestic savings rate and the capital/output ratio stay constant. A large part of the extra income can be pre-empted for extra saving, to finance investment domestically. After a period, the domestic savings rate will have risen enough to finance investment sufficient to sustain satisfactory growth without aid.[31]

It should be noted that the extreme crudity of this model can be softened, and that the softening process itself points to criteria for aid allocation that will improve its contribution to self-reliant growth. Let us consider some criticisms.

(a) "Population growth is not a constant". For each 1 per cent cut in population growth, there is an extra 1 per cent of income per head. This not only cuts the investment and aid needed for satisfactory growth of income-per-head. On the reasonable assumption that marginal savings rates are higher (or more easily raised by policy) than average rates—that people object less if saving or even taxation eats into *prospective* consumption than if it erodes *actual* living standards already enjoyed—this means a proportionately larger rise in domestic saving to finance ultimately self-reliant investment. Furthermore, since cutting population growth in practice means cutting birth-rates, it reduces the share in the population of infants who must consume but cannot produce, and increases the share of women freed from pregnancy, lactation or child-minding during seasonal peaks and hence able to increase farm output; both effects increase savings rates further. Finally and more familiarly, extra children divert public outlays towards health and education services with very long time-lags before extra output (if any) is induced; fewer children *ipso facto* free public resources for more productive uses. Both the savings and the income-per-head criterion[32] thus point strongly to associating aid with birth control.

(*b*) "The marginal capital/output ratio is not fixed, across projects or over countries or over time." There is a *prima facie* case for selecting for aid projects *and countries* where the ratio is low—or, if a country is clearly constrained *ex ante* by foreign exchange rather than total domestic-plus-foreign savings, where the marginal foreign-exchange/output ratio is low. It might be argued that such a policy, while good for short-run growth in that aid-financed capital will generate a lot of real income, is bad for long-run self-reliant growth in that the income is "wasted" in wages spent on consumption instead of going to profits that are saved and reinvested. This argument will be dealt with in detail in a forthcoming book;[33] its weaknesses can only be indicated here, by posing a few questions. (i) Do the people, on whose products wages are spent, themselves save or spend? (ii) Does extra consumption have no productive impact? (iii) Do we know that total profits rise as a result of picking projects with more capital but a lower marginal capital/output ratio? (iv) Do we know that *total* saving (company, plus personal, plus public revenue-over-expenditure surplus) rises as the profit/wage ratio rises? (v) In an open economy, how should we allow for the higher marginal propensity to import of richer people? These questions are designed to reinforce scepticism about the savings argument for pushing 88 per cent of aid, as has been done,[34] into the non-agricultural sector—when agriculture, allocated only 18-25 per cent of investment by the 22 poor countries for which figures are available for the 1950s and 1960s, employs—or underemploys—some 70 per cent of their population and hence enjoys a marginal capital output ratio typically one-third to a half of that of other sectors.[35]

(*c*) "Many types of non-investment outlay, not financed by saving in the usual sense, support growth and could be supported by aid." This is why I incline towards the older concept of economic surplus—what is available after consumer needs are satisfied. It is perhaps easiest to look at this income terms. Incomes of people producing consumer goods and services in the normal sense are not part of the surplus.[36] The surplus includes incomes received by teachers and doctors as well as by workers and profit-receivers in the conventional investment-goods sectors. It also includes incomes of members of the armed forces, politicians and civil servants. An adaptation of the Harrod identity still applies—

growth equals the *share* of income comprising surplus, multiplied by the *extra output* per unit of surplus. It is still a good first shot to put aid into those sectors where extra output per unit of surplus is highest. It remains true that *prima facie* agriculture and birth-control stand out as objects for aid that seeks to produce self-reliant growth.

(*d*) "There is not really a ratio, for any project, of extra output to extra capital; there is a series of output flows, over time; and that series will differ according to the other inputs associated with the extra capital." Ideally, it is true, projects should be ranked by their internal rate of return. In practice, enough information to do this for intersectoral aid allocations within or between recipients is seldom obtainable. Agricultural investment certainly, and (in income per-head terms) expenditure on birth prevention almost certainly, shows shorter gestation periods than most other outlays and hence even more favourable internal rates of return, as compared with crude marginal capital/output ratios.

(*e*) "What about income distribution?" By happy chance, the concentration of the economic surplus (including aid) on small farms is likely to benefit efficiency and equality in the same process —by providing income from work, usually from self-employment, to the rural poor. As for family planning, it is already likely to be practised by the rich, so that the extra benefits (and extra bargaining power in labour markets) from its spread are felt mainly by the poor.

V AID AND SELF-RELIANCE: BEYOND GROWTH

So we can locate sectors where aid will benefit self-reliant growth. But to what extent should growth be our objective? It is fashionable nowadays to denigrate economic growth. Most of the targets sought by its opponents—greater equality, a better environment, more satisfying work—cannot be met without more resources, both because they are costly in themselves and because of the power, in any social system, of the privileged to resist *absolute* impoverishment in the interest of the less well-off. Growth is indivisible; if the rich world stagnates in order to contemplate its own ecology, its imports from (and aid to) the poor world will at best stagnate also. Contempt for growth is also indivisible; it communicates itself readily between comfortable elites at international (growth-financed) conferences, and can too easily represent an intellectual transfer of rhetorical technology, justifying or excusing continued neglect of "the wretched of the earth" lest their proper feeding melt the polar ice-cap.

Nevertheless—here it comes—donors and recipients alike have noted that (in poor countries as in rich) growth is often *insufficient* for commensurate increases in welfare, and have sometimes jumped to the conclusion that it is *unnecessary* for them. One therefore applauds the Commissioners' attempt to set the record straight. The poor countries, and even their poorest people, have probably enjoyed more improvement in 'life-environment' in the past twenty years than in the previous two thousand. For the ordinary villager, "growth" increasingly sums up the resources needed to provide, out of the economic surplus, schooling for his children, a doctor in emergency, public distribution systems and food stores to prevent starvation when harvests fail, some sort of lighting in the village street and some sort of road to the town. Few of these items are valued, relative to others, anything like as highly in national as in individual estimations; almost all escape our measures of equality or inequality (though their ample and universal provision in rich countries is part of what we mean by calling them "developed" and an important though concealed component in their relatively high levels of equality); yet almost all are costly, and can be provided out of "economic surplus" only because part of that surplus is met by aid (and although, as its critics rightly point out, some of aid displaces private saving or seeks out low-yielding activities).

It is necessary to ask, though, whether the sequence by which aid—if sufficient and properly-directed—is supposed to produce. on the part of the recipient, self-reliant and sustained improvement applies to other aims than growth; and what sorts of allocation are required to do so. We pass here into a theoretical void. The remarks that follow are more than usually tentative.

Ultimately, there are only three aims of economic policy agreed on by, and within, almost all poor countries: faster growth, less inequality, and better composition of output.[37] (A fourth aim that I regard as basic, more and freer choice, is not generally agreed upon in most less developed societies or governments.) The three major intermediate aims, regarded in a developed context as necessary conditions for satisfactory attainment of the other four— long-run balance-of-payments equilibrium, containment of the rate of price increase, and high levels of employment—are also desired by most poor countries, though many recent discussions seem mistakenly to elevate employment from an intermediate aim (to provide efficient labour use for faster growth, and a larger share of employment income for greater equality) to an ultimate end in itself.

I shall deal briefly with only one non-growth area where aid can contribute to self-reliance: the complex of goals "equality—

prices—balance-of-payments". Poor countries can be set along the path towards greater equality by properly directed, self-eliminating aid to reduce the inflationary impact of expansion on prices or imports. The increase of inequality along many dimensions—above all urban-rural but also educated-illiterate, unionised-casual, employed-unemployed, racial and regional—has been a feature of post-war growth in most poor countries;[38] the poor have got slightly less poor, the rich have got much richer. Yet in rich countries rapid growth is usually associated with *declining* inequality.[39] There is something about development that turns growth from an unequalising to an equalising process. One reason is that the shortage of "growth poles" in poor countries causes new firms to cluster around them, and mobile and educated groups such as lawyers, doctors and engineers follow these sources of income to the few established centres of government, industry and communications;[40] while in rich countries labour scarcity *and mobility* means both that workers move in search of higher wages thereby (bidding them down where they are above average).

This is not the only reason, however. If it were, aid donors could safely concentrate on rapid growth in itself, and would soon create shortages of "growth poles" (and even of labour) turning the path towards greater equality; and such obvious equalising *and* growth-inducing measures as redistribution of big underfarmed land-holdings would have happened everywhere by now. There are two other important reasons why growth in poor countries has generally worsened inequality. Firstly, development policy is almost inevitably made by small and somewhat cocooned urban elites able, as in Ayub's Pakistan, to strengthen themselves by retaining the fruits of growth; here aid (especially from bilateral donors who are over-diplomatic or share interests with those elites) can do little, though it is notable that both the World Bank and the major US foundations are expressing, more and more publicly, a plainly sincere concern that their aid yield more benefits to small farmers and landless labourers.[41] Secondly, governments fear that increased equality will raise consumer demand,[42] thereby causing rapid rises in domestic prices and/or a balance-of-payments crisis and also eroding taxable capacity and marketed surpluses; this is closer to a classic self-reliance problem, in that the less developed country is, or believes it is, too poor to afford the means to greater equality, and to set itself on a path towards such equality needs outside help so given that the recipient can keep on course while dispensing with aid in the near future.

Many types of aid helpful to self-reliant growth paths—notably aid to tax-reform and to improved savings arrangements—

obviously help here too. Some employment-generating aid schemes (such as World Food Programme support for labour-intensive public works with, in effect, payment in kind for the employee) directly reduce the inflationary impact of egalitarian investment allocations—though such aid produces self-reliance only if the investment produced by the extra employment *itself* helps equality. At the extremes, food aid that permitted non-inflationary employment on drainage schemes that later allow double cropping by small family farmers clearly helps the recipient country to sustain equalisation even when aid stops; food aid to employ people who build a capital-intensive modern airport does not.

VI   A PROGRAMME OF AID FOR SELF-RELIANCE

One major illustration of the sort of aid promoting self-reliance in the recipient's path to greater equality, aid to land reform programmes, will illuminate some of the principles of aid for self-reliance, a target espoused by the Pearson Report with perhaps too little by way of concrete example. By "land reform" I mean the redistribution of land from large holdings to (*a*) farmers too small to support their families from their existing holdings, and (*b*) landless labourers. Both groups, in most parts of Asia and Latin America, are forced into dependence on local patrons, chiefly landlords and moneylenders, and thus prevented from finding the education, work or place of residence where they produce and earn most. Such stagnant patterns of hereditary dependence impede the development of any dynamic economic system, capitalist or socialist. In the shorter term, the case for land reform is that very large holdings, using much land and capital and little labour per unit of output, are unsuited to the conditions of poor countries, which are always short of capital and generally short of land (or, if not, then certainly of the sorts of capital and skill needed to develop new land).

Yet land reform, quite apart from its threat to the recipient élite's interests, presents serious short-run problems. The proportion of food output marketed (net of repurchases) from 100 acres is bound to be smaller if they are divided up among twenty hungry families than if they are farmed by one big commercial farmer; the ultimate increase in *total* output, from more labour-intensive cultivation after the reform, may well not offset the decline in the *proportion* marketed, so that the amount of food marketed (and hence the permissible rate of industrialization) is slowed down. Secondly, although small farmers in poor countries use a *given* endowment of land and equipment more labour-intensively and hence more efficiently than big ones, they are often less prone to improve that endowment, lacking either the resources (e.g. to buy a tubewell) or else the wish to sacrifice an already meagre present for a traditionally uncertain future (e.g. by diverting family labour from this year's weeding to dig an irrigation channel for next year's crops). Thirdly, disruption during the reform may well reduce farm output during a transitional period. Fourthly, the gearing of integrated credit-extension-marketing services to new and often inexperienced mini-farmers, essential both for efficiency and to prevent the re-emergence after the reform of the old immobilising patronage relationships, is administratively and educationally costly. Finally, compensation can present serious problems, especially of foreign owners, who can scarcely be left out of a reform, but who may be in a position to deny market outlets to plantation exports if seriously displeased with compensation terms.

Although land reform is often thought of as *par excellence* unaidable—as so institutionally complex and locally differentiated and politically sensitive as to be purely a recipient responsibility— all these five sorts of transitional problems can be substantially relieved by aid. If carefully run and allocated, such aid—both capital and technical—can place the recipient on a path, towards greater rural equality and more farm output, than can be proceeded upon well after aid stops. For all the five problems require economic surplus to pay both technicians and investment-workers (or, for another angle, to finance the expenditure of both) who can overcome them. How can aid increase the available surplus and help channel it to such purposes?[43]

If food marketings are to be sustained or increased during the reform, then facilities for transport, storage and co-operative processing must be provided for the small farmer, and managers of such facilities trained. If small farmers are to be encouraged to save and invest, their opportunities for doing so profitably and safely must be increased and explained; a careful and detailed survey of groundwater resources is usually the first step. If land reform, while raising long-run output, involves short-run disruption costs, those costs can be met in kind by temporary food aid (though great care is needed to avoid depressing food prices to the beneficiaries of the reform and discouraging them from marketing). Technical assistance can help to reduce the delay before the "new class" of viable small farmers receives properly integrated credit, marketing and extension services. Finally, capital aid, if handled with imagination instead of dogmatism, can be used for "compensation loans" to Governments faced with the political need to include foreign landholdings in an effective reform; such loans might even sometimes cover the leaks into imports from spending out of the compensation to domestic landed interests.

Land reform is obviously "about equality" first, but it is certain to disappoint unless it also underpins growth. It is indeed a central argument of this paper, and of the entire case for aid, that the relief of poverty and the acquisition of dignity in impoverished societies require growth as an absolute precondition, and that aid to enlarge the economic surplus is a way to help fulfil that precondition. In what ways can such help be most fruitfully and "self-eliminatingly" given? We have argued that birth-control is both a high-yielding use of resources and one which helps families to save (or bear tax); and that agriculture has been monstrously under-aided given the relative efficiency of capital and research there, a proposition that the so-called "Green Revolution", for all its patchiness and limitations, well illustrates. (The amazing thing about basic research into improved varieties of tropical cereals is that such research was so little and so late). To measures of aid with high yield might be added those designed to diagnose and cure, rather than to augment, excess capacity; before sending or lending extra tractors or steel mills, a donor would do well to ask if scarce aid might not yield more in repairing or providing ancillary inputs for those already out of production, or on general-purpose imports of wage-goods so that workers might be paid to be worked on a multi-shift basis. If we are concerned specifically with aid generating *self-reliant* growth, however, we have to ask how the recipient can be helped to increase the share of income it can itself devote to the generation of further growth.

Birth control, as we have seen, scores here. There are more direct approaches too, mostly in the area of technical assistance: assistance in raising the yield and income-elasticity of taxation, broadening its base, and reducing evasion and avoidance; in increasing the flow of private saving, especially from one rural area to another; and in developing methods of accounting and audit, especially for public corporations, that both encourage reinvestment and provide stimuli to ensure adequate returns on it. The real problem is less what to aid, but how to aid it. This in turn involves two questions: whether aid can be linked to performance in recipient countries, and how aid can be protected from inertial, commercial and political pressures in donor countries.

It is hard to disagree with the doubts about the psychology of subjecting recipient countries to performance criteria—doubts succinctly expressed by I. G. Patel at the Columbia-Williamsburg Conference.[44] The Pearson Commission rightly diagnosed a "crisis of will" among aid donors, but recipients are at least as disillusioned with some aspects of aid (notably the promotion of uncompetitive ideologies, and exports, with which it is too often associated). In this atmosphere the *imposition* of performance criteria might produce not better performance but countries that say "To hell with your aid" and subsequently go thither without it. Indeed, it is hard to see how "donors" of, say, tied five-year credits at 5 per cent interest earn the right to impose anything whatever. The increasing practice of gearing aid to a Plan, unambiguously the responsibility of the recipient Government but discussed in a World Bank consortium or consultative group, offers at best a partial escape from this *impasse*.

The real trouble about performance criteria is twofold. First, what happens if a recipient deliberately seeks goals different from those stated by the donor—say, equality even at the cost of growth? Second, what happens to non-performers? Repeated fluctuations in aid at the donor's whim, as the Pearson Report itself points out, greatly reduce the efficiency of planning. To use such fluctuations to punish poor performance is therefore to ensure its continuance. Moreover, the whole business of international reward and punishment in a field so imperfectly understood as development, and managed by donors whose own performances as regards both domestic development and external economic liberalism are so divergent and inadequate, is deeply distasteful. It is not quite neocolonialism, but it is certainly paternalism, and by an ignorant and imperfect parent at that.

Yet the argument that scarce aid must not be wasted, and that the past link to growth and self-reliance has been all too weak, has almost irresistible force. There are two areas in which donors could achieve many of the benefits of performance criteria while avoiding many of the costs: improved project analysis, and reduced bias by donors among recipients. The various techniques of benefit/cost analysis of projects submitted for aid—for all their drawbacks and dubieties[45]—make it possible for donors to assess a project in advance, instead of a nation in retrospect, and to allocate aid (to some extent at least) where it seems likely to do most good; certainly, however, the *distribution* of benefits from alternative projects, as well as the absolute size of such benefits, should be taken formally into account. Project appraisal is usually thought of as inadequate *ex ante* substitute for performance criteria *ex post*, largely because of the "marginality argument" that aid does not really finance the project on which it is spent (which would probably have been undertaken even without aid), but only the project which the aid just makes it worth the Government's while to undertake. However, this argument has been grossly overstated. For most poor countries, the balance of payments is such that almost any major foreign exchange outlay is very much likelier to take place if the dollars (or whatever) are made available on concessional terms. "If you don't pay, we'll do it anyway, and go to the Russians or finance it by ceasing to buy your exports of something else" is an increasingly unconvincing threat.

The assessment of projects *ex ante* instead of countries *ex post* could take some of the heat out of attempts by donors to reduce aid misallocation. As regards country allocation, however, donors might at least reduce some of the random biases in their own aid programmes: towards small countries, towards their own former colonies, towards nations that "kindly" purchase their inefficiently-produced and hence overpriced exports. The scale of British aid to Malta or Malawi, or French aid to Chad or Dahomey, cannot possibly be justified by these countries' poverty or by their use of aid: not, certainly, during an aid (and food) famine in Bengal. One of the most alarming parts of the aid scene is Britain's apparent readiness on joining E.E.C. to divert some 15 per cent of its exiguous aid programme to the European Development Fund, which effectively means *inter alia* even less aid to India, to pay even more to French firms in tiny dictatorships in Africa.

VII   DOES AID HELP?

The radical anti-aider, if he is still reading, is by now extremely impatient. Do I not realise that aid exists to serve donor interests, not recipient needs; that it aims to create dependence, not self-reliance; that cool project appraisal and reallocation away from client states would therefore be at best a dishonest facade? Well, all this is in part half-true, but not really relevant. The motive of one's action is only distantly, if at all, relevant to its consequences. Aid is much less of a gift relationship than its name implies, but much more than cynical donors intend. Even if I pay a man to keep him my servant, he may save up until he has enough to abandon me. Moreover, the cynical view of aid places much too little emphasis on what Sir Robert Peel termed "intellectual conviction, that priceless jewel of the soul". Nobody who knows the aid professionals—men who believe at least as deeply in Christianity and cost-benefit as in capitalism—can seriously argue that they would wittingly or unwittingly be used as pawns in a game of aid-as-exploitation. They must face, and often fight, the pressures of domestic commerce and short-run political gain; what they believe in is *efficient* resource transfer from rich to poor.

In this paper I have tried to show that the statistical case against the effectiveness of aid is not proven; and that the commonsense of "more means more" can in future be powerfully reinforced by allocative measures to associate aid with an increasingly self-reliant path to growth and the relief of poverty. Doubters will argue that aid is an inextricable part of the neo-colonial nexus that binds poor to rich, and that it is bound to be used by wealthy elites in poor countries to strengthen their positions. Let me ask those doubters two questions. Firstly, if aid *alone* were removed from the set of relations between rich and poor countries—leaving untouched the flow of profits on private capital, the determination of commodity prices, the brain drain, the cartel sale of manufactures—would poor countries be less exploited by rich ones, solely by virtue of the withdrawal of concessional resource flows? Secondly, in the thousands of years before aid appeared—and more recently in those poor countries such as Haiti which have been boycotted by the international donor community—has there been especially notable progress in replacing selfish and exploitative domestic elites by modernising democratic leadership?

The real choice is not between model and muddle, between free and decent international arrangements and the present set-up including aid. We shall anyway have a historically evolved set of rich-poor relationships, some exploitative, some mutually beneficial. The choice is to have these relationships with or without aid. Those who feel poor countries have a "clean-break" option—autarky—might ask themselves which countries, especially which small countries, have developed that way in the past; and what degree of *internal* exploitation in a poor country would be required to develop that way now. It must also be borne in mind that in many fields of rich-poor relationships exploitation can shade into mutual advantage. A lowering of tariff barriers by rich and poor countries to each others' goods is one such field. The Pearson Report contends that another is aid towards self-reliance, strengthening the recipient as an ultimately independent economic and cultural partner; and, implicitly, that the risks to poor countries from being left to stew in their own juice are immeasurably greater than the risks of exploitation. The whole history of development appears to support that contention. It remains to work out its implications through more rational project selection. But to undermine aid, unless one has clear proof that its effects are damaging to development (or can be replaced by transformed internal management), is really a rather unfruitful contribution to international relations or the relief of poverty.

NOTES

1 W. A. Lewis "The Purpose of the Pearson Report", in B. Ward *et al* (eds.), *The Widening Gap: Development in the 1970's,* Columbia, 1971 (the report of the Williamsburg-Columbia Conference of February 1970—hereafter referred to as *WG*), p. 6.

2 This comprises concessional intergovernmental capital transfers from developed to less developed countries (i.e. "gross aid"), minus capital repayments, but *not* net of interest repayments on past aid loans. It is shown below that either "net public transfer" (obtained by deducting, from net aid, such interest) or "grant equivalent of gross aid" is a more useful concept. Strictly it is the 1.0 per cent target, for "Flow of financial resources: public and private, including export credits but net of all *capital* repaid or repatriated", that the Commission aligns in the manner Lewis indicates.

3 Lewis, *WG*, p. 6.

4 See Note 14 below. The definitions of "aid", "development" and "self-reliance" cannot be ignored, of course.

5 *WG*, p. 6.

6 Ibid., p.. 7.

7 This is confirmed by data for the USA and the UK alike. W. B. Reddaway *et al, Effects of UK Direct Investment Overseas (Final Report),* Cambridge, 1968, p. 358; *Statistical Abstract of the United States 1970,* US Dept. of Commerce (Bureau of the Census) 1970, p. 766.

8 For Chile in particular and Latin America in general, see K. Griffin, *Underdevelopment in Spanish America,* Allen and Unwin, 1969, pp. 145, 146. For India, see M. Kidron, *Foreign Investments in India,* Oxford, 1965, p. 310. Indirect effects on visible trade *may* modify this.

9 A "net public transfer" or "grant equivalent" target would be still better; see below.

10 OECD, *Development Assistance: Efforts and Policies of the Members of the Development Assistance Committee* (hereafter DAC), *1970. Review,* p. 181. OECD donors account for over 95 per cent of world net aid.

11 OECD, *Press Release A (71) 22,* Paris, 28 June 1971, p. 1.

12 Ibid, p. 20.

13 UN, *Statistical Yearbook 1970,* p. 40; the index is for exports from developed countries, to which about three-quarters of all aid is tied.

14 Ibid., p. 28. Net aid grew by 3.2 per cent yearly in 1961–8, and only 1.9 per cent yearly in 1964–8; Pearson requires 14.1 per cent growth for this 1975 target (p. 382). See also M. Lipton, "Forward from Pearsonism", *Bulletin of the Institute of Development Studies,* December 1969, p. 12.

15 World Bank/International Development Association, *Annual Report,* 1970, p. 46.

16 The International Development Association, the "soft loan" branch of the World Bank. The USA, which does not like the fact that one of the International Labour Organisation's vice-presidents is a Russian (the first ever), is also in frank default on its subscriptions there.

17 T. W. Schultz has argued that the sale on the market of US wheat now given as food aid would cut prices about enough to leave total US receipts from wheat sales roughly constant. See T. W. Schultz, "Value

of US Farm Surpluses to Underdeveloped Countries", *Journal of Farm Economics*, 1960. Since then the US has imposed high transport costs on recipients; who is getting the "aid"?

18 Whether measured per head, as a proportion of imports, or as a proportion of GNP.

19 These low aid requirements *after* self-reliant growth is attained can then be correlated with such growth to "prove" that low aid and high growth are linked. This has been done.

20 H. B. Chenery, "Targets for Development", *WG*, pp. 39–41.

21 H. Leibenstein, *Economic Backwardness and Economic Growth*, Wiley, 1957, Chapter 8.

22 "External resources as a whole have only financed some 15 per cent of the investment of developing countries, and foreign aid probably only about 10 per cent" (Pearson, p. 14).

23 "The correlation between the amounts of aid received in the past decades and the growth performance is very weak" (p. 49). "Foreign aid has *not always* stimulated economic growth" (p. 14) "Aid . . . has *increased* the rate of growth in total production" (p. 48). Our italics. Examples could be multiplied, perhaps because "the Commission's first task was to satisfy itself that foreign aid serves a useful purpose and serves it well . . . (its) next task was to establish that foreign aid does contribute to economic growth" (Lewis, *WG*, pp. 4–5). To be fair, both Lewis and the Commissioners as a whole stress "performance criteria" to create a strong *future* link between aid and growth; comments on the efficacy of such criteria are made below.

24 F. Stewart, 'Comment", in Oxford *Institute Bulletin*, May 1971.

25 The very odd result in 15 (Brazil 1947–60) might be due to a strong positive correlation, during the inflationary period, between last year's income and this year's foreign deficit.

26 There is a risk that (*a*) and (*b*) will be collinear; if a suitable non-collinear proxy for one could be found, two-stage least-squares might be a solution; or the relationship between (*a*) and (*b*) could be sufficiently similar (or stable) for the countries (or years) under review that a regression of "growth" could be undertaken upon the linear combination of (*a*) and (*b*) giving the highest simple r^2.

27 Clearly, since a good or bad harvest can so enormously affect GNP in most poor countries, it is trend rates of growth (or, perhaps better, growth between comparable years) that should be considered. (In Table 1 it never is.)

28 Just before going to press, the World Bank's 1971 Annual Report made available, on pages 70–75, the information by recipients on the basis of which the latter of these proportions might be estimated.

29 H. Chenery and A. Strout, "Foreign Assistance and Economic Development", *American Economic Review*, September 1966.

30 Ibid; and V. Joshi, 'Savings and Foreign Exchange Constraints,' in P. Streeter, *Unfashionable Economics: Essays in Honour of Thomas Bologh*, Weidenfeld and Nicolson, 1970.

31 A similar picture can be drawn of growth without aid—on top of population growth—generating an import surplus. *Ex post* this is identical with the savings deficit. *Ex ante* (while the great majority of poor countries suffering import surplus do so mainly because they save too little to finance their rightly accelerated investment) it is possible that in a few cases rising import demands leave too little saving "over" to finance investment.

32　In India, extra income-per-head generated by birth-control outlays is at least fifteen times that generated by conventional investment. R. Cassen, "Population Policy", in P. Streeten and M. Lipton (eds.), *The Crisis of Indian Planning*, Oxford, 1968.

33　M. Lipton, *Why Poor People Stay Poor: Urban Bias in Under-developed Countries*, Temple-Smith, 1972, forthcoming.

34　OECD, *Aid to Agriculture in Developing Countries*, Paris, 1968, p. 11. The footnote suggests that this figure may be an over-estimate, but it excludes the manufacturing of agricultural inputs (13.5 per cent of total aid "to agriculture"), which is really no more aid to agriculture than assistance to cotton production is aid to industry, which after all processes the product. The *multilateral* aid share to agriculture has recently risen (World Bank/IDA, *Annual Report 1970*, p. 7).

35　E. Szczepanik, *Agricultural Capital Formation in Selected Developing Countries*, FAO Planning Studies, Rome, 1970, p. 2.

36　One might subjectively define a set of incomes, of producers of "unproductive" or "unnecessary" consumer-goods from yachts to haircuts, that comprised *potential* surplus (i.e. could be diverted to investment-goods sector rewards by determined policy).

37　By this last aim is meant an increase in the share of products satisfying each of the following relative to subsequent types: (*a*) physical needs, (*b*) wants genuinely chosen, (*c*) exogenously stimulated demands. Under certain circumstances, particular types of product (e.g. exports, if foreign exchange is undervalued; or products of sectors without monopoly power; or products satisfying the needs of the poor) should rise as a share of GNP. By "agreement on aims" is meant both that they or their implications would receive overwhelming voting majorities, and that decision-takers support them where there is no clash with self-interest. See M. Lipton, *Assessing Economic Performance*, Staples, 1968, Chapter 2.

38　G. Myrdal, *Asian Drama*, Pantheon, 1968, Vol. 1, Chapter 12.

39　*Assessing Economic Performance*, pp. 233–7.

40　G. Myrdal, *Economic Theory and Underdeveloped Regions*, Duckworth, 1957, Chapter 3.

41　Perhaps they are doing this to prevent the Green Revolution from turning red, but we are concerned with effects on the reduction of poverty, not purity of heart.

42　As is implicitly argued on p. 170 above, it is a misleading formulation to suggest that it would reduce saving, mainly because if I as a poor beneficiary of greater equality spend on your product and you save the income then the saving is postponed and not prevented. The problem is to keep down the price of the investment-goods to which your saving corresponds.

43　Some, not all, donor countries and multilateral agencies may be assumed to want to do this. The gradual removal of the land-reform commitment from the Alliance for Progress means that the US cannot be included at present.

44　I. G. Patel, "Aid Relationship for the Seventies", *WG*, pp. 295–311.

45　The most important is the use of world prices to value commodities, even if (*a*) sold on home markets and likely to alter world prices substantially if traded, or (*b*) subject to large price fluctuations or trends; I. M. D. Little and J. Mirrlees, *Manual of Industrial Cost-Benefit Analysis, Vol. 2*, OECD, Paris, 1968. Compare A. K. Sen—UNIDO, *Guidelines*, mimeo, 1970.

7

A NEW LOOK AT FOREIGN AID

by

Paul Streeten

Queen Elizabeth House, Oxford

A NEW LOOK AT FOREIGN AID

I THE ORIGINS OF OUR CONCERN WITH DEVELOPMENT

Social scientists rarely investigate the social origins of their own interests and doctrines. Yet, such investigations not only are intrinsically interesting but also contribute to purging research of bias and thereby to restoring perspective and objectivity. It is for this reason that I shall start by examining the social and political origins of our interest in development, which has culminated in the Pearson Report, hailed by some as the most important document on development of the postwar years or even the century.

Awareness of the existence of a problem of development is remarkably recent. The academic literature, the public debate, voluntary and official agencies and institutions and policies are not more than twenty years old. The Aid India Consortium, which marks the departure of a new approach to foreign aid, was created in 1958. There are, I believe, four quite distinct reasons for this rapid growth of interest.

First, awareness that poverty is not the inevitable fate of the vast majority of humanity is quite new. It is itself the result of the rapid and continuing postwar economic growth in the West and in Japan, combined with the spread of communications. The transistor radio in the distant village has brought home to millions of poor people that their poverty need not be their ineluctable fate. As a result of the education or propaganda of politicians and economists, economic growth has come to be regarded as a human right.

A second, quite different reason has been the cold war. Marshall Aid for Europe was aid to win and strengthen allies. Later, in the "third" world, the other two worlds, Western capitalism and Soviet communism, vied with one another for the goodwill of the "non-aligned". Growth, according to their respective western and eastern recipes, was held out as the reward for keeping out of the other camp. The second cause reinforced the first, by adding an element of competition to the propaganda that growth was a human right. It is a sad reflection, not only on the limits of economics, but on the limits of human generosity and wisdom, that the thawing of the cold war (if this is the right metaphor, bearing in mind its heating up in some places) in the sixties did not lead, as economists might have predicted, to more development aid. It might have been thought that resources previously devoted to defence could now be diverted to development. But availability is of no avail if the political will is absent. To say that nations that can afford to spend between 10 and 20 per cent of their national incomes on defence should be able to afford 1 per cent for development is raising an irrelevant alternative. It is like the story of the boy who announced proudly to his father that he had saved ten cents by walking home from school instead of taking a bus. "You fool," his father replied, "why didn't you not take a taxi and save two dollars?"

A third and again quite different reason is the radical change in the balance between men and resources created by rapid and accelerating population growth. World population grew from the dawn of human history to 1850 to 1,000 million. By 1960 it had more than trebled and by 2000 it will have reached between 6,000 million and 7,000 million. As a result of this stupendous change in the dimensions of the population problem, development became necessary to prevent a decline into abject misery. The problems raised by the introduction of modern death rates into societies with primitive birth rates are not primarily the result of pressures on land and food, though these can be serious in certain regions, but of the difficulty of generating a sufficiently high savings ratio for investment and allocating out of this smaller savings ratio enough to productive investment rather than to welfare investment—schools, hospitals, etc.

The fourth reason is the large number of countries that have achieved political independence and with it development aspirations. In the last twenty years sixty-five countries have become independent. In the past decade alone more than 200 million Africans in thirty-three newly independent countries are seeking nationhood with economic development as a main objective. UN membership has grown from the original 51 to nearly 140. Inevitably, this has produced new political pressures to concern ourselves with development and the structure of the UN system has been adjusted to handle these issues.

The psychological, political and even military origins of our interest in development have coloured the approach and the content of development studies. They are part of international diplomatic relations and hence polite and flattering diplomacy, intentionally or unintentionally, has entered not only the terminology ("developing nations", "take-off", "self-sustained growth", "the free world") but also the substance. Economic targetry can serve as a focus for political will. It can also serve as an escape mechanism.

II THE LIMITS OF PEARSON

The Pearson Report is, of course, a political document, to be understood against this background. Perhaps it is unfair to expect such a highly praised public document to come to grips with deep-seated intellectual and political difficulties. Perhaps the Commissioners had to be diplomatic and had to tread carefully. But can one make omelets in this particular kitchen without treading on toes? Effective policies create dilemmas involving choices. Private foreign investment creates a dilemma between, on the one hand, reinvestment of the foreign profits in the host country and consequential alienation of the capital assets of a nation, and, on the other, remittance home with the consequential burden on the balance of payments. The bilateral aid relationship creates the dilemma between doing only what national governments ask for (thereby avoiding the charge of paternalism or neo-colonialism) and what maximises the impact on development. Budgetary aid, considered necessary to prevent collapse, often gives rise to padding of unproductive employment in the government service. Aid to new industries, intended to save foreign exchange, gives rise to *larger* import requirements. Transfer of responsibilities to local staff may mean employing, for a time, *more* expatriates. There are gentle references in the Pearson report to these disagreeable dilemmas, but the main line of reasoning is not a presentation of the choice between sound and unsound uses of aid that arises from particular applications—a discussion which might have reduced resistance amongst the hard-headed if not the hard-boiled, on the left and on the right—but it is largely a confrontation of 6 per cent growth by recipients with 1 per cent contribution by donors in 1975.

Similarly, the chapter headed "Development Debts" does not draw a sufficiently clear distinction between *commercial* debts and *development* debts, between the problems of, for example, Ghana and India. Debt relief which does not draw such a distinction encourages the running up of commercial debts on hard terms in the expectation that relief will be given later. Such relief might then be at the expense of worthier aid recipients in favour of unworthy exporters and their bankers.

There can be no doubt that the spirit of the report is generous, the argument lucid and well presented and most recommendations sensible. But one is left with certain doubts. These do not relate to the lack of originality. It was right that the report should underline the conventional wisdom, particularly where it *is* wisdom. The doubts relate rather to certain presuppositions. Is it not naive and pious, as well as ultimately damaging, to assume that morality and national self-interest coincide? Is it not futile to build the case for aid on international interdependence? Is not the fundamental presupposition of the strategy of the report—that the need for aid should subside in thirty years—unrealistic, lacking in vision and inconsistent with the claim to reduce international disparities in income? Does not the enthusiastic support of a scheme of generalized, non-reciprocal preferences for manufactured and semi-manufactured products from underdeveloped countries, compared with a lukewarm hypothetical paragraph on the link between Special Drawing Rights and the replenishment of the International Development Association, display a curious lack of a sense of priorities? Are not aid, trade and private foreign investment treated in a political vacuum? Are not the targets of 6 per cent growth, 1 per cent capital transfer and 0.7 per cent official aid either meaningless or, if meaningful, unwarranted? (There is the odd result that in 1975 Japan is expected to contribute $2,062 million while Britain only $853 million, in spite of the fact that income per head will still be 50 per cent higher in Britain than in Japan. Should there not be, as with income tax, a lower exemption limit, or rates of contribution progressing with income per head?) Does not the preference for multilateral aid (the Commission calls for raising it from 10 per cent to 20 per cent of official aid) fail to take full account of the present limitations and deficiences of some of the international agencies spelt out in detail by the Jackson Report?[1] Are not the "Green Revolution" and private foreign investment oversold, inviting a backlash of disenchantment? The Commissioners and the secretariat are obviously aware of these dilemmas and difficulties. But a political document has to be diplomatic.

III   WHY AID?

The Report does not succeed in providing a good reason for rich countries to give aid to poor countries. It veers from moral duty to national self-interest and from there to the irrelevant fact of interdependence. But the Report does make an interesting start in attempting to reconcile national self-interest and moral duty.

"There is also the appeal of enlightened and constructive self-interest.... The fullest possible utilization of all the world's resources, human and physical, which can be brought about only by international co-operation, helps not only those countries now economically weak, but also those strong and wealthy."

But then the Report goes wrong. It does not explain how aid and international trade, which it specifically mentions, promote the harmony of interests.

A more promising approach might have been to point to the growth of applied and commercially exploited scientific knowledge as the factor which ultimately sets a ceiling on economic growth. Since the scientific revolution in the seventeenth century, it has been knowledge, applied in technically feasible forms, commercially exploited and spread through imitation, which has permitted the productive capacity of societies to advance. The basic knowledge from which economic progress springs is a free, public good. Its enjoyment by one does not deprive another. But its commercial exploitation is partly naturally, partly artificially, rendered scarce. Now it is clearly in the interest of humanity as a whole that no potential contributions to the stock of knowledge be wasted. It is not only a *moral* duty to enable human beings, wherever born, to develop their faculties, but it is in the *interest* of all that these human resources should be fully developed, so that, instead of being a drain on the world's resources, they may contribute to their growth. It is in this way that one might think that aid-giving can be shown to be in the long-run enlightened interest of donor countries, and not because it is a particularly effective form of export sales promotion, peace-mongering or democracy-promotion.

Unfortunately, this most promising line of identifying national self-interest with international solidarity does not succeed either. The direction and content of applied research has not contributed to a wide spread of benefits. On the contrary, it has been concentrated on the problems of the rich and much of it has been detrimental to the development efforts of the poor. It has also left vast gaps in our knowledge of how to solve the problems thrown up by development. Knowledge, like trade and capital flows, tends to benefit those who have and is either neutral or detrimental to the problems of the Have-Nots.

The point which few men in authority have recognized, or at any rate openly admitted, is that a disinterested concern with development and the promotion of national self-interest are incompatible. The current crisis in aid—the reluctance of the large donors, the USA and the UK, to expand or even continue the aid programme—is the inevitable result of false attempts to base aid on self-interest. When the Senators began to see, what others have known all the time, that aid does not buy gratitude, nor trade, nor democracy, nor peace, nor votes, nor military support, they were understandably disappointed. On the other hand, many smaller countries, such as the Scandinavian countries, the Netherlands, Canada and others, which based their programmes on moral and humanitarian grounds, expanded their aid in the late Sixties and early Seventies. Americans are no less open to moral and human appeals than Danes. But these appeals were not made sufficiently unequivocally in America and the programme is therefore in danger of collapse. A clearer sense of motivation and objective may lead to less aid, but it would be built on a firmer base.

IV   THE GAP

The treatment of the income gap between rich and poor in the Report is economically and logically unsatisfactory. The report opens with this sentence: "The widening gap between the developed and developing countries has become a central issue of our time." This proposition and the justification of aid that is built upon it is quite inconsistent with the emphasis on aid to get rid of aid and its anticipated demise in the near future. This emphasis again springs from a false bow to what is regarded as hard-headed American attitudes. In discussing "Why Aid?" the Report says: "What, then is the objective of co-operation for international development? It is not to close all gaps and eliminate all inequality. That would, in any case, be impossible. It is to reduce disparities and remove inequities. It is to help the poorer countries to move forward, in their own way, into the industrial and technological age so that the world will not become more and more starkly divided between the haves and have-nots, the privileged and the less privileged" (pp. 7-8).

But reducing the gap is inconsistent with aid to end aid by the end of the century. The gap in income per head today is at its extremes more than $3,000. Present projections show that it will widen to between $7,000 and $9,000 by the year 2000. Income per head in the USA is expected to reach then $10,000, in Brazil $500 and in India $200. This at a time when the Pearson Report envisages aid to cease.

The Pearson Report does not analyse the significance of the gap. It does not raise the question: does the widening gap matter? One can answer this question at three levels of sophistication. An immediate reaction is "of course: this is what aid, international co-operation and development is about". But, on reflection, it seems to be the need to eliminate poverty, rather than the need to reduce an income gap, that should guide our policy. If we could choose between, on the one hand, rich countries growing at 7 per cent and poor countries at 6 per cent, and, on the other hand, the rich growing at 2 per cent and the poor at 3 per cent, should we not all prefer the first alternative, even though the gap would widen, to the second, which would narrow the gap? Should we not hesitate to reduce the gap in income per head by recommending faster population growth in rich countries, which, after all, is one way of narrowing the gap? Do we not view envy as a deplorable emotion, not to be heeded by planners and policy makers? But at a third level of sophistication, we note that differential growth rates must not be considered in isolation. There are, for good and ill, numerous repercussions of higher growth rates of the rich on the prospects of the poor, depending upon whether the rich grow because their incomes *and* their numbers grow rapidly, or because their incomes per head grow rapidly. The demand for the staple exports and the new manufactured products of the poor, the availability of spare capital to be invested in the developing countries, the rate and direction of technical innovation, the flow of international migration, of skilled and unskilled manpower, and other forces crucially affecting the development prospects of the poor depend upon growth rate and income level differentials. Even if all dogs in the manger were kept on chains, gaps could not be ignored, because no country is an island, entire of itself.

V   THE IDEOLOGY OF AGGREGATION

It is a weakness of the report, which stresses the fact of international interdependence, that it neither probes into the specific economic problems created by the coexistence of rich and poor nor even, in any detail, identifies those problems in underdeveloped countries to whose solution international co-operation could make a particularly effective contribution. Much of the discussion is conducted in terms of vast aggregates of gross national products, savings, investment and their growth rates. Many sins can be concealed by such aggregations. They are sweet music to the ears of the vested interests which can shelter behind global expenditure ratios. A brief discussion early in the report of the need to eliminate *internal* inequality, as much as *international* inequality, is soon lost sight of when we move on to growthmanship. In order to eradicate the roots of poverty and in order to win the support of those who believe that aid is wasted, one must point to actually or potentially successful applications of aid (research, food, population, jobs, slums), as well as to ways of avoiding failure. As in Mr McNamara's speech to the assembled bankers in Washington in 1969, one must say what should *not* be done, as well as what *should* be done (for example, in education less "bricks and mortar" and more functional literacy for adults).

The arithmetic of the Pearson Report is simple. The target 6 per cent growth rate of the poor countries requires a contribution in aid and private foreign investment of 1 per cent of the gross national product of the rich countries. In 1969 the growth rate of the poor was 5 and the contribution 0.72. If the Pearson targets are hit, with population growth of, say, 3 per cent, income per head can then grow by 3 per cent annually. This means doubling income per head in twenty-three years. If population growth can be reduced to 2 per cent, income per head can grow by 4 per cent and double in eighteen years. This type of arithmetic is a source of comfort. Pour in the capital, turn the handle of the machine called capital-output ratio, and out flows sweet extra growth-juice.

This picture is false for three reasons. First, development is not a matter of aggregates such as financial flows, capital-output ratios and growth rates, but involves the painful transformation of social institutions and human attitudes. The link between a given volume of expenditure and an effective land reform, a policy of population control or the establishment of an honest and efficient civil service is tenuous. Second, the task of bringing about such a transformation can be tackled only if specific obstacles are identified and removed. This means digging beneath the aggregates. Third, while rich countries can make an important contribution to co-operative solutions, their contribution must be the net result of all their policies bearing upon the development efforts of the poor. To isolate financial flows is at best irrelevant, at worse escapism or hypocrisy.

All three criticisms of the arithmetical approach question the value of large aggregates and invite disaggregation and digging beneath the economic appearance to the human and institutional reality.

The Pearson Report contains much that satisfies the need to pay attention to social transformation, to identify specific problems and embark upon their international co-operative solution and to take other policies into account. But, being cast in the framework of target rates of growth and percentage contributions, the focus is on the aggregates and the picture of the reality is therefore blurred.

The framework cast in aggregates has been discredited by the lack of correlation between aid and development. Numerous excuses can be and have been advanced for this. The reason is inadequate insurance that aid is used for development because it was made the servant of too many other masters simultaneously. Confused objectives, bad selection of projects, allocation to the wrong sectors, and corruption are among the causes of the failure of aid. The policies other than aid pursued by the rich countries have often taken away with one hand what was given with the other.

The need now is to identify problems and set about solving them together. Rural development, population control, prevention of growing mass unemployment and underemployment and of the spread of slums and urban misery, improved nutrition and the right type of education—these are the issues to be tackled in the seventies; "1 per cent" can aggravate, as well as alleviate these problems.

Development has a Hydra-like characteristic. As fast as you cut off heads, they grow again. We reduce death rates and prolong mortality, a basic human objective, and we are faced with an unprecedented problem of population growth. We introduce mechanical contraceptives, and medical complications speed up the rejection rate of women. We introduce new high-yielding varieties of grains, only to find that rural inequality and unemployment, market surpluses and political riots result. We set up an educational system and find it leads to an exodus from the countryside, where the educated are most needed, and from the country, swelling the brain drain. Science may eventually present the solution to every problem. But each solution presents new problems.

The third deficiency of the Pearson Report is its emphasis on aid. Of course, even the Pearson Commission cannot talk of everything at once, and there is much talk of trade and investment. But targetry provides an easy escape from assessing the impact on development of the whole range of a rich country's policies—foreign policy, military policy, fiscal and monetary policies, immigration, as well as science policy, trade and private foreign investment. Just as private charity can be more than wiped out by a stroke of the Chancellor's pen, so the beneficial effects of aid on development can be cancelled out by military interventions or other acts of foreign policy, trade restrictions, restrictions on capital flows and migration or new technological inventions. Not until development enters as one objective into *all* acts of government that have a bearing on it, and is fitted into the *whole* development process, can we honestly speak of "partners in development".

VI LESSONS

The lessons that the sixties have taught us are different ones for the donors and the recipients. The donors must clarify their motives and objectives and abandon the notion that military, political or commercial ends can be bought through aid. Three conditions must be fulfilled: a sufficiently large quantum of aid must be transferred; it must be applied and used efficiently; and it should be removed from all the many frictions created by inter-governmental confrontation. In some way, the good will and the basic decency of the citizens of the rich country must be harnessed and backed by the powers of the state, without the intervention of diplomats. An imaginative proposal has been made by Hirschman and Bird.[2] Reform will have to be sought along such lines as these.

It is neither easy nor promising for recipients to appeal to the conscience of the rich. They must identify much more clearly where their bargaining power lies and exploit this power to the utmost. Instead of appeals to advanced countries to reduce their trade barriers and abolish protection, the interests of the consumers and of independent retail chains in low-cost products should be harnessed to the interests of low-cost producers and exporters from poor countries. The power to withhold the supply of minerals and tropical beverages, the power to withdraw money balances or default on debt, the power to tax private foreign investment, these and similar powers have hardly yet been used. Admittedly, the use of such powers requires solidarity between groups of poor countries and such solidarity is not common. But other powerful pressure groups have started off weak and disunited. Strength and success, like weakness and failure, are self-reinforcing.

NOTES

1 A Study of the Capacity of the United Nations (UN, Geneva, 1969).
2 Albert O. Hirschman and Richard M. Bird, *Foreign Aid—A Critique and a Proposal*, Essays in International Finance No. 69, July 1968.

Index